Also by KD Robichaux

The Blogger Diaries Trilogy:

Wished for You

Wish He was You

Wish Come True

Club Alias Series:

Confession Duet

Seven

Mission: Accomplished

Knight

Scary Hot (Crossover with Aurora Rose Reynolds's Until Her Series)

Moravian Rhapsody (Read Me Romance novella)

Doc

Standalones:

No Trespassing

Cowritten with CC Monroe:

Steal You

Number Neighbor

Dedication

To Chef Curtis Stone. The one-two punch of *Trading Spaces* followed by your *Take Home Chef* back in the day was all I needed to help get me through some rough times. I appreciate you, you Aussie cooking god.

Dishing Up LOVE

K.D. ROBICHAUX

Prologue

CURTIS

"TAKE IT FROM the top in five, four, three…" Martin, my director, finishes the countdown silently on his fingers then points to me, where I stand in the produce section of Heath's Healthy Food Market in downtown New Orleans.

With my signature smile in place, I look into the camera and deliver the lines always at the beginning of every episode of my cooking show. "I'm Chef Curtis Rockwell, and this is *Chef to Go*. I'll be surprising one lucky shopper with a chance to take me home with them—" I lift a brow, my smile momentarily morphing into a cocky smirk. Ninety percent of the viewers who watch my show are women and gay men just here for my good looks and flirtatious one-liners. "—where I'll teach 'em how to cook a gourmet meal."

I turn a quarter of a circle on my heel and begin strolling down the aisle of fresh vegetables, making sure to stop directly in front of the eggplants. I lean back against the display and cross my feet at the ankles. "Today, we're in gorgeous and history-rich New Orleans, also known as The Big Easy. Which is perfect, since it's my job to make tonight's dinner seem *easy* for our amateur chef." I lower my voice, as if it's a big secret, even though there will be a crew of eight people following me around the store with giant cameras, microphones, and lighting. "Follow me while I pick who I'll be going home with today." I flash a sexy grin at the camera before turning away and heading off in the direction of the meat department.

One

Erin

I STARE INTO the dark abyss that is my empty freezer and curse myself for not going to the grocery store on the way home from work. I could've sworn I at least had some leftovers, dreaming all day about the southwest chicken egg rolls I had brought home a couple nights ago. I even drew little pictures of them in the corners of my notepad as I listened to Sally Stewartson drone on and on about how she hasn't been able to go out on a date in the past four months because her freaking dog has such terrible separation anxiety that she would come home to her entire house being wrecked. I quirked my head at her like a puppy myself when she asked me if I'd ever shrank a dog before, since clearly her furbaby needed therapy. I'd managed to answer, "Sorry, I'm merely a human psychologist," without then prescribing Sally a fucking lobotomy.

But alas, I must've gotten the drunk munchies last night and eaten the eggrolls in the middle of the night when I got home from my favorite little bar down the street from my creole townhouse here in New Orleans. In all actuality, it's not technically mine, per se. It's my best friend Emmy's family home. But seeing how her world-renowned archeologist parents left it to her when they moved to Egypt, and now she travels the world, cohosting the super-popular travel documentary show *No Trespassing* with her husband, it's now basically mine. I had offered to move out once they got engaged, but Emmy wouldn't even let me finish the thought out loud, stating I had grown up here as much as she had. We've been BFFs since we were kids and were inseparable. Plus, she didn't want to just leave it abandoned for three-quarters of the year while they were off filming their explorations.

I close the freezer with a huff. I had skipped lunch today, so there's no way I'll be able to sleep if I try to go to bed without eating dinner. With no other choice, I trudge up the staircases and into my room. When I got home from work a little earlier, I shed my professional outfit of black pencil skirt, a tucked-in, sleeveless, floral button down top, and black pumps, trading them for an oversized tee, sighing with relief as I'd pulled the thong out of my butt and covered my buns with the most comfortable thing I owned: surgery panties. It's what Emmy and I had dubbed the white mesh boyshort-cut underwear they'd put me in after my surgery last year. They were so freaking comfortable that I asked for a few more pairs before I was discharged from the hospital. And as long as I washed them in my lingerie bag on gentle cycle, they didn't unravel. My good ole surgery panties.

I pull on a pair of leggings and tie my hair up in a high ponytail, not even bothering to put on a bra, because I plan to just run in and out after grabbing something to eat for tonight. I'll do an actual grocery run tomorrow. Maybe.

Snatching my purse up off the bed, I gallop down the stairs, out the front door, take the time to lock it really quick, and then head down the sidewalk on foot toward my favorite store. There's actually a grocer a little closer in the opposite direction, but I like Heath's better even though they're a smidge more expensive. They always seem to have everything I'm looking for. And I never run into anyone I know here, so I won't have to worry about being embarrassed by my… comfortable appearance.

A few minutes later, I welcome the cold shot of air conditioning as I walk through the automatic doors. The sun may be on its way down, but the temperature on a gorgeous summer day like this doesn't usually get the memo until well into the wee hours of the night. And even then, it's still hot as hell with the humidity to match.

Glancing to my left, I see a crowd of people near the produce section, and it makes me wonder about the last time I ate an actual fresh piece of fruit or vegetable. Probably the last time I saw a crowd of people in the produce section and wandered over to see what was going on, which was a few months ago when the first shipment of cotton candy grapes came in. But I ignore the draw of the hoard and turn to the left, toward the freezer section. I'll take my chances and hope they'll have whatever healthy but yummy deliciousness still in stock tomorrow. When I come actual grocery shopping. Maybe.

My cell rings just as I turn onto the frozen pizza aisle, and I glance at my smart watch, expecting to see the name of one of my patients. Instead, it's Emmy and I pull my phone out of my purse with a wide grin. "Well, good evening, Mrs. Savageman," I say as a way of greeting.

"Good evening to you too. Um... Erin. Are you sober?" she asks, sounding surprised, and I can't help but chuckle.

"Wow, talk about making me feel like an alcoholic, bee-otch."

She scoffs, and I can practically hear her rolling her eyes. "Oh, shut your face. It's Friday, your favorite night to go to our pub, drink three-dollar you-call-its, and then flirt with the hottest tourist in the place."

"Dude. I'm totally an alcoholic ho," I hiss, as if it's the first time I'm realizing this.

"Um, excuse me. No talking about my best friend that way. As you've always slurred, 'What's the point of living in a party place like New Orleans if you're not going to party?'" she asks, and I twist my lips in thought.

"Says the gal who'd only had sorta-sex with one guy before she met her now-husband." But she's right. For several years, I'd made it my mission to speak to as many people who came through town as I could while out, sampling all the different personalities as if they were foods at a Mardi Gras festival. Being a psychologist, I have a thirst for reading people from all over the place and all walks of life, which isn't hard at all when there are so many tourists in The Big Easy. My favorite are the men—guys visiting for a bachelor party weekend spent on Bourbon Street, or the occasional world traveler here to check off an item on their bucket list.

I get to have an awesome get-to-know-you conversation, the excitement of learning a bit about a complete stranger, and no matter how the night ends, they go back to where they came from, and I'm left with a new personality to mull over after secretly shrinking them. But never locals. It's just better this way, no chance of getting attached.

"So... why don't I hear crazy commotion from the bar in the

background?" Emmy prompts.

"Ah, no big deal. I just had a late patient today who bored me to tears, like to the point I just wanted to go home. But then I realized I didn't have anything to eat for dinner, so my ass is currently scoping frozen pizzas at Heath's."

There's a pause, and then Emmy's teasing tone changes to one more concerned. "You feeling all right? More tired than usual? If you need me to fly home and go with you to the doct—"

"Em, I'm fine. I swear. It was the dog lady who had the late appointment." I share stories with my best friend, but I never tell her their names. She's the most trustworthy person I've ever met, so I know the tales I share would never be repeated. "She had to postpone her usual morning appointment for one in the evening because she had a spa day with—"

"Let me guess. Her dog," she cuts in, and I bite my lip to keep from giggling. I try my best to be nonjudgmental when it comes to my patients, but I'm only human.

"Ding, ding, ding! She asked me today if I had an available opening in my schedule to see her beloved Fifi, as in to shrink the fucking dog," I grumble.

She laughs, making me purse my lips. "I mean, I could give you Cesar Millan's number if she's serious. Our network just picked up his show."

"Oh, she's serious, all right. But as much as I love that man's gorgeous salt-and-pepper hair, there ain't no way I will be whispering anyone's freaking dog." It puts me in a sour mood to think about it, and my best friend must hear it in my tone.

"You sure you're okay, Rin?"

I sigh. "Yeah. I just... I always wanted to be a therapist to help people. To really help them with their problems and be able to watch them go from their lowest of lows to happy and succeeding in overcoming whatever obstacle they needed me for."

"But?" she prompts.

"But... I feel like we're all stuck right now for some reason. Not falling behind in recovery, but also not making any progress either," I tell her, opening the freezer and pulling out a personal-sized supreme pizza.

"We?"

"Huh?" I ask, confused.

"You said, 'We're all stuck.' You included yourself in that statement, not just your patients," she points out, and I straighten, closing the freezer door and catching my tired reflection in the clear glass.

"Hey, who's the shrink here?" I joke, my usual line when conversation directed at me turns too heavy. A great listener, yes, but a talker I am not when it comes to myself. I turn and lean my back against the freezer door, the world feeling too heavy for a moment. While my body slouches and I allow the coolness to seep into me through my clothes, I keep my voice perky even if I feel anything but. "Anyway, I promise I'm all good. I'm going to take my bomb-ass pizza back to our bomb-ass house, and then I'm going to watch my bomb-ass BFF in her newest episode of her bomb-ass show. I'll actually catch it live for once instead of watching it on the DVR. You should feel loved."

She obliges me with a little chuckle. "Uh huh. I feel loved, all right. Well, I guess since you don't need our traditional good luck toast over the phone tonight, enjoy your pizza and I'll talk to you soon. If you need me for anything—"

"I will call you and you'll be on the next flight home. I know, Em. And I love you too," I tell her, knowing exactly what she was going to say, since she ends every one of our calls the same way. We say our goodbyes, and I end the call before slipping my cell back into my purse.

Two

CURTIS

GLANCING UP AND down the aisles as I walk across the grocery store, I scan for the perfect candidate to be on the show. The highest rated episodes so far have been ones featuring moms with small children, and men who want to impress a date. The moms are easy to spot for obvious reasons, but the men I can always tell, because they're either holding a bouquet of flowers or a bottle of wine, or both.

I spot a mom with kids who look around three and six, but seeing the older one punch her mother in the leg before taking off down the aisle, I decide to pass. It's best to stick with better-behaved children for the purpose of the show or filming can be disastrous. We learned from experience.

I pass up a grandmotherly type, knowing they tend to want to take over the cooking instead of learning something new. There's a pretty lady in the bread aisle I consider, but when she turns around to place a loaf in her cart, I see she has a cover over her shoulder and her front, with tiny feet sticking out from it near her waist. Not wanting to make a momma breastfeeding her baby feel awkward by approaching her with a camera crew, I smile at the sweet scene of her pulling back the cover for a moment to coo at the little one before I move along.

Just when I'm about to lose hope in my mission, I spot her.

My sights zero in on an angel.

The florescent lights above shine down on her like a sunbeam from the heavens, making her dark hair gleam when she spins in the opposite direction, her ponytail swinging out around her narrow shoulders.

I stand there dumbly, probably looking like a creeper just watching her as she animatedly chats on her phone, hypnotizing me and making me grin like a loon at her facial expressions and gestures. She talks as if whoever the lucky bastard she's speaking to can see her, and I'm struck by the force of overwhelming jealousy that hits me as soon as I picture a man on the other end of the line.

I have a moment to wonder what that weird growling sound is before one of the cameramen, Carlos, hisses, "Yo, Curtis. You good, bro?" And I realize the sound was coming from me.

I clear my throat, shifting on my feet. "Yeah," I whisper. "I think she's the one." My heart does an impressive high-dive, gold-medal-winning flips and all, into my stomach. *The one*, a voice repeats inside my mind. *Mine*. But I shake it off, because that's just crazy.

I don't believe in love at first sight. Maybe lust... Actually, definitely lust. Because as I watch this stranger as she reaches into a freezer and pulls out a pizza, all I can think about is what her nipples might look like pebbled from the cold.

Yet, when she spins again, this time to lean her back against the freezer as if the weight of the world is on her shoulders, all the lively animation gone from her limbs, it's not lust that makes me take a step toward her. It's the urge to comfort her and take every ounce of whatever is bothering her away so she can stand up tall again.

She must tell the person goodbye—I'm still too far away to hear the sound of her voice—because a small smile crosses her beautiful face before she hangs up and tosses her phone into her bag. When she stands up straight, taking steps toward me but not looking up as she reads the pizza box, my body leaps into motion of its own accord.

Sweat breaks out on the back of my neck, and the hair on my arms stand on end as we near, adrenaline making its presence known. I usually get a little zing of excitement and anticipation whenever I'm about to approach a target, but never anything close to this pulse-racing, almost jittery feeling I have right now. I feel like a fucking teenager about to ask his crush to prom. What the hell is wrong with me?

I'm so into this unfamiliar feeling that I don't realize just how close I've gotten to her. And when I stop in the middle of the aisle to say my usual opening line, nothing comes out, and since she's still looking down reading the pizza box, she doesn't see the idiot human roadblock until it's too late. She runs right into me, the pizza getting smashed between us, as she gasps. From the coldness of the frozen dinner now pressed against the nipples I was imagining only moments ago, or from running into me, or from the group of several people holding cameras and microphones surrounding us, or from—and I like this option the most—finding me incredibly attractive as she looks up into my eyes with shock, or a combination of all of them, I have no idea.

All I know is she's got the most beautiful, unique eyes I've ever seen. I supposed one would call them green if they were being general, but up this close, they're pure gold. Not just flecks throughout the irises, no. They're solid gold, with a dark ring around the outside, keeping the gorgeous color contained as it surrounds pupils I watch with fascination as they dilate when she seems to recognize my face.

"Oh hell," she breathes, and then those golden eyes peer around me, spot the crew, and then glance down at herself as one hand lifts to pat her messy hair. "Ah fuck," she murmurs even quieter, so low only I can hear.

"I…" I start, but then I can't help but chuckle at her potty mouth. When her eyes shoot to mine, with both an annoyed and worried look, I give her my best, winning smile. "I'm Chef Curtis—"

"Curtis Rockwell. And you want me to take you home," she cuts me off and finishes my line.

You have no idea, dollface.

I grin widely. "I take it you watch my show."

"I do. You come on right before my best friend and her husband's show," she replies, surprising me.

My eyes widen, and I turn my head with a shocked face toward Carlos, who is filming the entire exchange. "Well. This… this is new." I glance back down at her, still so very close, as if it hasn't occurred to her to take a step back. It occurred to me… but I just didn't wanna. "Small world. I'm good friends with Dean Savageman, host of *No Trespassing* here on The Adventure Channel." I wink over my shoulder at the rolling camera.

"Yeah. Crazy." Her small voice pulls my attention back to her. "Ummm… I'm probably not the best candidate though. I'm just grabbing something quick for myself to eat while I watch their newest episode airing tonight." She shrugs.

And that's my cue. A genius idea hits me.

"Actually, you're perfect." Her eyes meet mine, her breath catching at my words. I clear my throat and continue, pushing aside the way that look makes me feel. "Oh, first, what's your name?"

"Erin." She shifts from one foot to the other.

"Why shouldn't you eat like a queen, even if you were planning to eat alone, Erin? I can help you prepare something quick and simple yet delicious, while making it a meal for one."

She nervously bites her lip, clearly thinking about my offer. Finally, the tension in her stance releases a bit as she visibly gives in. "What the hell. YOLO, right?"

I smile genuinely, knowing I get to spend the next several hours with the beauty still so close I can smell her floral perfume. "Right, exactly. YOLO. You only live once, and what better place to exercise that way of thinking than in New Orleans?"

She nods, taking a step back, and then holds up a finger before spinning around. I watch as she walks back to the freezer she'd been scouring when I first spotted her and replaces the pizza where she found it. When she returns, she tells me sternly, "This food better be good or I'm sending you for takeout."

I throw my head back and laugh. "Yes, ma'am."

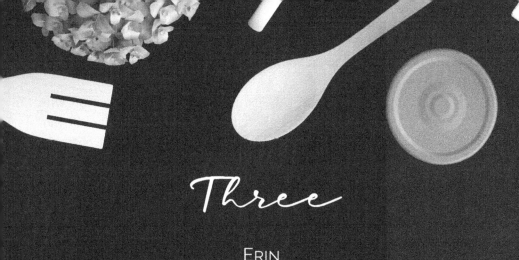

Three

Erin

Okay, Let's be honest here. I'm normally a pretty good-looking gal. On a scale of one-to-ten, I'm a solid 7.6 on any given workday. When I actually put in the effort to look my best, that jacks up to about an 8.4. I hit the jackpot with good genes. My mom's gorgeous and my dad's equally as handsome. They met on a photoshoot for a JC Penney catalog in the early '80s, where they had to play a couple with two kids who looked nothing like them. Apparently, there were instant sparks as they sat around the fake Christmas tree, pretending to be a happy family opening presents, and they've been inseparable ever since.

But I digress.

Workday, 7.6.

Maximum effort, 8.4.

But when I shed all my shit and throw on my comfy clothes to make a grocery run after a hard day of shrinking, that number dive-bombs to about a 6 thanks to the dark designer bags under my eyes and the hangry look I'm sure I have on my face. Still a point above average, because of nice bone structure and being mostly healthy, but I sure as hell don't warrant the way Chef Curtis Rockwell is looking at me… like he wants to put me on one of his buffet tables and eat me.

He, on the other hand, I'd like to put on a plate and sop up with a biscuit. Because dear Ayida-Weddo, Voodoo goddess of fertility and rainbows, my lady bits woke up the second I slammed headfirst into the brick wall of his chest. And then when I looked up and saw who it was,

I was mesmerized by the fact that he was even more gorgeous in person than he is on TV.

But I, Erin Bree Bazzara—my parents had a weird obsession with Tolkien—am not some cowering kitten. I am not a shy, wilted flower. I don't back down, and I didn't back away. Well, that last part was because he just smelled too damn delicious and was so warm in this cold-ass freezer section. But still, even so, I wouldn't have turned into a blithering mess either way. That's just not who I am as a person.

So even though he's so towering-tall that my head only reaches the center of his muscular chest, and his jaw was sculpted by Roman gods, and his eyes are as blue as my September birthstone, and his hair is the perfect shade of light blond that I can see is natural and not out of a bottle, coiffed in a way that looks like he had mind-blowing sex and just "woke up like dis"… I threw my minor tantrum after being caught looking like a hobo and quickly got over it.

I've always wondered if the food he cooks is actually good or if they pay the people they find to say it's super yummy. Like, is it in the contract I'm sure I'll have to sign to release the footage? *Even if the food tastes like twice-baked dog shit, you must act like it's the best meal you've ever eaten.*

But at his wonderfully infectious laugh and the confident look in his beautiful eyes as he politely said "Yes, ma'am" when I told him it better be good, I somehow have a feeling his skills are as fine-tuned as the viewer is made to believe. And the way he continues to look at me like he wants to devour me makes me wonder what other skills he might be really good at.

"So, I know you had your heart set on frozen pizza," he starts with a mischievous tilt of his sexy mouth, "but how would you feel about a dish more traditional to your… hometown?"

"Yes, I was born and raised here, and that sounds really nice but definitely a challenge. The dishes here have all sorts of spices and ingredients, and you promised me it would be a simple recipe for one." I raise a brow.

He smirks, and my surgery panties go up in flames. "I've got a plan." I nod once and give him the universal gesture for *let's hear it*. "We're going to do a gorgeous traditional pot of red beans and rice."

My stomach instantly growls at the thought. I fucking love red beans and rice. But… "Doesn't that take like… forever?"

He shrugs. "It can, if you do it on low and simmer it all day or overnight. But you're actually giving me an opportunity to do something I've been wanting to try for a while now." He grabs my hand, when normally he'd take the reins of the shopping cart the participant would be pushing, and it feels like static zings up to my elbow from our connected palms, making me shiver. He must feel it too, because he stares at our hands with fascination before seeming to snap out of it and pulls me up the aisle.

I don't say a word as he takes me three rows down to the utensils aisle. I just follow along and wonder what we're getting as I try my best to ignore the intense feelings radiating from our connection. A steady *zing, zing, zing* matches the rapid beat of my heart, filling me up until I'm ready to burst with energy.

"Here." He stops, and I'm barely able to halt before I run into him again. I look to where he's pointing, and an overwhelming sense of loss takes over when he lets go of my hand to reach for the item on the bottom shelf. When he stands, holding it out for the cameraman to see, I tilt my head in confusion.

"An Instant Pot? Aren't those for like… making big family meals really fast?" I question.

"Or one meal really fast, if you don't put in as much." He winks. "But I think I'm going to teach you the art of meal prepping. That way you can make your individual meals that are ready to eat ahead of time, which will taste much better than something that's been flash-frozen and boxed in cardboard for months."

I pooch my lips out, not really sure how I feel about the idea. "You do know that anyone with an ounce of Cajun blood in them would rather die before considering using an Instant Pot to cook an authentic Cajun meal, right?"

"Do you have Cajun blood?" he asks, tilting his head to the side with curiosity.

"Not technically," I admit.

"Then that means you'll survive." He grins.

I lift a brow, giving him just a little more shit, because I love this banter. "Isn't meal prepping for body builders or people on a diet? I'm not about that life." I may go to the gym a few times a week just to keep my muscles a little toned, but most of my exercise comes from walking around my beautiful city. I rarely have to use my car.

"That's what comes to mind for most people when they hear the words meal prep, but in all actuality, it's just a fancier version of reheating leftovers and packing your lunch for the next day," he tells me with a smile, and dear God I have never seen such a beautiful smile on a man. I need to ask him his teeth-whitening regimen, because his perfectly straight grill is blinding.

When I snap out of the spell he put me under with his grin, I finally reply, "Well, when you put it that way, it sounds pretty nifty. Let's do it."

At the sexy quirk of his eyebrow, the one only I can see since he's turned profile toward the camera, I bite my lip and hold in the giggle that wants to escape. He obviously wants to jump on my "let's do it," but is forced to stay professional while the cameras are rolling.

Oh, this could be fun.

He must see the mischief playing in my eyes, because he gives me the slightest shake of his head, to which I give him a second's flash of a smirk.

Challenge: Accepted.

"So, we should probably get a buggy, huh?" The words are barely out of my mouth before one of the crewmembers returns with one and lets go as she pushes it toward us. Curtis catches it with his one empty hand before swooping it around to take hold of the handle, placing the Instant Pot into the empty shopping cart.

"Your 'buggy' awaits, *cher*. God, southern girls are adorable," he says, using his fingers to make quotation marks around the word buggy, and also impressing me with a decent attempt at the term of endearment. Most people want to say it like the singer's name or "share," but a true Cajun pronounces it "sha," meaning dear or sweet.

I know Curtis is from California from conversations he's had with other participants on the show, so I tell him, "Nice accent," as I take the handle of the cart.

"I had a Cajun sous-chef once. I used to love hearing him talk and would spend our time cooking together trying to mimic his accent," he explains. "I'm surprised you don't have much of an accent, since you said you were born and raised here. You sound more... southern."

"My parents were from Virginia. But the Cajun accent you're thinking of is more southwest of here, a place officially known as Acadiana, where a bunch of Canadians settled back in the day," I explain elementarily.

He claps his hands and gives a little jump of excitement, making me smile. "Oh! A history lesson. If you're a fan of the show, you probably know I love hearing all about the history of the place I'm in each episode. So please, tell me all about it while I grab our ingredients."

I give a small nod and start to follow him up and down the aisles as he picks out each item we need. "Well, Acadians are the descendants of the French colonists who settled in Canada back in the 17th and 18th centuries. The area is now like... Nova Scotia and that creepy Prince Edward Island place."

"Creepy Prince Edward Island place?" He chuckles.

"Yeah, well, I guess it's not really creepy to most people, but my best friend Emmy went to check out some abandoned and supposedly haunted spots there while she and Dean were visiting for their show. She told me some stories that were *creeeeeeeepy,*" I singsong. "Anyway, the Acadians got kicked out because the British thought they were fighting for the wrong team, and they ended up settling down southwest of here along the Gulf of Mexico. The accent is Louisiana French and a crapload of dialects of North American English." I shrug. "Here in New Orleans though, we have a huge mix of accents, since we're in the middle of a bunch of different parishes—or counties, as the other states call them. But what's interesting, at least to me, is the majority of the people from here sound almost like a perfect mix of Southern and working-class New Yorkers."

He seems to think about it for a second, and then smiles. "Now that you mention it, that is exactly what they sound like. Hm!" He stops in the middle of the aisle, looking back at me. "Lafayette really nailed the accent on *True Blood*, huh?"

I pout my lip. "Rest in peace, Nelsan Ellis. He was seriously my favorite character."

"Right? That actually made me really sad when I heard he passed away. Like, most of the time you hear about a celebrity dying, and it's like, aw, that sucks, and you kinda just go about the rest of your day. His made me genuinely sad that we wouldn't see him around anymore," he tells me.

I'm nodding my agreement before he's even done speaking. "Same."

We just stand there staring at each other for long moments, basking in the fact that we totally get each other in this conversation, and it's not until someone who I assume is the director yells "Cut!" that we snap out of it and turn to look at him.

"Y'all went off on a bit of a dark path there for a lighthearted cooking show. Can we get back to the happier shit please, Casanova?" he aims at Curtis, and I bite my lip to keep from giggling.

Curtis rubs the back of his neck before nodding. "Yeah, sorry. That was kinda weird, huh?"

The director just shakes his head and points at him. "Action."

"Okay, so let me show you everything I've collected so far," Curtis says, coming to stand next to the cart. "In the spice aisle, I grabbed bay leaves, garlic, cayenne pepper, black pepper, thyme, and salt. And down a ways on the same aisle, I got some vegetable oil and chicken broth." He holds up each item for the cameraman to zoom in on. "I also got a bag of red beans and a bag of white rice. Now we just need to hit the produce section and the meat department."

As we start up the aisle, I murmur for only Curtis to hear, "Hm... I thought we were already in the *meat* department." And when he turns wide eyes to me, I smirk, glance down at his ass then back up, and wiggle my eyebrows, and he throws his head back and laughs. As many innuendos as he usually throws out on the show, I've never once seen anyone do anything but get red-faced and flustered around the man. I'm happy to be the one who finally dishes them out to him—pun intended.

When we're standing in front of the pork section, he gestures toward some gnarly looking hunks of meat wrapped in clear plastic. At my sneer, he smiles. "This is a ham hock."

"Looks like a prop out of one of the *Saw* movies," I comment, and he bites back another laugh.

"This is what gives the otherwise bland red beans and rice that delicious smoky and hearty flavor. Those little bits of meat you get in every bite comes from the pork literally falling off the bone while it cooks," he explains.

"Hm," I chirp with interest. "Learning has occurred."

He takes a few steps down and gestures at the many different varieties of sausage, and at my evil grin, he clears his throat and bites his lip, visibly collecting himself before stating, "There are literally hundreds of different sausages to choose from, but only one is just right for this dish." He sends a heated look directly to my pussy, and I swear to God my leggings nearly melt down my thighs.

Touché, motherfucker.

CURTIS

I HAVE A hard-on in the sausage section of a health food grocery store like some kind of twelve-year-old pervert, and there's absolutely nothing I can do about it. Any attempt at readjusting would not only be seen by the impish beauty in front of me, but it would also be caught on camera and live on, archived for my humiliation for years to come.

So I do what any rational man would do in this situation.

I grab hold of Erin and pull her in front of me, facing the sausages and turning our backs to the camera, even though that's a no-no in TV Hosts 101. I hear her little intake of breath when she feels the… pickle I'm in, pressing into her lower back, but I try to recover the scene and point to the ingredient we need.

"That, I'm sure you know, is the only sausage for the job, being a NOLA native and all," I tell her, and she coughs into her fist and nods, sending her ass back into me as she bends over to grab one. My knees nearly buckle at the feel of her round globes encased in tight black material pressing against the front of my thighs. And it takes every ounce of self-control I have not to grab hold of her hips and grind into her. I only pray that the angle we are to the camera makes it impossible to see just how close we are. When she stands again, she turns to face me, my throbbing erection now pressed into her soft stomach.

"Andouille," she states, and I nod.

"Super delicious, and even more fun to say. An-dooo-wee," I singsong, and she giggles, her stomach muscles flexing and making me groan. I literally cannot take anymore.

I take a step back and say without looking toward my crew, "Cut. I need a bathroom break." And glaring at Erin's muffled cackle, I turn on my heel and head toward the back of the grocery store, the tented front of my jeans leading the way.

I return a few minutes later after tucking my cock into the waistband of my jeans, since the fucker refused to go down no matter how many times I chanted the National Anthem or thought of saggy old lady tits. Because in my mind those saggy old lady tits would suddenly morph into Erin's perfect, perky handfuls inside her oversized tee with a David Rose quote from *Schitt's Creek*, my favorite TV show of all time. Which means she must really love it too, if she owns a shirt with a quote from the show. And then all I could picture was her and me cuddled up in my big-ass bed binge-watching all the seasons, which led to me imagining doing all sorts of other things in said big-ass bed. So Operation: Get Rid of My Fucking Hard-On was a big, fat fail, and all I could do was hide him away behind my belt buckle.

"Feeling better, princess?" Carlos asks as I approach, and I shoot him the bird before taking my place in front of the sausages once more. Erin still sports a cute all-knowing smile, and I narrow my eyes at her.

I roll my head around on my shoulders to release a little tension and then nod at Martin, my director, letting him know I'm ready. After he calls action, I pick up where we left off.

"So, all we have left are a couple things in the produce section, and then you get to take me home," I say, the usual flirtatious line I use on the females at this point in the show.

But instead of the normal reaction from the participant—a stuttered response and pink cheeks—Erin throws the sausage into the cart, grabs hold of the handle, and starts sashaying toward the produce, tossing over her shoulder, "I don't suppose you're going to come up with a way to add cucumbers, squash, and eggplants to the red beans and rice, because I'm starting to sense a theme here." She turns just enough to eye my ever-present but hidden erection before meeting my stare with a smirk.

I hear Carlos bark out a laugh before covering it with a cough, and Martin murmurs, "Make a note to edit that out," to his assistant.

My poor, throbbing dick will soon turn into a terrible case of blue balls at this rate, so I quickly snatch up the remaining ingredients without any more banter. "A yellow onion… celery… green onion… a green bell pepper… and fresh parsley. Boom, time to party," I say, and hightail it toward the checkout.

Four

ERIN

WHEN WE EXIT the grocery store, Curtis turns right toward the small parking lot just as I turn left to head home. I hear his feet stop abruptly on the asphalt, and then he calls out, "Did you park somewhere else?"

"Nope, I walked. I'm only a few blocks this way," I respond, turning around to face him.

"We have all our equipment and vehicles, so uh…." He looks at a loss, and I tilt my head to watch him with interest. I've never seen him like this—on TV, I mean. He's always sure-footed and perfectly together in every episode. It's amusing to see him so… fish out of water.

Usually on the show, Curtis rides shotgun in the person's car. There's a cute little getting-to-know-you type scene before they get to their house and start cooking. I guess I've thrown a wrench in that plan.

The cameraman speaks up. "Why don't you walk home with her? I can follow with the camera while everyone else meets us at her place with the cars. That way we still get the footage between the store and the participant's home," he suggests.

"Good thinking, Carlos," the director says, and as I'm giving them my address, a tiny woman wearing a headset attaches a small microphone inside the neck of my tee and then does the same thing to Curtis. Martin and the rest of the crew minus Carlos head to the parking lot, one of them pushing the shopping cart full of our groceries.

I point over my shoulder with a small smile. "It's just right up here."

When we hit the sidewalk, Curtis takes hold of my arm and tugs me toward the building so that he's the one walking next to the street. When I look up at him, he doesn't seem to realize what he's done, and I find it ridiculously charming that the chivalrous act was just part of his nature. Say what you will about girl power, feminism, et cetera. I, for one, always thought it was a shame I missed out on the era of gentlemen.

I don't realize I've let out a small chuckle until I feel his eyes on me and he asks, "What's so funny?" with a little smile on his kissable lips.

"Nothing, really. You're just… not what I expected you'd be like in real life," I admit.

"Oh yeah? What did you think I was like?" he questions curiously.

We stop at an intersection and push the button to cross the street. "No offense, but you come off kind of cocky on the show."

He lifts a brow. "And I don't in person?"

"Well, sort of. You're more playful than cocky. And I wouldn't have thought you to be the kind of guy to take the time and conscious effort to make sure you're the one walking closest to the street instead of me," I confess.

He smiles broadly. "My yaya would love to hear you say that."

"Your yaya?" I prompt.

"My grandmother raised me," he replies quietly, and oh how I'd love to dig deeper into that, but now doesn't seem like an appropriate time, with the camera rolling and all.

"She taught you well then," I say instead, grinning up into his gorgeous blue eyes, and they twinkle back in the setting sun's light.

"I even open doors and pull out chairs," he adds, playfully puffing out his chest, and I giggle.

"The opening doors thing is nice, but I never understood the chair thing. Like, when is the lady supposed to sit? Does she sit down after he pulls it out and he has to like, shimmy her forward until her legs are under the table, or like, is it perfectly timed to where he pushes it under her butt just as she's sitting down? You'd think that could be quite the gamble if the timing was off." I pooch out my lips in contemplation.

He laughs loudly. "How about I show you once we cook this meal?"

I nod once. "Deal."

We cross the street, and the sidewalk narrows, his muscular bicep bumping into me as he avoids the many posts along the way. "Sorry." He reaches out and steadies me. "The balconies of all the buildings are gorgeous, but the sidewalks aren't quite wide enough to share with guys like me," he says, looking up at the cover above us.

"Galleries," I correct absently, hopping over a crack in the cement.

"What?"

I meet his curious face. "A balcony doesn't have these posts or columns and doesn't stick out as far from the building. A gallery sticks out about as far as the sidewalk and has these to support them," I explain, pointing to the iron poles that go from the ground up to the second story.

"Learning has occurred," he repeats my earlier words with a crooked grin. "What else you got?"

I bite my lip, thinking of some fun facts to tell him about the area. "Well, back in the day, people could tell how wealthy you were by the number of posts you had holding up your gallery." At his lifted brow, I continue, "They charged a tax for every post you had, since the sidewalk was owned by the city. So if you had enough dough to pay for a shi— crapload of poles, then you obviously had lots of money to blow." Carlos is so stealthy behind us I totally forgot he was there until my potty mouth almost showed her ugly head.

"Hm! You're full of cool information. I seriously wanted to take one of those ghost tours while I was here, but I might just ask you to be my tour guide instead," he says, nudging me gently with his arm, and the contact instantly hardens my nipples to a painful degree. I'd been trying my best to ignore the physical reactions my body was having to his accidental bumps, but this purposeful one cuts through my defenses.

"Psh! Those ghost tours are fun as hell. Let's just go on one together. I know a couple of the guides with the best stories, and like ninety-eight percent of them are true." I lift my brows with excitement before understanding I basically just asked him out on a date.

And that's exactly what he thinks too, because the next words out of his mouth are "It's a date."

Thankfully, I don't have to awkwardly find an excuse to correct my blunder before we reach my house. "This is it," I tell him, and he looks up, then at the door, and then takes a few cautious steps out into the middle of the narrow road after looking both ways even though it's a one-way street. He takes in the glory of Emmy's and my home, eyes and mouth wide open.

"This is where you live?" he asks with awe in his voice.

"Yep," I reply, popping the P.

"Like… is it like in New York, where it's offices or a storefront on bottom and then your place is a super tiny apartment above?" He tilts his head, his eyes on the second story.

"Nope." I pop the P again, pulling out my key and unlocking the front door.

I turn to watch his head bob up and down as he counts, his eyes going from the left side of the building to the right. "One, two, three, four, five, six, *seven*. You have seven posts holding up your gallery. You must be *loaded*," he jokes.

I shake my head. "Nuh-uh. Corner lot, baby. We got thirteen of these bitches." I grimace and cover my mouth. "Oops, I mean—"

"Bitches is fine. We're a cable network." Curtis chuckles, jogging back up onto the sidewalk and coming to stand behind me in the doorway just as a van and two cars stop in front of the building.

Martin rolls down the window of the van. "Where should we park?"

"On that side of the street wherever you see open spots. Hope you're good at parallel parking," I answer, and he nods, giving a little salute before he pulls forward slowly to find somewhere to park.

The last car stops next to us and the trunk pops open, showcasing all our paper bags. Following Curtis's lead, I grab two bags as he grabs the last one and the cardboard box containing the Instant Pot before using his elbow to shut the trunk. The car then pulls forward to find parking as we head inside the front door.

CURTIS

"THIS PLACE IS incredible," I murmur, taking in the bottom floor of Erin's home. The décor is a museum's worth of architectural finds, pictures, and paintings, and I instantly recognize photos of Amelia Savageman's parents.

"Have you met them before?" Erin asks, obviously reading the recognition on my face.

"Yes. Fascinating people. I met them when they came to watch Dean and their daughter accept a network award for their show. But the question is, why do you have all their stuff in your house?" I ask, taking in all the Egyptian artifacts around the foyer and living room, still holding the grocery bag and Instant Pot in my arms, because I haven't made it to the kitchen yet. There's just too much to take in.

"Emmy and I are roommates. Well, sorta. We've lived together since we graduated high school. Her parents relocated to Egypt when she was little and she lived here with her grandma. And when she passed away, I promised I'd stay here so Emmy wouldn't be alone. But when she met and married Dean and joined his show, she basically demanded me not to move out. So I guess I'm the groundskeeper of the manor," she says the last bit with a put-on British accent, and I grin.

"So ancient Egypt isn't your décor of choice?" I ask, my eyes meeting hers.

She scrunches her nose with a shake of her head. "Definitely not. Em gets irritated with me when I don't remember half the shit she tells me about all this." She gestures toward a photo of a statue that looks like a dog head on a human body. "If it were my house, it'd be Joanna'd the fu—reak out." She side-eyes Carlos still standing in the foyer, his camera aimed at us.

"Joanna'd?" I prompt.

"Joanna Gaines? *Fixer Upper*? She's like, my ultimate girl crush. Oh crap, wait. Different network. Sorry." She shrugs.

I wave my hand, dismissing her worry. "That's like, farmhouse stuff, right? Shabby chic?"

She nods. "Exactly. I love it. All whites and grays, black-and-white buffalo plaid, silver tin canisters, shiplap *everythiiing*," she singsongs. "But, alas, this isn't my house, so pyramids and hieroglyphics it is. At least down here. My room looks like Joanna herself decorated it. I've tagged her ass in like, fifty-eight thousand Instagram posts, but she's never responded. By now she probably thinks I'm some creeper stalker and is ready to serve a restraining order if I show up in Waco, Texas. And I totally wouldn't blame her. After all, I did start growing my hair out and parting it down the middle, so it'd be just like hers." She puts her pointer finger up to her lips as if it's a secret, winks up at me, and then spins on her heel, leaving me to follow after her while my brain is still stuck on the mention of her bedroom.

We enter the open concept kitchen with a big island in the center that's lined with barstools along one side. I set the bag and Instant Pot next to the two bags Erin brought in and vaguely notice as Carlos moves to the far corner of the room with his camera on his shoulder.

"So, what now?" Erin asks, glancing between the grocery bags and me.

"Normally, this is when most women would go into panic mode and go change their clothes and put on as much makeup as humanly possible while the crew gets everything set up for the kitchen scenes," I tell her, and I watch as her nose scrunches adorably.

"I always thought that looked funny while watching the show. One minute, they look like normal people who just went grocery shopping, and the next, it's as if they're cooking dinner dressed for a night out on the town," she admits, and I chuckle.

"Yeah, and that's just what actually aired. We've had women come down dressed in straight-up ball gowns, because they thought they needed to put on the nicest thing they had in their closet. Luckily, we got them to change before we started shooting again."

She looks up at me with curiosity. "Do you think I should go change?" She brushes back a strand of her long hair that's fallen over her shoulder in her ponytail.

I immediately shake my head. "And miss replaying one of my favorite episodes of *Schitt's Creek* in my head every time I look at your shirt for the remainder of the evening? I think not."

Her eyes light up as if I just told her she won a million dollars. "David Rose is my spirit animal," she breathes.

"I love David, but Moira's accent and vocabulary give me life," I confess with a grin.

"Such an underrated show. Like, I wish everyone in the world watched it so they could experience how amazing it is, but at the same time, I kind of love that it's just got a cult following. Like… it's our dirty little secret."

She giggles, and it's the sweetest sound I've ever heard. I can only imagine how great her full-on belly laugh would sound, laughing out loud while watching the riches-to-rags family figure out simple tasks like how to "fold in the cheese."

"I would have a field day shrinking them if they were real people. The way they grew as people from the first season to the last, oh my God. It was a beautiful thing. At first, you thought there was no hope for them. They were… spoiled and selfish human beings with absolutely no relationship between the parents and their two grown children. But then losing all their money and being forced to live in adjoining rooms in a rundown motel in a town Johnny bought David as a joke because of its name—Schitt's Creek—it was such a pleasure to watch their fish-out-of-water story. Pure genius."

I'm nodding the entire time she's speaking, watching the passionate expressions play across her beautiful face. And when she's done speaking, I latch on to something she said. "You'd enjoy 'shrinking' them?"

Her head bobs once. "I'm a psychologist. It's kinda my thang."

My eyebrows shoot up in surprise.

She smirks and props a hand on her hip. "What? Don't I look like a highly respected doctor of the mind?" She gestures to her messy hair then her leggings.

I almost swallow my tongue trying to reel in my shocked look. "No, no, no… it's not tha—"

"No, no, no, I don't? Wow, Curtis. Way to make a gal want to go throw on one of the ball gowns she has just lying around…."

Before I realize what they're doing, my hands are cradling her delicate jawline, tilting her head back so she looks up into my eyes as I bring our bodies almost as close as they were when she ran into me at the store. "I'm sorry. I made the poor, sexist, chauvinistic judgment that a woman as incredibly stunning as you wouldn't choose a job as difficult and consuming as what I imagine a psychologist to be. I would think it'd take extremely hard work and dedication to become a highly respected doctor of the mind, as you so eloquently put it, which in my experience, women near your beauty tend to avoid or choose an easier route in life, like a profession that utilizes the way they look, not how great their minds are."

Her eyes dilated not even halfway through my little apology, and the weight of her head in my palms grew heavier as she melted against me. My lips twitch as she whispers, "I was just fucking with you," but she doesn't move away, seeming hypnotized. "And you've been in California too long if that's what you believe beautiful women do."

I say only loud enough for her to hear, "If there wasn't a Virgin Islander with a camera standing fifteen feet away who loves nothing more than to make gag reels and give me shit for things that happen while recording the show, I'd kiss you like you've never been kissed before."

Her throat moves near where my hands still cup her jaw as she swallows deeply, and my eyes watch her mouth as she speaks. "While that kiss sounds wonderfully tempting, it's the mention of a gag that makes me want to meet you in the pantry for a round of Seven Minutes in Heaven."

My knees nearly buckle as my cock stands at full attention when I see her face morph instantly from its drooling hypnotized state to a wicked smirk as she finally takes a step back.

Holy. Fuck.

Is she still fucking with me?

I can't tell for the life of me if she's playing some sort of game or if she really is a naughty minx who wants to meet me for a quickie.

Her quick glance to my once-again-tented pants and then her satisfied smile tells me it may be a little of both.

At the sound of everyone coming through the front door, I don't follow her retreat, narrowing my eyes at her chirped "Moving along!" as I continue to wonder about this confident, sexy, and flirtatious woman. She's so different than any of the other participants I've had on the show. Hell, she's unlike *any* woman I've ever had the pleasure of meeting before.

I don't do relationships. With all my traveling for the show, plus spur of the moment trips to cook for celebrity dinner parties, or cater weddings for socialites and royals, I have zero time to give to a person I feel would deserve my devotion. I love what I do. I worked fucking hard as hell to get to where I am today.

I'm no celibate saint, but I am also not some love-'em-and-leave-'em fuckboy who lets a woman fall for him before dropping her as I hightail it to the next city. I especially never show any kind of interest in the guest I choose for the show. Ninety-nine percent of the time, they're in a relationship, wanting to cook a meal for their significant other. More often than not, they're married. But occasionally during my visits to different cities, someone will come along who I want to spend an evening with, but I make it completely clear that night is the only one we will spend together. I have gotten really lucky not to end up with a stalker or two, and I count my blessings nothing has happened to me like my friend Dean, who ended up in the tabloids when that chick claimed she was pregnant with his baby. Not once have I ever had a scare like that, thank God.

I've never met a woman I could see a future with. I've never met a woman who made me want to learn her every opinion, her every motivation, her every thought. And I've certainly never met a woman who affected my body in the ways Erin does—keeping me on my toes as much as she makes my dick hard. It's a mindfuck, and I'm enjoying it immensely.

And it's during this realization I decide…

She's mine.

Five

ERIN

CURTIS PULLS ALL the groceries out of the bags, displaying them neatly across the island before looking around with an expectant look on his face. Spotting the butcher block by the microwave, he chooses one of the knives in order to cut the tape holding the box closed then reveals what's inside.

Hefting the gadget out, the silver pressure cooker gleams under the kitchen light as he sets it on the countertop, cutting off all the plastic bubble wrap and tossing it back into the box after finding the instruction manual inside. He takes the time to wash the interior, which is super impressive for any guy if you ask me, before plugging it into the outlet on the side of the island.

Grabbing the bag of red beans, he finally looks up at the camera and begins to speak. "Some people would end up using canned beans if they didn't have time to soak their dried ones. But canned beans are full of not-so-healthy things like way too much sodium and preservatives. Normally, you'd want to soak your dried beans overnight to use the next day, but there's this handy little feature that allows you to quick-soak your beans in the Instant Pot in half an hour."

Before he can start rummaging through my drawers, I hand him a pair of scissors out of the pencil holder by the old-fashioned rotary phone sitting on the edge of the counter beneath the cabinets. He smiles at me then snips the bag open, and after requesting a colander and rinsing them off, he pours the beans into the pressure cooker.

"Put the beans inside, and then fill with water until the level is one inch above the beans," he instructs, so I pull down a measuring cup, turning on the tap.

"Does it matter if it's hot or cold water?" I ask over my shoulder.

"Nope," he replies, so I nod and begin the processes of filling the cup with water, turning to pour it into the pot with the beans, and repeating until there's enough inside.

"Very good. Now, I got you the Instant Pot Ultra. There are a few other models, but I wanted you to have the quickest one to cook your meals with, so you'd be less tempted to choose a frozen meal." He winks, and internally I melt, but on the outside, I stick my tongue out at him, making him chuckle. "We close the lid, select Pressure Cook mode, and set the timer for five minutes." He does all of those things, and then gestures toward it like he's a model on *The Price is Right*. "Would you like to do the honors?" he asks, pointing toward the Start button when my face is confused.

I shake my head at his antics then give in to the smile wanting to break free across my face. "Why not," I murmur and reach across him to push the button, my forearm brushing against his rigid stomach, which makes my core clench just thinking about what it must look like beneath his stark-white polo shirt that does amazing things for his surfer boy good looks. I try to put my hormones in check, knowing I'm having a natural reaction as a woman to his obvious virility.

I don't realize I'm staring until he asks gently, "You okay?"

I blink, clearing my throat. "Uh, yeah. The whites of your eyes are just... really, *really* white," I say, facing the island and grabbing the empty plastic bag to have something to do with my hands.

"Ummm... thanks?" He chuckles, and I look up at him once more, seeing the curious look.

I roll my eyes, propping my hip against the island and facing him, crossing my arms over my chest before I explain, "I'm a psychologist, as we established earlier. And I was momentarily distracted by your many features that completely explain why most of the women on your show end up tripping over themselves and stuttering in your presence. You have one hundred percent of the attributes associated with virility."

"Virility? Like... what? Manliness?" He puffs out his chest and then runs his hand through his blond hair, making it stand in all different directions but somehow causing it to be even sexier than it already was.

"Sort of. It's the quality of having strength, energy, and a strong sex drive. Masculinity in its purest form. It's associated with vigor, health, sturdiness, and one's ability to father children. It's the male equivalent to a woman's fertility," I explain, my heart doing its usual pang when I refer to the subject.

Suddenly, he steps closer, his hand reaching out to lift my chin when otherwise I'd be looking away in order to hide the twinge of pain he obviously saw in my eyes. "You all right, sugar?"

One side of my mouth quirks up at the sweet endearment. "Yeah. Totally."

He has mercy on me in front of the crew and more importantly the camera, and drops the subject, a look of promise in his eyes telling me that he will be bringing this up in the future if he gets the chance.

The timer goes off, saving us from any awkwardness. "It's done already?" I ask.

"Not quite," he replies. "Now we wait for the Natural Pressure Release, or NPR. When this little float valve drops that means it's safe to open it."

"Safe? What, is it just like... really hot or something?" I ask. A cook, I am not. I have no clue how any of these fancy gadgets work. A microwave is about as technological as I get in the kitchen.

"A pressure cooker works by literally building pressure inside of it as the water begins to boil. The boiling water produces steam, and since it's trapped inside, completely sealed off, it causes the temperature to rise. The high temp and the pressure cause everything to cook quickly. So if you suddenly just busted open a pressure cooker without letting it release slowly, it could cause an explosion. And all that hot liquid inside plus flying parts could cause burns and all sorts of injuries and damage," he explains.

My eyebrows shoot up. "Hm. Noted."

"Since we have time while we wait for the NPR, why don't you tell me what these other virile features are?" he asks with a grin, propping his hip against the island and turning his towering body to face me.

"Well, there are the obvious ones. A narrow waist, a V-shaped torso, broad shoulders, and the fact you're just... stupidly tall. But then there are smaller details, like the facial features that are built by testosterone.

The strong, square jaw, a prominent brow ridge, high cheekbones. It all points to a healthy male who can make babies. Men with higher testosterone tend to be healthier, which women are biologically more inclined to be attracted to. So features indicating health point to a virile male as well. Nice, straight, white teeth, super clear eyes, clean and groomed hair, including facial hair, those sorts of things," I clarify.

"Fascinating," he murmurs, and he truly looks interested in everything I'm telling him, not just trying to fill the wait time with mindless chatter. "I've always been interested in psychology. As a matter of fact, cooking started out as a form of therapy for me." The moment the words are out of his mouth, his eyes close, he slumps for a moment, and then says over his shoulder to the crew, "Fuck, edit that out, would you please, Martin? The last thing I need is tabloid reporters delving into my past more than they already try to."

"No problem, Curt," he replies, pointing at his assistant to make the note, which surprises me.

One would think tidbits like that would garner more attention for the show, causing higher ratings and in the end more money, and that someone like Martin wouldn't want to cut something as valuable as that out. It speaks volumes about this team, and even more about Curtis himself, if they are willing to protect him at such a high cost.

"Man," he murmurs, running his hand through his hair. "Been a while since I had to get them to cut something for me. You're just… so easy to talk to. I forgot we weren't alone for a minute there." He gives me an almost shy smile.

"Well that's a good thing, I guess. Seeing as it's my job to get people to open up to me." I reach out and squeeze his forearm in reassurance, since he still looks somewhat flabbergasted he spilled something he obviously usually keeps close to the vest. When his eyes glance down to my hand wrapped around his sinewy arm, I let go, using my still-tingling fingertips to tuck a stray piece of hair back behind my ear.

"So… what do you do as a psychologist? I assume you're a therapist, but what is your specialty?" he asks. He picks up the package of sausage and cuts open the wrapper, and I immediately grab the cutting board for him from on top of the refrigerator.

"I'm a clinical psychologist. So I meet with patients to diagnose their problems, whether it's emotional, mental, or behavioral. Some, I send to other doctors in the practice I work for, like if I believe they have a certain disorder, but some I keep for myself, if it's emotional support they need. I'm not a psychiatrist, so I can't prescribe meds if they need that type of help. But if I believe I can help their issues through therapeutic methods, they become my personal patients," I explain.

He begins slicing the andouille into bite-sized disks, making the task seem effortless. When he gets halfway through the first link, he holds the knife out to me by its blade, and I hesitantly take hold of the handle. When he sees how awkward I am, trying to slice it the way he was doing, he steps up behind me, wrapping his long arm around mine and placing his giant hand around my much… *much* smaller one. I nearly whimper at the feel of his hard body pressed against my back, his heat seeping into my bones and instantly calming me while at the same time my heart feels like it's going to leap out of my chest.

"Let the knife do the work," he says gently, and I can feel his voice rumble in his chest where it rests against the back of my shoulders. He guides my hand to make three cuts, and when he lets go, I try it myself, succeeding in the effort and feeling proud I got it right.

"Whoa, that *is* much easier. Usually I end up just sawing through a steak or whatever." I glance up at him over my shoulder, excitement taking over my expression until I see just how close our faces are to each other. If I suddenly stood up on my tiptoes, we'd end up in that kiss he mentioned earlier, the one he promised would be like none I've ever experienced before. And being this close, seeing in high-definition and zoomed in to 200%, I can see just how plump his lower lip is. I can tell that not only are his teeth perfectly straight and white, but his breath is pure spearmint. His hint of a five-o'clock shadow promises just enough roughness to counter the softness of his mouth, and I have no doubt his promise would hold true.

His eyes are almost turquoise, and they're focused on my own mouth. And it's not until his head begins to descend, that the director clears his throat and says loudly, "I saw a porno that started like this once," that I finally snap out of my Curtis-induced stupor.

My head whips around to face forward and my body straightens, and Curtis steps to the side, but his hand that was wrapped around mine and the knife gently trails along my arm before resting on the small of my back, sending goose bumps along my skin. The heat from his big palm seems to sink into me then pool directly between my thighs, making them clench together in an attempt to soothe the ache beginning to make itself annoyingly known there. But I try to ignore it, instead focusing on the task at hand. I finish slicing the sausage the way he taught me, placing the knife down next to the pieces of meat on the cutting board.

"Perfect," Curtis murmurs, his voice like butter. "I'd like to point out that this is smoked andouille sausage. If you don't have this available in your area, any smoked sausage will work. This one has a little kick to it, so if you don't like things spicy, you can always use any other smoked sausage you prefer."

As he takes hold of the onion, I hurry over to the refrigerator to grab another cutting board off the top, knowing he'll probably try to make me cut the evil tear-inducing vegetable myself. That ain't happening. Instead, I choose the bell pepper from out of the lineup of ingredients, pull out another knife, and try to imitate the way he's dicing... on the opposite end of the island, as far away from the onion as possible.

I see his grin even though he tries to hide it. He's so tall even ducking his head can't disguise it from my shorter height. He knows exactly what I'm doing, but again, he shows mercy and doesn't make me cut the onion. He's finished dicing it in warp speed, before I'm even halfway done with the bell pepper.

"Bowls?" he asks, running his pointer finger along the flat sides of the knife to clear off the remaining pieces of onion before setting it down.

My head nudges toward the cupboard above the microwave. "Bottom shelf of that cabinet."

He opens the white wooden cabinet door and collects several bowls we usually use for ice cream. When he comes back to the island, he scoops the onions into one bowl, the sausage into another, and then begins to chop up the green onion. He's starting on the celery as I finally finish with my bell pepper. It took me even longer because I kept stopping to watch with fascination how effortless he made it all look. If I tried to do it as fast as him, there would be a little part of me in every dish, and I don't mean a figurative piece of my heart.

I couldn't even catch what he does with the little bulbs of garlic. One second they looked like the fake white roots in net bags they have hanging around Italian restaurants for decorations, and the next, they look like off-white almonds. And then he took the flat of the knife and smashed them before mincing it all up.

"I didn't even know you could use a knife like that," I say, my face contorted in puzzlement, I'm sure.

"You'd be surprised all the different ways you can use kitchen utensils, other than their normal purpose," he murmurs, a teasing smile lifting one corner of his lips as his eyes meet mine for a split second, long enough for me to catch the naughty gleam in them.

Visions of him spanking me with a spatula immediately come to mind, followed up by a weird one of him moving a rolling pin up and down my back. I shake my head. Obviously, I'm not creative enough to come up with anything remotely sexy the way he seems to be able to, if the chuckle he tries to hide is any indication.

Just then, the Instant Pot goes off, letting us know the NPR is finished. "Now, we just press the Cancel button, and we can open the lid safely." He pushes the button, and then he carefully lifts the lid. "Drain, and then they're ready to cook." Which he does, pouring the beans in a bigger bowl I set on the counter for him.

"Next, we set this bad boy in the Sauté mode. We're going to brown the sausage in two tablespoons of vegetable oil." At that instruction, I hand him the little set of measuring spoons connected together with a plastic ring, but he winks at me, shaking his head. "What kind of teacher would I be if I did all the work for you? The rest is all you, sugar."

My nose scrunches up as I pout. "Fiiine," I drawl, grabbing the bottle of vegetable oil and filling the largest of the measuring spoons before dumping it in the pot. I take the bowl of sausage we cut up, and put that in as well. When I go to close the lid, he stops me.

"We don't have to close it just to brown the meat. We leave it in for about five minutes, continuously moving it around so it gets cooked evenly," he explains. "When that's done, we'll use a slotted spoon to remove just the sausage, leaving all those delicious juices in the bottom of the pot for our other ingredients to cook in."

No one could ever describe me as graceful if all they had to go by was watching me brown the meat inside the pot. I am pretty proud I don't spill anything or burn myself when I move the sausage from the pot to the bowl though.

"Now, add in the onion, celery, bell pepper, and garlic we prepared while the beans were soaking," he instructs, and when I'm finished, he tells me to use the same motion I did to brown the meat to now sauté the veggies until the onions are translucent, which takes another five minutes. "Perfect. Now, add one teaspoon of dried thyme… half a teaspoon of cayenne pepper… a teaspoon of salt… and one teaspoon of black pepper." He pauses between each ingredient, allowing me time to measure everything out with my handy little spoons. "And then we'll just stir that up for about thirty seconds to get the veggies nice and coated in our concoction we've created here."

"I didn't realize we'd actually like… cook inside the pot. I thought it was more like a crockpot, where you just toss everything inside and forget about it for a few hours," I admit, looking up at him as I stir. "But I have to say, it smells amazing, and it hasn't been hard at all."

"I think we both know that's a lie," he says quietly through gritted teeth, his lips not moving as he smiles back at me, and I have to clamp my teeth around my lips to keep from bursting into laughter. "Now…" He claps his hands, glancing down into the pot. "We're going to add in a fourth of a cup of chicken broth, and then use your wooden spoon to scrape up all the brown from the bottom of the pot. That's the good stuff, where we get a ton of the flavor. Also, we have to make sure we scrape everything off the bottom of the Instant Pot. They call it deglazing, and we need to do it before starting the pressure cooking."

"What'll happen if we don't deglaze it?" I ask, because that's just who I am as a person.

"It'll give us a burn message and won't work," he replies simply.

"Fair enough." This time, I do mess up a little, the liquid sloshing a bit as I try to do what he said. But he cleans up the little drops with a paper towel, his big body folding around mine so I don't have to stop what I'm doing. It takes everything in me not to press myself against him, an overwhelming urge to be as close to him as possible filling me up.

It confuses the hell out of me.

I haven't been in a relationship since I was twenty-three, almost a decade ago. With the way things ended with my ex, I've had zero aspiration to get close to a man, only for him to break my heart when he finds out I can't give him everything out of life men instinctively desire. Max and I had been together three years, engaged and two months away from our wedding date, when the doctor delivered his heartbreaking news. He left me a month later. With barely enough time to contact everyone to let them know the wedding was off so they could cancel all their travel arrangements. I'd never been more embarrassed and hurt in my entire life, and I swore to myself I'd never let that happen again, essentially swearing off any and all relationships with the opposite sex.

I haven't had a single problem with this deal with myself in the last eight years. So why, all of a sudden, am I wanting to rub up against Curtis like a cat in heat? Why do I want to nuzzle into his tall frame that makes me feel so extra small and feminine? Why do I want to curl up together and see just how many TV shows we're both obsessed with? And why in the world does a sense of loss take over my chest when I think about him leaving once we're done cooking?

I immediately regret him choosing something that would cook so quickly.

His deep voice snaps me out of my thoughts. "Next, we're going to add the rest of the four cups of broth the recipe called for, two large bay leaves, the beans we quick-soaked, and the ham hock." As I add the first three ingredients, he removes one of the ham hocks from the packaging, setting it delicately into the pot once I've stirred everything together. "*Now*, we get to set the pot and forget about it for forty-five minutes to an hour. Select Pressure Cook mode, set the timer for thirty minutes, and press Start. The rest of the time will be fooor…?"

"Natural Pressure Release?" I guess.

And he gives me a wide grin. "Exactly. See? I knew you'd get the hang of this. No more microwave meals for you, sugar."

I roll my eyes but can't help my genuine smile at his praise.

Dishing
~up~
Love

Six

CURTIS

HER SMILES ARE addictive. I'm beginning to crave them the way I used to crave admiration and praise in the cooking community. That's not to say I don't still enjoy all the attention I get for my abilities as a chef; I don't think anything could feel better than being wanted above all others for an important benefit dinner. I mean, how cool is it to think "Man, these people think my food is so bad ass they believe it's worth a thousand dollars a plate to bring in charitable donations for a good cause."

It's the same feeling of pride I get when I can make this beautiful yet closed-off woman smile. She's got some pretty sturdy walls built up around her. I don't know enough about her to make any assumptions. But I plan to change that starting now.

"All right, everybody, we've got about an hour break. Get yourself some dinner; you know the drill," Martin calls out, and I see Carlos put down his camera for the first time in hours.

Normally, everyone would immediately head for the front door, going out to the vans and cars for lunchboxes and smoke breaks. And everyone else sticks to the routine. But I stay behind, wanting to finally spend a moment alone with Erin to see if she may open up a little more without a camera and crew watching her every move.

She slumps onto a stool next to the island, sprawling her arms across the marble countertop as she puts her cheek to the cold surface. "I'm staaarviiing. I was just running to the freakin' store to grab a heat-up meal that would've taken three minutes and thirty seconds in the microwaaave," she whines, making me chuckle.

"Good Lord, woman, the least you could do is heat up a frozen pizza in the *oven* instead of the microwave," I say, moving toward the refrigerator. "Is there nothing you can snack on while we wait for it to cook?"

"The oven takes too long. Preheating sucks the life out of me," she replies before adding, "and all I have is random crap and condiments that don't go together."

"We'll see about that," I tell her, biting my lip as I take in all the "random crap" she has in her fridge and cabinets and spotting the perfect combination. She sits up at my "Ah-ha!"

"What did you find? Be careful not to poison me with rotten food. It's been a decade since I cleaned those condiments out. Does mustard even expire?" she asks, making me laugh.

"You have cream cheese… that's still good until the thirtieth," I say setting that on the counter. "Raspberry pepper jelly that hasn't even been opened yet…"

"Blech. That was in a gift basket I got from a patient. Who the hell eats a peanut butter and jelly sandwich with peppers? I just didn't have the heart to throw it out," she grumbles, and I chuckle once again. Has a woman ever made me laugh as much as she does?

"And a box of Wheat Thins that are, in fact, expired but—" I toss one into my mouth, testing the crunch. "—are still good. Not even stale yet."

She looks at me blankly. "Congratulations, Curtis. You've now discovered how a single woman lives in her bachelorette pad."

I purse my lips and hold her stare as I take out a Pyrex container I found in one of the cabinets, unwrap the cream cheese from its silver foil paper, place it into the container, and then heat it up in the microwave for just a few seconds, enough to soften the brick but not enough to melt it. I then pour the pepper jelly on top of it, sliding the combination and the box of crackers across the island to Erin and her scrunched face with its adorable wrinkled up nose.

"Dafuck is this?" she asks, and my nostrils flare with my effort to keep a straight face.

"Trust me" is all I say, and she narrows her eyes.

After a stare-down that lasts a full minute and eventually makes my dick hard once again—randy fucker—she finally gives in, pulling a single Wheat Thin out of the box.

"Do I fold in the cheese?" she asks, lifting a brow, and my whole face spasms trying not to laugh at her *Schitt's Creek* reference. She dips out a tiny bit of the jelly and cream cheese, using the corner of the cracker.

"Here goes nothin'," she says, acting more like she's on an episode of *Fear Factor* than in her kitchen tasting something made with simple ingredients. She squeezes her eyes closed and tosses the cracker in her mouth, chewing with a scared look on her face. Which quickly dissolves as she opens her eyes, a look of pure bliss coming over her every feature. "Holy shit!" She takes out another Wheat Thin and dips it into the mix, this time scooping a lot more onto the cracker before placing it in her mouth, her moans of pleasure making my balls draw up as she reaches for yet another cracker. "This is amazing!" she breathes, and I shake my head at myself, feeling overwhelming pride fill my soul at her reaction to something I made for her.

It's more than the regular feeling of achievement I get when someone praises the meal I've made. It's almost primal. My woman was hungry. I made her something to eat. She ate it, and not only is she getting the sustenance she needed to end her discomfort, but she thinks what I provided is "amazing."

Me Curtis.

You Erin.

Oo-oo, ah-ah.

Caveman grunt.

What. The. Fuck?

When she pours several crackers right onto the counter in order to make the process of dipping and devouring a little more streamlined, I laugh and take hold of her hands across the island.

"Don't fill up on snacks, sugar. You still have a whole meal coming in just… fourteen minutes," I tell her after glancing at the timer.

Her bottom lip pouts out as she whimpers with her mouth full, "Plus NPR time," giving me puppy dog eyes.

And I fall for her right then and there.

This sexy yet adorable, playful, spirited woman will be the end of Curtis Rockwell as we know him. From this moment forward, if I have anything to do with it, it's gonna be Curtis and Erin. Like that one song says, *"When they think of me, they think of you."* When everyone thinks about me, they're going to instantly think of her. If I go anywhere without her, the first thing out of anyone's mouth is gonna be "Where's Erin?" Never in my life have I ever wanted an attachment like that. Not once have I ever craved an association between me and another person. Sure, it's pretty nice having my name come up when people are talking about "the greats" of the chef world, but even being associated with the likes of Gordon Ramsay and Wolfgang Puck doesn't compare to the idea of pairing up with this beauty, currently making her lip quiver in an attempt to make me let her hands go so she can eat another cracker dipped in cream cheese and pepper jelly, acting as if it's the finest caviar.

And I can't deny her. I let her go, and she chomps down on the snack as if she thinks I might steal it out of her hand, grinning at me before pushing the container away.

"Put a lid on that sorcery, please, before I eat the whole damn thing," she requests, rolling the bag of Wheat Thins before closing the box. "I have so many regrets right now."

I lift a brow. "Did you eat it too fast?"

"No. I regret I never knew about that deliciousness. Do you know how many jars of jelly with peppers I've kept over the years, just waiting for them to expire so I could finally throw them out without too much guilt? At least like… twenty. All this time, I could've been enjoying this journey, Curtis," she says, her face twisted dramatically like she's actually disappointed in herself.

"Well, from now on, I'll make sure you don't miss any more food-related journeys. As long as you trust me, I'll take those taste buds on a magic carpet ride you'll never want to end," I promise, and I watch her face soften for a long moment before I see the window behind her eyes board itself back up.

During the rest of the break, she signs the show's standard contract giving us permission to air footage of her, and I teach her a quick and easy way to make rice—without burning the bottom half of it, as she warned me she has a habit of doing. I pull bits and pieces of information out of her, enough to learn this girl has walls around her like a fortress. They're incredibly high and armored, probably after years of reinforcing them. When I try to nonchalantly ask when her last relationship was, she immediately shoots me down with a change in subject, but not before

I see a flash of pain in her eyes. Whatever or whoever hurt her must've really done a number on her, which makes me admire her more for her profession, wanting to help others even after she'd been hurt herself. It makes me think she's pretty selfless, but at the same time, I wonder if she might be using her job to distract her from her past instead of dealing with it. To be honest, it makes her even more intriguing that I'm having to work to get to know her. Normally, the women I come into contact with can't *stop* talking about themselves.

When everyone comes back from break, we pick up where we left off making the meal.

"Taking our big spoon, I'm going to remove the ham hock from the pot—" I follow my own instructions as I say them out loud. "—and place it on our cutting board." I put the spoon back into the pot so it doesn't make a mess on her countertop, since I didn't see a spoon rest when I was going through her kitchen earlier. "Now, I'm going to chop it up into bite-sized pieces. I'll do it this time, just because our student here looks like she's about to fall out and shouldn't be wielding a knife." I wink at the camera and then grin at Erin, who looks grateful even as she sticks her tongue out at me. "When that's done—" I finish the last three cuts. "We throw away the bone, and then take about a cup of the beans out of the pot and put them into a bowl."

Erin hands me a bowl before I've barely gotten the words out. She's been doing that this entire time, practically reading my mind and producing everything I need. It's been a dream to cook with her, like a dance in which we both know the choreography. The editing process for this episode should be a piece of cake, since usually they have to cut out long minutes of rummaging through drawers and cabinets and such. This time, they'll only have to worry about making sure it reaches our TV-PG rating, assuring the footage of the constant boner I've had takes its final resting place in the cutting room garbage can.

"Okay, now my lovely assistant is going to take a fork—" I hand her one out of the drawer I'm standing in front of. "—and mash the beans."

She takes the bowl from my hand and makes quick work of smashing the red beans up. When she gives it back to me, there's a slight tremor to her fingers, and suddenly teasing her about being hungry is the last thing on my mind. I set the bowl down on the counter, ignoring the camera and other people in the room, my only concern being the woman I take hold of, forcing her to look up at me.

"Are you all right, babe? When you were saying you were starving earlier, I thought you were just playing around and being dramatic." I search her eyes, discovering surprise there along with a bit of discomfort.

"I skipped lunch today and took on an emergency patient," she tells me.

"And what did you have for breakfast?" I demand.

Her face turns guilty. "I don't normally eat breakfast."

I feel my face heat with anger, and it startles me. She must read the look though, because she tries to make a joke.

"Those clever millennials. They took skipping breakfast and made it into a fad, calling it 'intermittent fasting.'" She snorts, her mouth smiling but her eyes looking uncomfortable.

I hate that expression almost as much as I hate that she hasn't eaten all day, so I give in to her joke for just a moment. "Aren't you technically a millennial, sugar?"

She scoffs. "I prefer Generation Y. I sleep with a top sheet and have beautiful cursive handwriting, thank you. But they were totally onto something when they invented avocado toast. That shit is gooood."

I ask as calmly as I can, "So what you're saying is the only thing you've eaten today is the little snack I made you during the break?"

She shrugs. "Hence why my ass was at the grocery store getting a quick heat-up meal."

I shake my head. "Unacceptable."

She gets a haughty look on her face, but before she can tell me off for my bossy tone, I cut her off.

"From now on, you prepare yourself meals in advance using this handy appliance I just gifted you with. When you get down to the last day's-worth of meals, you take one hour of your time to run to the grocery store, grab the list of ingredients I'm going to leave you with for several different recipes, and cook them before boxing them up the way I'm about to teach you. You take one to work with you, so you don't even have to leave your office in order to grab lunch. You heat one up when you get home and eat it for dinner. That means, during the day, you'll only have to fix yourself one meal. Breakfast. The most important meal of the day. You are obviously a very intelligent woman, one who needs fuel for her brain in order to help her patients throughout the day.

Your brain runs on carbohydrates. It does not run on an empty freaking stomach. So now, sit your ass on the stool and let me feed you."

Her mouth opens and closes a few times, a look of shock in her beautiful eyes, but finally she just nods, pulls herself out of my hold on her, and sits on the stool Martin brings around from the other side of the island.

"All right, Carlos. Keep up. I'm going to make this fast," I say, taking hold of the bowl of beans Erin mashed. When he points at me, I begin. "We return the chopped ham hock and mashed red beans to the Instant Pot, and then add our sausage we browned in the beginning. If you want the dish less spicy, leave the sausage out and you can just add a few of your slices to the plate."

I begin to mix all the pieces together with the spoon once more. "Stir everything together, cooking in Sauté mode, and then let it all thicken to your desired consistency, about five minutes." I turn around, pulling two bowls out of the cabinet behind me. I dish out some of the rice I prepared during our break into both bowls, setting them on the counter near the cutting board.

"I'm going to chop up our parsley, the last ingredient left in our recipe, so we can garnish with it and more of the green onions we prepared in the beginning," I say, mindlessly cutting up the herb while keeping one eye on Erin just to make sure she's truly okay. The way she talked about not eating today was way too nonchalant, as if it's a frequent occurrence. The thought sets my ass on fire, making my hackles rise. I don't like the idea of her not taking the time to care for herself while focusing all her energy on other people. Yes, that just adds to my reasoning that she's a good and selfless person, but it makes this feeling of protectiveness overwhelm my every emotion. I don't understand it, but I go with it. My instincts have never steered me wrong before, and because everything inside me has been screaming this woman belongs with me since practically the moment I laid eyes on her, I'm pretty sure it's just part of wanting to protect what is mine.

"Alrighty. It's time to taste the fruits of our labor, sugar," I tell her, trying to put on a more cheerful tone than I had minutes ago, knowing the camera is rolling and wanting them to have actual usable footage. I don't want to have to reshoot anything. When we're done with this, I want to kick everyone out, share our first meal, and then devour every last inch of this woman next to me. Whether it be physically or mentally. I want to learn everything about her, and I can't do that unless I have the opportunity to get her truly alone, without the worry of my crew walking in at any minute, and chip away at her walls.

I dish out the red beans mixture on top of the rice in each bowl, sprinkle the parsley and green onion on top, and then angle the bowl toward Carlos so he can zoom in on the contents. When he gives me a thumbs-up, I grab the fork, stick it in the rice and beans, and hand it to Erin, giving her a pointed look that clearly says "Eat."

As she stirs and blows on the food inside the bowl, I make my own plate then pull the other stool around the island to sit next to her there at the counter. Normally, I would've had the guest make place settings at their dining table for whoever they were cooking for. But like all things with Erin, this episode is different. We were cooking for just the two of us—for just her, really—so this laid back ending just… fits, even though it makes me a little sad to think about the gorgeous woman eating here alone every night.

But if I have my way, she'll never have to worry about eating dinner alone ever again.

Dishing
~up~
Love

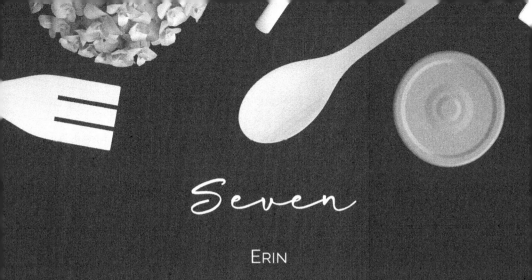

Seven

Erin

"DEAR SWEET BABY Jesus in a handbasket, this is amazing," I groan, closing my eyes and tilting my head back as I chew the next bite. "Sweet, sweet nectar of the gods." I swallow.

I feel Curtis's eyes on me, but I don't look over as I shovel more red beans and rice into my mouth.

"So, you think all the Louisiana natives would forgive me for using an Instant Pot if they could taste this dish?" I hear the smile in his voice.

"Never. But if we took it to a potluck in a different serving dish, they'd never have to know," I reply, making him chuckle.

"I'd call that a win in my book." After a pause, he puts on his TV host voice, the same one I've listened to during countless episodes while waiting for Emmy's show to come on. "Another successful meal after taking a Chef… to Go."

After a beat, the room goes from perfectly quiet to bustling as Martin calls "That's a wrap!" and everyone starts packing up their equipment. The lighting comes down first, the room instantly dimming to its normal soft light, and as I look around, wondering if I'm supposed to do anything, Curtis rests his hand on my thigh, shaking his head.

"Finish eating, sugar. They'll take care of everything else," he tells me, and I watch as I take another bite.

One of the crew members begins cleaning the kitchen, and I halfway feel bad about it. It's feels weird having someone clean up after me when I've done it all alone for so long. When she gets to the Instant Pot on the island next to Curtis, he holds up his hand to stop her, swallowing his bite.

"Don't worry about that, Rachel. I've still gotta teach her how to meal prep," he says, and her eyes widen.

"Oh crap. Were we supposed to film that? Carlos already has his camera and stuff packed up. But I can run to remind them if you—"

Curtis shakes his head. "Don't even think about it. We're done for the day."

I don't see the look he gives her, because she's on the other side of him, his head turned in her direction. But the way her eyebrow lifts before her eyes come to me then back to him lets me know he gave her a signal indicating he wants everyone out so we can be alone.

The idea is both stimulating and worrisome.

Curtis is unlike any other man I've come across. He's not intimidated by me whatsoever. Which is admittedly refreshing. I go out all the time and spend evenings talking with all sorts of men. But the second they find out I'm a psychologist, you can see a steel wall come crashing down from its hidden spot in the ceiling of their mind, immediately shutting me out. They never want me picking them apart, which I assume they think I do by having a deep and meaningful conversation with them in a dimly lit bar at my favorite two-top table in the corner.

Not only does Curtis keep himself open to me, but he also had to catch himself from revealing too much in front of the rolling camera. Not only is Curtis unintimidated by me, but he also has no qualms being all bossy and putting me in my place. I *know* I should take better care of myself. I just don't have anyone around to keep me in check when I get lazy and put everyone else's needs before mine. I can't help it. I'm a nurturer by nature. And knowing I'll never get to put that part of me to use for what it was made for, I direct it onto my patients and my friends. And since my only real friend ran off and got married and travels the world, I confess I get a little depressed and don't worry too much about my own well-being—hence why I put off things like… eating until I feel like I'm going to die.

When the bustling ends, the room is deafeningly quiet as I hear the door shut behind the crew. I scrape every last grain of rice and every morsel of the beans and meat into the spoon before savoring the very last bite.

"I swear I could lick the bowl," I say before lifting my eyes to Curtis, who has been watching me with a little smile on his face. His eyes twinkle as they catch my every movement, and I squirm on my stool. "I'd say you could take a picture to make it last longer, but you have hours of footage of me now, so what's the point."

"How is it that a person such as yourself, whose job it is to help people better themselves and teach them ways to take care of themselves, doesn't apply it to their own life?" he asks. But it's not in a scolding, accusatory way. He doesn't give off any vibes of judgement. His tone is purely curious, as if he wants to understand me.

I place my bowl down on the counter, putting my elbow there as well to lean my temple on my fist as I think about my answer. "I guess there's a reason someone came up with that saying 'practice what you preach.'" I shrug. "I use up all my energy on everyone else until there's none left over for myself. That way I can sleep at night." I sniff out a sad little laugh. "Wow. That went dark." I smirk.

He nods, looking down into his bowl for a silent moment before setting it on the counter next to mine and glancing at his watch. "It's 9:28," he murmurs to himself, pulling out his phone from his pocket. "What's the name of the best haunted tour company you were talking about?"

I give him the name and watch him google it, pulling up the website and clicking on the Buy Tickets link.

"You don't have patients on Saturdays, right?" he asks out of left field.

"No, I'm just always available to them by phone," I reply, and before I can stop him, he purchases two for tonight's tour at eleven. "Uuummm…"

"Shhh… just go with it," he whispers, putting a finger to my lips, and my automatic reaction takes over. I bite him.

He jumps a little in surprise, pulling his hand back before his eyes go wide. And then he throws his head back, letting out a laugh that makes me smile before I'm suddenly squealing as he lifts me into the air. I feel like I'm flying he's so tall, and my heart races until my ass meets the countertop of the island.

"Did you seriously just bite me?" he asks, and we look down at his pointer finger between us and see the little teeth marks.

Up on my counter, I'm able to be eye-to-eye with him, and I make out the mischievous twinkle there mixed with the shock.

"Yeah, my bad. It was my first response to something being in my face," I reply, grimacing a little in apology.

He lifts a brow. "So, note to self...."

My lips pooch out at that as I lift my own brow. But before I can comment, he inserts, "We need to prep all your meals. You wouldn't happen to have a food scale, do you?"

I tilt my head to the side, my expression clearly stating "Really?"

"That's a no. Okay, well, we need to get you one of those in order to do this properly in the future, but for now, we can just guess. If I were Tupperware, where would I be?" he asks, and I try to ignore the bit about the future. He said it so casually, as if he knows for a fact he'll be around past tonight.

I look him up and down for a moment, deciding he might be right. I may let him stay until the morning.

"Cabinet down there." I point to the one beside the stove and watch as he turns to squat in front of the open cupboard. When he stands and turns back around to face me, he's holding an unopened package of small containers, his expression full of unasked but unsurprised questions. "I got them one year to make cookies as Christmas presents, but then ended up just getting everyone boxes of chocolates. And I don't cook enough to ever have leftovers."

He shakes his head but there's a lift at each corner of his lips. "Why didn't you bake the cookies?" he asks as he opens the package and begins washing and drying each of the containers.

"That would've required a grocery run." I shrug.

"Didn't the boxes of candy require a grocery run?"

"Costco. My weakness. I had to go grab my economy size batch of K-cups and saw the pretty boxes of different Belgian chocolates. They were even already wrapped up for Christmas. All I had to do was write names on the already provided tags," I explain, flipping my ponytail over my shoulder.

"How... personal of you," he teases.

I pout my bottom lip. "Hey. Those chocolates were freaking delicious." At his raised brow, I mumble, "I might've gotten myself a couple boxes for Christmas too."

"Have you ever made it past the coffee section of Costco? They have an amazing grocery section."

"No. I figured it was all like... family sized, giant portions of food, like everything else there," I admit.

"Negative," he tells me, bringing the containers over to the Instant Pot before grabbing a ladle out of the drawer of kitchen utensils. "They may give you a shitload of food, but most of it is separated into individual portions. And a ton of it is already prepared. You just have to either stick it in the oven or heat it up in the microwave."

"I thought you frowned upon heat-up meals." I cross my legs, leaning onto my right butt cheek to watch what he's doing more closely.

"I frown upon *frozen* meals. A lot of their stuff is made from scratch and never frozen. Their hand-pulled rotisserie chicken is da bomb." He pulls the lid back off the Instant Pot and explains, "Okay, so this—" He holds up the silver ladle that's been here since Emmy's granny was alive. "—is an eight-ounce ladle. Eight ounces equals one cup, which is a serving size of the red beans. So you need to fill the ladle only halfway for the right amount of rice."

He does just that, scooping out enough rice to fill just half the oversized silver spoon before dumping it into the freshly washed plastic container. He does this several more times until all six have rice in the bottom of them. He then takes a whole ladleful of the red beans and meat concoction and pours it on top of the rice, lining them up next to each other once more before putting the ladle in the sink.

He makes quick work of snapping the lids on all the Tupperware, looking like he's done this a few times in his day. He stacks them all up then slides them toward himself and off the ledge of the counter, balancing them by placing his chin on the top one as he moves toward my fridge.

"Wherever will I find the room to put these?" he asks in a dramatic tone as he looks inside the mostly empty space, making me giggle.

"Asshoooole," I sing, and he closes the fridge, grinning when he turns back to me.

He winks as he passes by, picking up the Instant Pot that's had enough time to cool, since he unplugged it after he served us while everyone was still here. Moving over to my sink, he starts washing everything left after his crewmember did everything else.

I brace my palms on the countertop, ready to hop down, but he stops me with a simple "Nope," and I freeze in place.

"You just chill and let someone take care of you for once," he tells me, and my heart does this weird little thump and dive I've never felt before, making me squirm.

I use my foot to hook the top rung of the stool and scoot it over to me to then place both feet on the seat, resting my elbows on my knees while I watch him work. His every movement is full of masculine grace, and it's almost hypnotic, a calm settling over me as I take in the way his hands grip and flex, the way his forearms clench and relax, the way his back and shoulder muscles bulge beneath his white shirt.

I let out an unconscious sigh at the view, and when he looks at me over his shoulder, I blush just a little at the knowing expression on his face. I make a joke to cover up my sudden blip of embarrassment. "So, is this what they mean by wife porn? I totally get it. No wonder y'all leave this part out of the show. You'd have to change your rating to TV-MA, for mature audiences only. You'd lose your status as a family show for sure," I ramble.

He chuckles. "I don't normally wash my participants' dishes. That's one of Rachel's jobs. You're the first to get this royal treatment."

My eyes widen at that. "I suppose that makes sense. You're a big, fancy chef who has minions to do his dirty work. You sure you don't want—"

His hands are full and covered in soap suds, so all he can do is narrow his eyes at me. "Don't. Move. You need to relax." After a beat and seeing my discomfort, he asks, "It's like… physically paining you to let someone do something nice for you, isn't it?"

I grimace. "It's not that. I just feel guilty when someone else is doing work in front of me while I just sit there and do nothing."

He seems to ponder on that for a moment before nodding once. "Well, if it makes you feel any better, there's nothing else to be done, and there's no room for your luscious little body over here, because mine takes up the whole sink area. So chill."

My face heats for an entirely different reason this time, and I can't help the smile that pulls at my lips as I feel myself relax. The tension in my body melts as I sink down onto the stool to rest by back against the island, watching as he dries our bowls before putting them back in the cabinet where they go. The Instant Pot is next, and he searches out a spot to put it. He rearranges a few things on the counter next to the stove, placing the butcher block of knives on the other side of it to make room in the corner. And the Instant Pot finds its new home there, where I'll think of Curtis Rockwell every time I see it when I enter my kitchen.

"Out of sight, out of mind, sugar. It's going to live right here, so you might actually remember to use it," he says, patting the top of it before he slowly prowls toward me. As he comes right up to me, my breath catches when he leans down, placing a hand on the counter on either side of me and bringing his face oh-so close to mine.

Is this when he'll give me that kiss he threatened me with? Is this the moment he'll erase the memory of every kiss I've ever had in my life, overshadowing all other intimate moments I can ever remember having and replacing them with the feel of his flawless lips on mine?

My eyes shutter, and everything disappears around me except for the man just inches away from me. When my lids completely close, all I sense is my breath rushing in and out of my lungs as I anticipate his kiss, all my nerves seeming to rush to my lips, awaiting the press of his mouth to mine. They've grown so sensitive I can feel his breath mingling with mine where the air passes through my slightly parted lips. I can barely stand the anxiousness of it all, adrenaline pumping through me as if I'm at the top of a roller coaster ride. I've never felt such excitement, not even at one of the Comic Cons Emmy and I attend, in line about to meet one of my celebrity idols.

Sorry, Jensen Ackles, but you've got nothing on the man currently hovering over me, making every hair on my body stand on end, my nerve endings doing the same, reaching toward him as if they all want to latch onto him *Venom*-style and never let go.

And just when I think I may come unglued and launch myself at him, he dips his head to the side and nuzzles my ear, making me shiver. "Our haunted tour awaits, sugar," he whispers there, and my pussy clenches at the same time I want to cry out in frustration as he stands up straight, reaching his hand out for me to take. There's an evil little glint in his eye I catch before he smothers it with his excitement. "You think they'll tell the story about Kathy Bates's character in *American Horror Story*?" he asks, spinning around as I take his hand before tugging me out of the kitchen.

"Most definitely. It's on every tour I've ever taken," I reply, trying to get my body to calm its tits… especially my tits. My nipples could cut glass, and it reminds me I never put on a bra after we got home from the grocery store. "Holy shit."

He stops in his tracks. "What's wrong?" he asks, hearing the worry in my tone.

"I never put on a freaking bra, and we just recorded a whole fucking episode of your show. The entire world is going to be staring at my boobs when the show airs," I squeak, starting to hyperventilate.

He doesn't look fazed and shakes his head. "Nah, you're all good. I kept an eye on them the whole time, and your nipples didn't make their grand entrance until about three minutes ago when you were basically fapping to me washing your dishes." He smirks.

For the first time in my entire life, I'm speechless.

There is no comeback to that.

Instead, after my teeth click shut, I spin on my heel and rush up the stairs to my room, hearing him laugh behind me. I rip my shirt over my head and scramble around, looking for the bra I wore to work today. When I find it tangled up in the shirt I'd been wearing, I flap it around in the air until it pulls loose, hooking it in front before spinning it around my body then sticking my hands through the straps. I hike my boobs up inside the cups then scramble through my dresser drawer to find a cute tank top. If I'm going to be walking around in the humid evening air, I'm going to need less fabric on my body.

I change my leggings out for jeans shorts in record time, just in case the sexy chef decided to follow me up the staircases while checking out all the stuff Emmy's parents have collected during their excursions.

Catching a glance of myself in the dresser mirror, I let out a squeak and yank the ponytail holder out of my hair. This time, I actually take a second to brush it to get it somewhat smooth before piling it on top of my head in a messy bun. I slap on a fresh layer of deodorant and spritz on a little bit of my One in a Million body spray from Bath and Body Works, because I will no doubt be sweating my tits off soon. It just won't be clear whether it's from being around Curtis Rockwell, celebrity chef, or because of the NOLA heat.

Eight

CURTIS

"BUT… THEY'RE SUPPOSED to be the best in New Orleans. In the world, even," I pout as Erin takes hold of my wrist and drags me past Café du Monde.

"That they are, *mon ami*. But they're also open twenty-four hours. And we've got just eight minutes to meet up at the tour spot. You see that line?" Erin asks, and I glance back as her little body continues to haul me down the sidewalk in Jackson Square heading toward the French Market.

"You mean the one that's about sixty-people deep and reaches all the way to where the two guys are break-dancing and sliding across the makeshift dance floor on the top of their freakin' *heads*?" My jaw had dropped when I saw the first performer do it, sliding fifteen feet across what I assume is plastic. Otherwise, I have no idea how he could've slid… On. His. Head.

"Yep, that one. The line goes pretty quickly, but not quick enough that we can wait in it, find a table, order our food, receive and eat it, and then make it to the tour," she explains, looking back and up at me. She reads the disappointment clearly on my face, and hers softens from the sternness it's been harboring since we left her house, as I've wanted to stop to oo-and-ah over every little thing like the tourist I am. She sighs. "I promise after the tour you can treat me to some beignets and café au lait."

I grin. "I can treat you, huh?"

"That's right. You're the one who dragged me out tonight, when all day today I had dreams of an early bedtime after eating my easy frozen meal. So I will go on this tour with you and eat the beignets and coffee you provide, and then I guess I'll finally get some sleep. I'll just do something I never, ever do tomorrow," she says, and I lift a brow, fully planning on keeping her out way later than what she's expecting. It's NOLA on a Friday night, after all.

"And what's that?" I prompt.

"Sleep in." She shrugs.

Visions of spending all night with her then curling up to sleep all day together flash through my mind. I can't think of a better way to spend a Saturday.

"You don't usually sleep in?"

"Never. I'm very… routine-driven. And if something throws me off course, it takes me forever to get back into my flow. I mean, I'm pretty laid back and easygoing, as long as things fit into the allotted times," she admits.

"Is that why you're manhandling me right now?" I grin.

"Yes. That is one thing I cannot stand—not being punctual."

I chuckle. "I don't mean to shrink the shrink, but have you considered you might be just a teensy bit OCD?"

"A teensy bit? Bruh, I've got it bad. Everything but the tics. Mine manifests as anxiety attacks," she confesses, and I nod.

"I had a sous chef who had OCD. Like… with the tics. Cleanest kitchen I ever worked in, but goddamn it took forever to cook a meal. He always had to measure out ingredients seven times before he ever added it to the dish. Poor guy." I shake my head.

She slows as we reach a door opened at the corner of a building, and I glance up to see a sign with the name of the tour company.

"There are medications and therapies for that. Did he ever see anyone about it?" she asks, and I lower my gaze to hers, seeing the look of concern there. Concern for someone she had never even met before, who I mentioned at random. God, what an angel.

I can't help but lift my hand to trace the line of her delicate jaw, and my stomach dips at the way she unconsciously leans into my touch. "He chose not to. Kinda like how Freddie Mercury never got his teeth fixed even after he became rich and famous. He thought his four extra incisors were part of his instrument, what made his voice what it was, so unique. My sous chef thought that if he got his OCD treated, it might take away some of his qualities that made him such an excellent cook. He was well on his way to becoming a head chef himself."

"Sous chef. What does that mean exactly?" she asks curiously, finally seeming to relax now that we made it to the destination with... three minutes to spare.

"It's like the second-in-command, the Vice President if the chef is President. The literal translation is under-chef," I reply.

"Gotcha. Well, we can either go inside and chill in the waiting room to be lined up for our tour or we can just hang out here." She turns to wave at the gal sitting at the desk inside, who waves back and seems to check off something on the paper in front of her. "We're all checked in."

"Wait." I tilt my head, my brow furrowing. "I was the one who bought our tickets online. How did you just check us in?"

"I sent my buddy Ronnie, our tour guide, a text letting him know I was coming and to give us the extra special tour, since I had a certain celebrity chef with me. He told me he'd let Jamie, the girl sitting at the desk, know I would be here and gave her your name as the person on the tickets." She shrugs.

"The extra special tour?" I smile. "You did that for me?"

She rolls her eyes. "Well duh. You're sober and it's your first time taking a haunted tour in New Orleans. Gotta make sure you get all the cool stories instead of the easy lame ones they give to all the drunk tourists who aren't really going to remember it the next day anyway."

I burst out laughing at that. "Speaking of which, I was told I need to try a... Hurricane, is it?"

I nod. "Ah, yes. The drink NOLA is famous for. But in all honesty, it's the Hand Grenades that are so freaking delicious."

"How about both? Do we have time to run into that bar really quick to grab one of each, or will your OCD spaz out for not being star student and first in line for the tour?" I tease and she sticks her tongue out at me, her nose wrinkling in the most adorable way.

She leans around me and glances into the bar right next door. "As long as we make it quick. They look dead, so it should be fast."

And it is. Within five minutes, we have our drinks and are standing back in front of the tour spot, a small group starting to line up both inside the small room with chairs I see through the open doorway and a couple people outside, everyone with a drink in hand.

"Guess it's a good thing we grabbed these. Looks like everyone brought their own form of hydration," I joke, tapping my large plastic cup to her green one shaped like a grenade. "This one is damn good. Pretty strong too. Let me see." I take a sip, rolling it around my tongue, letting the liquor pool in my mouth as I inhale through slightly parted lips to get a good taste of the flavor. "I saw him pour in the light rum, dark rum, and grenadine, but I'm tasting… passion fruit?" At her amused face and nod, I continue, "Orange and lemon juice?"

She nods again. "And one more thing," she hints.

I take another sip. "Those are pretty tart and sour ingredients, but this is mostly sweet. Sooo… simple syrup?"

Her smile lights up her entire face. "Ding-ding-ding! Wow. That's a pretty cool trick. Do this one," she says, trading her drink for mine. And it's ridiculous how proud I am of the fact that I've impressed her with my taste-testing abilities.

I use her straw, finding the act somehow intimate sharing something that's been in her mouth instead of taking a drink from the brim of the plastic bomb-shaped cup. Again, I roll the liquid around my tongue. "Mm." I nod. "Mm-hm. I think… I think I've got it," I say, taking another taste. "Definitely gin. Everclear." She nods, lifting an eyebrow and biting her lip in anticipation. "I saw him put in vodka and rum… but the other bottle didn't have a label." I pull in air through my lips, concentrating on the flavor. "Is that… *melon* liqueur?"

She hops a little, holding her arm out away from her so she doesn't spill the drink in her hand. "Yes! That is so freaking cool! I'm going to have to take you to my favorite restaurants so you can tell me all their secret ingredients in my go-to meals."

I grin, watching the realization cross her face as she understands she just told me she wants me around for more than the next couple hours. I'm not dumb. I can tell she's trying to keep me at arm's length, trying to stay detached for some reason I plan on figuring out and soon. But I can also see she can't deny this palpable connection we have.

I decide not to tease her about that little slip as we trade drinks. "Sounds like a deal. I'll be your own personal copy-cat. But I'll raise your deal and bet that I can probably take whatever dish you want me to

68

copy for you and make it even better."

She tilts her head to the side and narrows her eyes. "I don't know. It'd be pretty hard to top the meatloaf and mashed potatoes at Mia's Table. I swear, I think their secret ingredient is crack, because I am addicted. I ate there three times in one workweek once."

I burst out laughing. "Sugar, my meatloaf and whipped potatoes will make Mia's taste like dog food. You wait and see." I cheers her cup with mine once more.

"We shall see, *mon ami*," she replies, and it's the second time she's called me *my friend*. I wonder if it's a conscious thing she's doing in order to remind herself to place me in the friend-zone or if it's a common thing in this area to call people, like a generic term of endearment.

I don't have time to ask her though, as a tall, lanky man with shaggy brown hair and a goatee claps his hands, gaining everyone's attention. When I finally take my eyes off Erin for the first time in several minutes, I notice our group has gotten larger. In all, there are about eighteen to twenty people ready to take the tour and learn some NOLA history.

"Good evening, everyone. My name is Ronnie…" He gestures with his arms out, waiting for the small crowd to greet him.

Everyone else mumbles a hello, but by the grace of crazy coincidence, Erin and I both give him a warm welcome.

"What's up, Ronnie!" Erin shouts, just as I call out loudly, "Hey, man! How you doing?"

Ronnie grins at us near the back. "Ah, *c'est bon*! Nice to see you again, my friend," he directs at Erin before his eyes meet mine. "Very good, and thank you for coming." He points at me briefly with a wink, letting me know he's not going to call me out aloud.

No one seems to recognize me, or maybe they're just too buzzed to notice me, so I relax even more and pay close attention to our tour guide.

"It is very important that we stay together as a group. If you aren't from around here, it is easy to get lost in the Quarter. All the streets can look alike this late at night, especially if you've imbibed a little of that dranky-drank," he tells us, and everyone lifts their drink in the air and lets out a collective "Woohoo!"

"In addition, most of the stops on the tour are private property. The owners are pretty cool about letting us tour companies stop and tell their stories, so please be respectful of their generosity by not touching anything on their property. Nooo touchy," Ronnie explains, and everyone gives him a nod.

"This is a walking tour. We will be walking approximately two miles from start to finish. We will have one bathroom break in the middle of the tour, so if you need to break the seal now, please hurry and use our facilities before we get going." He gives all the tourists an opportunity to speak up, but when no one does, he claps once more and says, "All right. Follow me!"

Erin and I stay toward the back of the group as Ronnie leads the way down a side street, and I can't help but admire my surroundings. Everything is just so… festive. The shops are all brightly painted in Mardi Gras colors, and everything is so authentically New Orleans, from the mask and bead stores to the random Voodoo shops we pass by. If I could, I'd wander through each and every one of them.

I hear Erin chuckle beside me, and I glance down at her. "What's so funny?" I smile.

"You. I don't think I've ever seen a guy such as yourself look so longingly at storefronts before," she says.

"A guy such as myself?" I prompt.

"Ya know… straight." She shrugs.

I laugh loudly, apologizing to the people right in front of us that I startled. "I don't like just any old shopping. I only love touristy shopping. Like those beach shops with all the souvenirs, and the places everywhere that have the name of the city on everything. But this… this is awesome. Voodoo shops? Where else in the US could you find a voodoo shop on every street? Only New Orleans, Louisiana. And Mardi Gras masks? I bring one of those babies home to my yaya, and I won't even have to tell her where I got it. You only get stuff like this here."

She nods, giving me a sweet smile. "Yeah, it's one of the reasons I never left. There's nowhere in the world like it."

The group comes to a stop, and we break our gaze at each other when Ronnie speaks.

"The first stop on our tour is Ursuline Convent, which you can see across the street." Ronnie gestures toward the massive structure. The left side looks like a church, while there is a wall surrounding what I assume is a courtyard to the right. There is a huge three-story building attached to the church, windows lining the entire top floor.

"The year is 1704, and the few cities that existed in what is now the United States are mostly along the coasts. They're brand spanking new, and most of the colonists are men. It was hard to get women to make the long voyage from Europe, which was obviously a problem. These guys needed wives. They needed to make babies and establish roots here, to start the first generations of Americans."

At this, Erin makes a little grunt that brings my eyes briefly down to her before she looks up at me, seeming to pretend like she didn't make the noise. Ronnie draws my attention back to him as he continues the story.

"At first, the city officials recruited these potential wives for the men of NOLA within their actual town limits. They even went shopping for these girls in jails and brothels. They didn't care, as long as they had a vagina."

One of the drunk tourists in the group holds up his beer in the air and yells out, "Wooo! Pussaaay!" making most of us chuckle. One doesn't come on a ghost tour in arguably the biggest party city in America and expect it to be a serious lecture similar to a class in college.

"Needless to say, these women didn't make the greatest wives for what were mostly religious colonists," Ronnie says, to which the same tourist yells, "Prudes!" before his friends shush him. He hisses, "Sorry!" allowing our guide to go on. "So, they had to look elsewhere.

"Over the years, a lot more people besides the original colonists were sent over to populate the new world. Tons of them were convicts and prostitutes who made the journey against their will. Instead of the leaders putting them up in their jails or dealing with them in other ways, they decided just to ship them off and get rid of them altogether, using the new world as sort of their own personal human dump. But in 1704, the first of three groups of girls arrived in what is now Mobile, Alabama. They had one purpose—be the fresh batch of women to choose from to become the wives of the colonists.

"These girls were all between the ages of fourteen and nineteen— the average marrying age of females back then—and they were mainly chosen because they were virgins. They'd been recruited from France, from their convents and orphanages. But there were also rumors that even more were sent over after being picked up off the streets. Another group was sent to what's now Biloxi, Mississippi in 1719, and another to our beloved New Orleans in 1728. Unfortunately, the journeys on the ships were anything but luxurious, and many of the recruited would-be wives didn't survive the trip across the Atlantic. Over the years of this practice, things changed a little, and the women who survived the trip were now allowed to mingle with the male colonists and choose husbands from them. Unlike the previous settlers, the journey itself was now consensual, and so was their choice in hubby," Ronnie says, making the women giggle.

"Once the ladies in the New Orleans group got here, they experienced crazy culture shock. And the established colonists had quite the shock of their own. The young women, who were sometimes called 'pelican girls' because of the ship they arrived in, were super pale. Many of them were coughing up blood. And they carried little bags with all their belongings." He drops his voice low, making the next part seem ominous. "The New Orleans residents couldn't help but notice these bags looked a hell of lot like... coffins."

The drunk guy from earlier lets out a screech, making most of the women scream then laugh. Admittedly, I jump a little, and Erin tries not to laugh at me. Her plump lip is pulled between her teeth, the tiny gap in the two front ones making my blood run hotter, but the crinkles in the corners of her eyes let me know she's holding back laughter.

I lean down a little to whisper in her ear, "Oh, you wanna laugh at me. How 'bout you keep me safe, my big, bad ghost huntress?" With that, I pull her in front of me, her back fitting snuggly against my front, and I wrap my free arm around her, just below her breasts, taking a drink of my Hurricane with the other. I can feel the weight of her tits resting on my forearm, and I swallow a groan.

Ronnie continues, "Thanks to these bags, the girls came to be known as *fille à la cassette* or 'girl with a suitcase.' They were also called 'casquette girls,' with a Q-U-E-T-T-E on the end. And since the word casquette was also spelled casket, with a K-E-T on the end, these girls have most notably been called the 'casket girls.'

"The year before the casket girls came to NOLA, a group of nuns arrived in our fair city. These nuns established a school here that housed the *fille à la cassette* as they looked for husbands. When Ursuline Convent was opened up for the nuns in 1734, the girls were moved to the third floor as they continued their search. The nuns would often arrange marriages for the young women, basically a one-stop shop. 'We'll put you up until we find you a man and can kick you out.'"

This provoked a couple laughs around the group, everyone riveted to the story, because by his tone of voice, we all know the other shoe is about to drop.

"But NOLA peeps were suspicious of the casket girls. Unlike most of the houses in the city, the windows along the third floor were shuttered, even nailed shut. Not only that, but after their arrival, the death toll in the city *doubled*. Add their pale skin, coffin-shaped bags, tightly locked and nailed shutters in a city that rarely had them—to the residents of New Orleans, it was obvious these casket girls *must* be vampires!

"New Orleans is known as a hub for all things paranormal. It is possibly the most haunted city in the country. So, it's no surprise legends spring up from locals' encounters with girls who were, from their perspective… just plain weird.

"Quite a few of the girls had trouble finding husbands. That is, if they lived through the yellow fever or tuberculosis that was ravaging the area. The ones who finally married often didn't see their hubbies for extended periods of time, since many of them were fur trappers or traders, which were jobs that required lots of travel."

"Man, that sucks," I murmur and squeeze Erin tight at that, realizing this would be similar to us if I were lucky enough to be in a relationship with her. Lots of travel and time away from her. I shake my head at myself. No, we'd figure it out. If she didn't want to travel with me, then I'd come here to live in her city. Open a restaurant, maybe.

"According to the legends, the king of France grew tired of the young women he sent over here not fulfilling their duty and instead being forced into prostitution to earn their keep, so he ordered them to be brought back home. But… once the nuns got up to the third floor of this convent to get the girls—" Ronnie points up to the windows along the top floor of Ursuline Convent. "—they were *gone*. The nuns looked everywhere for them, but as the story goes, the windows had been sealed shut the whole time. *This,* ladies and gents, is when the vampire legends really kicked up a notch.

"The nails sealing the windows shut were blessed by the pope himself! So how in the world did these young women disappear?" Ronnie asks dramatically, and Erin tilts her head back to look at me and waggle her eyebrows. I grin down at her, enjoying being so close to her and loving that we have yet another similar interest. This woman was made for me. I can feel it to the depths of my soul.

"More than two hundred years later, in the year 1978, two paranormal investigators came and visited the convent to see if the legends were true. They were kicked off the property for loitering but secretly returned anyway to stay the night and see what happened. While they slept, the security cameras showed the windows opening and shutting several times before stopping. And the next morning—" Ronnie points to the few steps leading up to the front of the church. "—the bodies of the investigators were found... ravaged and drained of blood."

"Whoa," I breathe, taking another look at the building that suddenly seems way creepier than it had before.

"At this time, I'll give you a minute to take pictures and read the placards if you'd like," Ronnie says, and a couple of women take off across the street toward the steps in front of the church. I feel Erin's body shake a little with laughter as we watch one of the women lie across the steps, apparently pretending to be drained of blood except for her huge yardstick margherita she holds in the air while her friend snaps pictures. When she stands, she takes a swig from the straw before trading places with the other woman, who seems a little more creeped out being that close to the convent. She just stands next to the sign and holds up her finger to point at it while she gets her photo taken.

As they make their way back to our group, we hear the excitement in their voices as they check the photos on the phone for "orbs."

"If we're all ready, we'll head to stop number two," Ronnie prompts, and everyone gives an affirmation.

"We are named Louisiana because at the time we were founded, King Louis the Fourteenth was the ruler of France. So we are the 'Land of Louis.' We had two major fires that ravaged our beautiful city, so what you see now is nothing like it looked when we were first built up over three hundred years ago, the French Quarter being the first neighborhood here. The first fire was in 1788, on Good Friday. We had eleven hundred buildings, and eighty percent of them were burnt to the ground. That means it burned down eight hundred and fifty-six buildings in one night. The next fire was in 1794, and it started just a block away from the first fire, meaning we hadn't even had time to rebuild all the ones that had originally burned down. It burned down two hundred more," Ronnie tells us.

"Most of the French colonial buildings that were here to begin with were built out of cypress, and you might've seen all the cypress trees all over the city. It's oily. It's amazing for hurricanes, but oil... is used to burn. Which is why we lost nearly the entirety of New Orleans in just one fire, two—no pun intended—just added fuel to the fire. The town was devastated. But we loved our home here, so rebuilt we did. This time, we built everything out of the brick and stucco we are now known for. All these buildings, all the beautiful courtyards, it's all Spanish architecture from when we were taken over. But more on that history later.

"These days, we only have three of the original French buildings left. Three out of the original eleven hundred. Now, if you take a look at this building we're standing in front of, this green and white structure was a place of residence. Notice how it looks completely out of place, like it doesn't belong. Sort of looks like a giant version of the old man's house in *Up* when they built the skyscrapers around it when he wouldn't sell, right?"

"Saddest movie in history," I murmur in Erin's ear.

She turns wide eyes to me. "Right? I cry through the entire thing, even when I fast-forward through the first fifteen minutes."

"It's the only one out of the three original French buildings that was a place of residence. Its style is called a raised French colonial," Ronnie explains, which makes sense. The bottom floor looks like a five-car garage, and above that is a wraparound balcony encasing the second floor, where the home actually sits. "Some fun facts about this place. It was used in the movie *Twelve Years a Slave* and also the coffin scene in *Interview with the Vampire*."

"Oh, shit. No way! I love that fucking movie," I whisper, and Erin nods excitedly.

"Me too! I could show you all the places Anne Rice owns around the city," she tells me, and I grin internally once again at her wanting to keep me around a little longer. Could this be my "in" with her? Could I possibly use her love of the city to get to know her more? I wonder just how many days I could get her to spend with me, showing me around and telling me stories of all the rich history of this fascinating place.

"Here's some awesome NOLA lore for you. After all, this is a haunted tour, right? In that scene, Anne Rice was super accurate in her portrayal of how funerals were done down here. It was pure chaos, everyone going in different directions, no one taking the same route. It probably looked strange if you were paying close attention to this, because nowadays, we have a funeral procession. Everyone heads to the graveyard in an organized line, flashers on, even police escorted. We've grown up showing respect for the dead by pulling over to the side of the road when we see a procession coming from the opposite direction. Back then though, they purposely mixed it up. They never went straight from the funeral to the graveyard for a very specific purpose." He lowers his voice and we all lean in. "It was known as 'spirit confusion' and it was done so the evil spirits couldn't follow you into the cemetery."

"Ahhh," a couple people in our group, including me, murmur, and Erin smiles up at me, seeming to enjoy my enthusiasm for gaining cool knowledge.

We make our way down the street, stopping momentarily for Ronnie to point up at a random building. "If you look up, do you see those upward-facing spikes?" I tilt my head back and squint to see several metal spikes circling each of the poles Erin gave me the lesson about on the way to her house before we recorded the cooking part of the show. "We call those Romeo spikes. You could always tell which homes had residents with daughters, because they'd have these spikes." A few of the tourists chuckle, but I don't get it. Luckily, Ronnie explains further. "If the young Romeos tried to climb the poles to Juliet's room, they were soon met with these very painfully sharp spikes. And if they did make it past them, they returned down the pole as Juliets themselves."

It dawns on me what he means then, and I burst out laughing.

I shake my head, finishing off my drink, and I see Erin is done with hers as well. As we continue walking, I toss both of our empty cups into a trashcan. When our hands brush, having to walk so closely on the narrow sidewalk, I take the opportunity to casually slip my fingers through hers, lacing them together. I purposely don't look down at her to gauge her reaction, choosing to not make a big deal about it as I glance up, noting more of the Romeo spikes on various buildings we pass by. I can feel her eyes on me, but fighting my urge to lock gazes with her, I feel her limp fingers finally tighten around mine, and something inside me eases, an anxiousness I didn't even realize I had before, suddenly gone.

We continue to hold hands even as we come to our next stop, and don't let go throughout Ronnie's next fascinating yet tragic tale.

"Here's where our tour takes a darker turn. I've told you a fun vampire story, some cool architectural history, and a pretty humorous tidbit about spikes along the galleries. But the farther along we get in the tour, the more obvious the reasons why our little town is known as one of the haunted places on earth will become. If you look across the street, this boutique hotel, now known as the Andrew Jackson, used to be a private boarding school for boys. And yet another fire broke out here, killing everyone inside, including the children. But don't worry, the boys still live there."

There's collective nervous laughter from the group, but more importantly, I note Erin wrapping her free hand around my bicep as she steps closer to me. I look down to see she's not part of the uncomfortable chuckles. She has a distinctively sad look on her face I want to ask her about, but Ronnie starts up his story once more.

"People, for decades, have reported the sounds of children laughing, playing, running up and down the halls. But when they open their door to tell them to quiet down, to go back to the room they surely share with their parents while visiting the city, there's no one there. Also, for a lot of years, this was an adults-only hotel, so the sound of kids playing out in the courtyard was especially ominous."

I shiver a bit, a reel of every creepy movie starring ghost children playing through my mind, freaking me out a little. And I damn near scream like a little bitch when Erin uses the hand previously wrapped around my bicep to tickle up my side.

"Woman," I growl after jumping almost a foot away from her but never letting go of her hand. I use our connection to pull her tight against me. "You'll pay for that, sugar."

"Oh yeah?" She grins.

"Yeah. No one makes me pee a little and gets away with it."

She squeezes her eyes tightly closed and doubles over laughing, causing several people to turn and look at us.

As she continues to laugh uncontrollably, I tell our confused audience, "She's one of those people who laughs at inappropriate times. Like at funerals and… during stories of a bunch of people dying and haunting a hotel." I shrug. "But we still love her."

At this, Erin's laughter fades and she looks up at me, surprise etched into her face, I assume at my use of the L-word. Again, acting casual, I tell Ronnie, "Sorry, bro. Keep on going, please." I gesture for him to resume his story.

He shakes his head, a smile twinkling in his eyes. "No need to apologize. It's very nice to see my friend enjoying herself and laughing so much."

By his tone, I pick up that maybe that's not a regular occurrence, but not wanting to embarrass her in front of all the people now with their attention riveted on us, I deflect. "So they still report hearing ghost kids at this place?"

Ronnie nods. "Yes. Not so long ago, back when we had to get our camera film developed before we got to see the pictures we took, several people wrote to the hotel once they got back home, complaining someone had snuck into their room while they were sleeping and took photos of them. But upon closer examination, the photos seemed to have been taken from above." His voice takes on his favorite creepy tone. "As if they were floating above their bed."

Another collective shiver.

"Also, lots of people say the TVs like to flip through channels on their own."

Our next stop is pretty crowded. Across the street is another tour group, the guide gesturing to our side of the road, so I put two and two together, discovering we're right outside the door of a haunted hotel. Furthermore, from what I overhear Ronnie telling a couple at the front of the group, this is where our bathroom break will be. There's a bar inside on the first floor that we'll be able to get a drink refill if we choose to. Once the other tour leaves and the area quiets down a bit, Ronnie starts the story.

"A few hundred years ago, the building that stood in the place of this one—the lovely and extremely haunted Le Richelieu Hotel—was a Spanish barracks during the war. Not too far away, where the jazz museum is, was the French barracks. It was called Fort St. Charles. Some of you might've guessed that the reason the architecture went from French colonial to Spanish is because we were taken over. The

French and Spanish obviously didn't like each other.

"The first governor that was sent here by Spain wasn't very effective and we ran him out of town. But unfortunately, the next one they sent, they sent with an army. Even though he was Spanish, his name was O'Reilly. As soon as he got here, he came over to Fort St. Charles and put to death twenty-four of their highest-ranking officers. And then he proceeded to make a jail out of the barracks for the rest of the soldiers. If you're here, you probably love legends and ghost stories. So most of you probably know who Vlad the Impaler is. Much like the ruler who inspired Dracula and how he'd line the streets with heads on stakes, O'Reilly would periodically hang soldiers from the flagpoles right in front of their families, thinking it would deter anyone from trying to start a revolution. The Spanish ended up ruling us for forty years and when the French won us back, we only stayed on top for twenty days. But in that twenty days, we certainly didn't forget about what Riley did to our men.

"We immediately marched down here to this block, which used to be the Spanish barracks, gathered up all their officers, and returned the favor out in what is now the parking lot.

"There have been several ghost sightings here. Most of them are of soldiers, for apparent reasons, out in the courtyard. And like a lot of places especially around here, whenever someone renovates a room upstairs, there is a lot of paranormal activity."

And with that creepy revelation, he gestures for us to enter the haunted building.

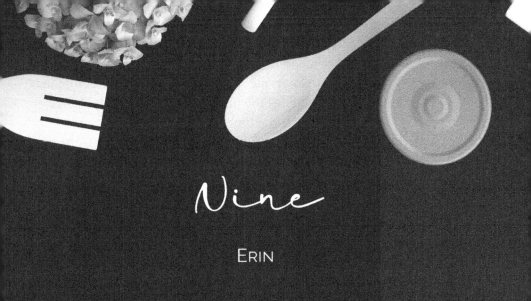

Nine

Erin

Inside Le Richelieu Hotel, I take a seat on one of the barstools to wait for Curtis to return from the restroom.

I try to gather my rampant thoughts while I'm out of his presence. The longer I'm with him, the more time I want to spend with him. And that is not good. Normally, after holding a conversation with a man I meet, whatever happens that night, it's no big deal just to either go home alone or kick them out soon after getting to know them in a physical way. But Curtis…

Curtis, I want to take home with me, introduce him to the sanctuary of my room, and for him to never leave. I want to let him pull me to him like he's been doing all night, curl up against his tall, strong body that makes me feel oh so safe, even in the presence of what could be evil spirits along the tour in the dead of night, and just stay there for hours, days, weeks even. I want to binge watch our favorite shows, let him cook me any meal he can think of, and then make a dessert out of his deliciously masculine body. He makes me feel a hundred percent all woman, even though a very vital part of what makes me female does everything in its power to make me feel less than.

I love and hate a certain part of Curtis I've picked up on with my psychological brain. He's very, very observant. I can tell when he catches a peek behind my strategically placed defenses before I can reinforce them. But thankfully, he hasn't questioned me. He's smart, choosing to let it go, probably building a list inside his beautiful mind so he can ask me about them when we're alone or whenever, if ever, I choose to open up to him. Even with his towering size, there's a definite gentleness about him, in the way he handles me physically and mentally. It makes me appreciate him, but at the same time, it scares the shit out of me.

I have very strict rules I've placed on myself. I don't get close to men. I don't let them get close to me. There is no depth to the time I spend with any of them. It's just better this way. Then my heart doesn't have to get broken when I'm not good enough, just me.

"Sugar, sugar." Curtis's hot breath sends chills down my neck as he whisper-sings in my ear before taking the stool next to me.

"Oh, honey, honey." I shake my head, using the lyrics to the oldie as I cross my arms on the bar top and lay my head down, facing him. "You think we have enough time for me to take a powernap?"

"You think you could sleep in this haunted creepy-ass hotel bar? Go ahead and we'll catch up to the tour group later." He chuckles.

"I'm so tired I probably could," I say, and he reaches over to rub my back in soothing circles. I fight with all my might not to purr like a fucking cat in heat.

"How about… another drink? This one with a pick-me-up," he suggests, and I nod. When the bartender makes his way over to us, I order a Red Bull and vodka, even though I can't stand the taste of the energy drink.

"Which flavor?" the bartender asks.

"Flavor? You mean which flavor vodka?" I ask, confused.

He shakes his head. "No. Red Bull."

I sit up straight, my eyes widening. "Red Bull comes in flavors now? O-M-G, this is a game changer."

"Did you just say O-M-G out loud?" Curtis questions next to me, and I use my fingertips to gently pinch his lips closed.

"Shhh," I direct at him, but my eyes don't leave the bartender's. "What flavors do you have?"

"Well, there's original…" He opens the sliding door on the refrigerator in front of him behind the bar and takes a closer look at the cans inside. "Cranberry, grapefruit, blueberry, tropical fruit, orange, kiwi-apple, coconut berry—"

"That one!" I interrupt his list.

"Are you sure? I have a few more."

"Yep. Positive. Nothing beats out coconut," I reply, and I feel and hear Curtis sniff out a chuckle, his breath coming out of his nose and hitting my fingers where I still have them clamping his lips closed. I let him go, take a moment to gently pat his cheek before reaching for the drink the bartender was kind enough to pour for me quickly.

"So coconut, huh? I'll have to remember that. I have a damn good coconut cake recipe that will blow your mind," Curtis murmurs close to me before turning to order another Hurricane.

"You shut your filthy mouth, Curtis Rockwell. Don't you talk dirty to me in public," I scold, taking a sip of my drink. My head tilts back and I close my eyes. "Holy shit. This is amazing. Can I get one of these in a to-go cup please, good man?"

"Sure thing, dollface," he says, grabbing a large plastic cup from the wall behind him and mixing me up another Red Bull and vodka. I pour the rest of my glass I'm working on into the cup and mix it all up with my straw.

"That's one thing I could definitely get used to about this place," Curtis tells me, and I lift a prompting brow at him. "Getting to walk around with open containers of alcohol. So weird, but oh so cool."

"But you're a California boy. Don't you make frequent trips to Las Vegas? You can do it there too," I ask him.

"Nah, I don't go to Vegas much, and if I do, I don't really do anything but cook for celebrities who flew me in for a special dinner or something," he responds.

"Not a big gambler?" I take a sip of my drink, toying with the straw as I look into his eyes while he speaks.

He shakes his head. "Not a gambler at all. I'm actually quite the hoarder when it comes to spending money all… willy-nilly."

"Willy-nilly?" I laugh.

"I don't blow what I earn on senseless crap," he explains. "I have this… fear, I guess. As quickly as I was able to earn it, I'm scared I could lose it just as easily."

I lean closer, taking a sip from my straw. "If we were in my office, this is when I'd pull my reading glasses down off the top of my head and start making notes," I whisper, and when he looks at me with a raised brow, I smile at him jokingly.

"There are no cameras, sugar. Whatever you want to know about me, just ask. I'm an open book… at least, with you I am," he confesses, and for some crazy reason, it makes me want to open up to him as well.

What. The. Fuck?

The drinks must give me loose lips. "Probably because you know you'll never see me again after tonight. And you've caught on I'm a good person who would never sell your story to a magazine or some shit, so you find me safe to vent to." I nod in conclusion.

Next thing I know, my drink is no longer in my hands, and I barely have time to let out a squeak of protest before I'm letting out a silent scream as my body flies through the air, floating… floating… before I'm suddenly facing Curtis, my ass no longer on my bar stool but perched upon his muscular thighs. I'm incredibly aware of the way the zipper of his jeans lines up perfectly with the seam running up the center of my denim shorts, and it all presses right up against my clit that is more aware of the situation than my mind is. Because it takes me a moment for my brain to catch up with the arousal I'm feeling, finally figuring it out that it's because I am sitting on Chef Curtis Rockwell's lap in a crowded bar… not in a dark corner we've snuck off to, but right. Fucking. Dead. Center. Of the bar itself. People surrounding us on all sides. I can only imagine the bartender's face right now.

Who am I kidding? He's a bartender in New Orleans. Nothing probably fazes him anymore.

But back to the situation at hand.

My pussy throbs at the closeness of his now extremely hard cock. The poor guy has had so many boners today from our horsing around I feel sorry for him. Blue balls are no joke, I'm told.

Before I can continue assessing my new position, Curtis's deep voice in my ear as he leans forward to press our bodies flush against each other brings me back to the conversation we were just having.

"If you think I'd never see you again after the day we've had together, you are mistaken, sugar. I've already made the decision for us," he murmurs, and my head jerks back to look him in the eye, a haughty expression on my face, I'm sure.

"You've made a decision for *us*?" I sass. "Sorry to inform you, homeskillet, but no one makes decisions for m—"

He cuts me off with a single, subtle pump of his hips beneath mine, the seam of my shorts rubbing against me in the most delicious way, making me gasp and forget what I was saying.

"Tell me when you've *ever* felt this way with another person. Tell me, and I know you'll be lying. Because I know for a fact that I've never come close to feeling like this before." He leans ever closer, one of his big hands going to the edge of the bar behind me before he pushes my body against the back of his hand. Even in the heat of this intense moment, he thinks of everything to keep me safe, even if it's just from a bruise.

He pulls only his head back and just enough to look into my eyes. And it's the stormy look I see there, the complete seriousness I've yet to see in this usually lighthearted and carefree man's eyes until now, that stops me from blowing off his words.

The joke I had locked and loaded dies in my throat, and my words come out almost strangled as I can't look away from his beautiful irises. "I… I can't."

His other hand tightens on my hip, sending sparks up my side. "Don't tell me you can't, Erin. There is nothing stopping you from being mine—"

I shake my head at his misunderstanding. "No, I mean… I can't. I can't tell you I've felt this way with someone before. Because I haven't. And it's scaring the ever-loving fuck out of me," I tell him honestly, and his tight hold on my hip relaxes just a smidge.

He dips his head to press his forehead against mine, a lazy smile pulling up a corner of his lips. "Nah, sugar. That's just the haunted tour we're on getting to you. Because you have nothing to be afraid of with me."

And with that line floating through my mind on repeat, the entire bar… street… city… fuck—the world… disappears around us as he makes good on his promise and presses his lips to mine. With my body trapped between the bar top and the solid brick wall of his torso, my legs dangling on either side of his hips, I feel his free hand wrap around my lower back to pull our lower halves ever closer before it briskly moves up to bury his fingers up the back of my hair. He tugs on my ponytail just enough to make me gasp and swiftly dips his tongue inside my mouth for a taste, his groan rumbling inside his chest and tickling my nipples pressed against him.

I let go of all control, allowing him to tilt and bend me whichever way he wants, and the limper I become against him, the better it feels, just letting him mold me into a ragdoll of pure desire.

I don't do this. I don't make out in public. I don't straddle laps of men I just met out in the open for the whole Quarter to see. And I one hundred percent do not give up control of a sexual nature. I keep that shit on lock so I can stay completely focused on the physical aspect of it, the pleasure it brings my body, never allowing it to penetrate my mind or heart.

But with Curtis, in this first kiss we share—which was absolutely no lie when he swore it would be unlike any I've ever felt before—I relinquish my hold on all power and give it all over to him. And by God, it's the most addictive feeling in the world. I melt against him, my body feeling heavy and like it's floating all at the same time. And when he lifts his hips just a little, it's instinct, not my conscious mind, that has me grinding against him, making me whimper at the sheer pleasure of it all.

He overtakes every one of my senses—the sound of his breath and light groans, the scent of his intoxicating cologne, the taste of his Hurricane-laced tongue, the feel of his perfect body against my much smaller one—as the kiss goes on and on, and I never want it to stop.

How long has it been since I've made out like a teenager? Probably not since I was an actual teenager more than a decade ago. But Curtis's kiss is the best sexual experience of my life thus far, and he has yet to even touch me intimately with his tongue, hands, or cock.

If I rocked forward just a tad… as his tongue continues to glide against mine… as I continue to breathe in his amazing scent… as I continue to listen to his unconscious sounds of desire while he brings me unsurmountable pleasure with just the press of his lips and dance of his tongue, I have no doubt he'd make me come, right here and now, in front of everyone in this bar. And at this point, with just the little bit of alcohol floating through my veins, I wouldn't care one bit.

Dear God, this man has turned me into a dirty little exhibitionist with just one kiss.

I pant as his steel pipe of a cock pushes my seam against my aching clit, and just as the last star is about to align and make me explode in the bar of a haunted hotel, I nearly scream in both terror and frustration as a heavy hand lands on my shoulder, and Ronnie's voice says loudly, "Time for our next stop! Girl, damn. Get a room. We're in a hotel, after all." And as I pry my lips from Curtis's, I glance over his shoulder to see my tour guide buddy shaking his head and chuckling as he makes his way out the front door.

"Motherfucker," I exhale, as the entire world slowly comes back into existence. And it's then I realize Curtis still hasn't spoken a word. I timidly look into his eyes, and what I see there is completely breathtaking.

He looks like a man possessed.

And I know my assessment is spot on when the first words out of his mouth after our first kiss are "Never letting you go, sugar. Not. Ever."

My whole body goes warm thanks to the heat in his eyes, and something in me believes him. In this moment, I truly believe he'll never let me go.

But a little voice in the back of my mind warns me, *Don't get your hopes up. He's saying that without knowing the whole truth.*

Yet, I can't help but think this is different. *Curtis* is different. This feeling between us—different. Could this man possibly accept me, just me—broken, imperfect, Woman Card rejected… me?

I have no time to ponder it further before he wraps his arms around me and stands, allowing my smaller frame to slide down his deliciously rigid front until my feet are planted on the floor. I breathe in his scent when he leans into me to reach behind me and grab our drinks, and when he hands me mine, I smile up at him, feeling more drunk from his kiss than the alcohol we've consumed.

"We'll continue this later, little one," he purrs, and the promise in his eyes sends an excited shiver of anticipation through my every nerve ending. He takes hold of my free hand and guides me through the packed hotel bar until we make it out onto the sidewalk with the rest of our group.

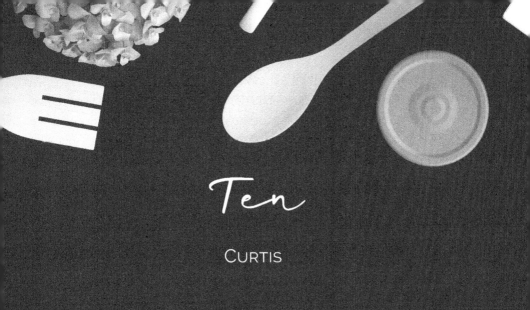

Ten

CURTIS

"Is THERE ANY voodoo on this tour?" a woman asks while we're walking to the next stop.

"Actually, no. There is a specific voodoo tour you can choose to take, because there is just too much information and too many places to see that pertain to it. But it's guided by an actual practicing voodoo priestess if you're interested. Also, if you sign up when we return to our home base, you get fifty percent off a second tour. I highly recommend that one and also the cemetery tour, because it is now the only way you're allowed into St. Louis Cemetery #1, which is where Marie Laveau's tomb is."

Erin nudges me with her elbow, and when my eyes meet hers, she winks up at me. "It may be where her tomb is, but it's not where her body iiisss," she sing-songs, making me grin.

"Why, Erin. Are you referring to a certain discovery your best friend made with her now husband slash baby-daddy?" I put my hand to my chest as if I'm clutching my pearls.

Her jaw drops. "You know? But… it's totally classified. Only the people who were at their ceremony in Paris know exactly what they found. And we all had to sign non-disclosure agreements."

"I was there, sugar," I tell her, and her head jerks back in surprise.

"How the hell…? I certainly would've noticed you. At least, I think I would've. Well, that was actually before I watched your show, since it wasn't until after that when Emmy joined *No Trespassing*," she ponders aloud.

"Did you like the food?" I ask nonchalantly.

"Oh my God. Yes! It was seriously delicious. I was a little nervous, since it was traditional French dishes, not the creole and Cajun yumminess we have here, but for real, I ate all of mine and most of Emmy's, since she wasn't hungry. She gets a nervous belly," she explains enthusiastically.

"Good to know. I catered that dinner. As well as Dean and Emmy's wedding reception," I tell her, and she slaps my arm.

"Shut. Up. Are you serious? We were in the same place twice and never met." She pouts, and I chuckle. This second drink and that world-shattering kiss must be loosening her up a bit if she's not hiding the fact that she's disappointed we could've known each other this whole time.

"Everything in its own time. I guess we weren't meant to meet until today," I tell her, taking a sip of my drink.

We listen as Ronnie gives in to the woman who clearly really, *really* wanted to hear a story about voodoo as we continue walking.

"Voodoo is likely the most misunderstood and misrepresented religion there is. It came to New Orleans from the slave trade from Africa and also from ten thousand refugees sent here from Haiti. Since France owned us and they also owned Haiti, when the Haitian refugees got here, there was a large number of free people of color. There are three types of voodoo here in New Orleans. There is African voodoo, there is Haitian voodoo, and there is what is known as New Orleans and plantation voodoo. The last one is a combination of both Haitian and African voodoo mixed with Catholicism."

"Catholicism? Those don't seem like they'd mix very well," the woman inserts, and Ronnie nods.

"Misunderstood and misrepresented, remember? New Orleans was the most Catholic place in the United States. At the docks when everyone would be getting off the boats, there would be priests there to convert everyone coming into the city to Catholicism. It's the only religion people were allowed to openly practice at the time. Voodoo has just one all-powerful being, one creator. It is a monotheistic religion. But much like Catholics and their saints, voodoo people have their ancestral spirits. For the people whose religion was voodoo, in order for them to practice, they had a genius idea to disguise their spirits as the Catholic saints.

"You might've heard of a woman named Marie Laveau. She is hands-down the most infamous voodoo priestess who ever lived. She was a Catholic her entire life, brought up her children as Catholic and everything. They were all baptized at St. Louis Cathedral in Jackson Square. To this day, eighty percent of all voodoo practitioners here in New Orleans and in Haiti are Catholic."

"No way. That was so smart of them!" the woman says, and before she can ask any more questions, we all come to a stop as Ronnie turns to face us and holds up is hands.

"Now, here is probably the one most of y'all have been waiting for." He gestures toward the massive corner mansion we're standing next to, and everyone starts to mumble to each other, obviously confused.

Erin winks up at me, smiling and elbowing me gently as she lifts her chin toward Ronnie, who begins his tale.

"Looks a little different than the home they used in *American Horror Story*, no? If you look just across the street there—" He points to a familiar looking building. "—that is actually the place they used as Madame Marie Delphine MacCarthy Blanque LaLaurie's house in the show. Easily one of the cruelest and most sadistic women in American history, she was played pretty much spot-on by the amazingly talented Kathy Bates in Season 3, Coven." He drawls out the last word, and I get chills of excitement, glancing down at Erin with a giddy grin on my face like it's Christmas morning.

"The real Madame LaLaurie was born in 1787. She was part of New Orleans's elite, wealthy beyond compare. As many manipulative sociopaths are, she was known to be kind and sweet. That is, to her social equals. According to British writer Harriet Martineau, *The lady was so graceful and accomplished, so charming in her manners and so hospitable, that no one ventured openly to question her perfect goodness.*

"Not too long after her third marriage to the less wealthy Dr. Louis LaLaurie, she had built a lavish, two-story mansion on Royal Street in New Orleans in her own name. This home—" Ronnie sweeps his arm out to the gray monstrosity next to us. "—which is actually the rebuilt version, quickly became known as the grandest in all of the French Quarter. But on the opposite end of the spectrum, her slaves were noted to look haggard and sickly.

"Rumors started to spread about her cruelty to her slaves, and not long after, multiple complaints were filed. This happened across several years. One infamous story about her was when she flew into a rage when a twelve-year-old servant girl named Lia accidentally pulled on a tangle while brushing Madame LaLaurie's hair. As Lia ran from her uncompromising, whip-wielding owner, Lia chose to jump from the roof to her death."

There's a gasp throughout the crowd, including one from me, and when I glance down at Erin, she's watching me with an amused glint in her eye.

"How are you smiling right now? You have no soul. She was twelve," I hiss quietly.

"I've heard this story so many times I could tell it forward, backward, and upside down. I guess I'm jaded. Also, I'm a tad tipsy. But it's fun getting to see your reaction to hearing it for the first time." She shrugs.

I shake my head at her before my eyes are drawn back to Ronnie as he continues his tale.

"Witnesses later reported seeing LaLaurie burying the girl's mangled body, so she was given a fine of $300 and was forced to sell her other nine slaves. This was actually a big deal back then. Seeing as this was the South during slavery times, punishments against owners who treated their slaves badly was extremely rare.

"But alas, like rich people everywhere during that time, she was able to buy her way out of trouble. And that wasn't the end of her slave ownership. Obviously, or we wouldn't be standing here nearly three hundred years later, telling these stories about her. Marie's family members simply repurchased the slaves and, to the slaves' utter horror, they got sold back to LaLaurie." Ronnie shakes his head, a sad look crossing his face. "Can you imagine being one of those slaves? You think you've finally escaped this evil woman, hoping to be sold to anyone else, because anything would be better than this crazy bitch. And just when you believe your luck has changed… you're sold back to the one person on earth you'd rather die than be owned by."

I lean sideways to whisper to Erin, "Damn, that sucks."

She giggles. She actually… giggles, and I turn my shocked face toward her.

"Just wait," she says ominously, and gives me an evil grin.

"You know, you're a little scary right now," I tell her, even though secretly I think she's fucking adorable. I'm sure the first time she heard these tales, it freaked her the hell out, but living here in New Orleans and hearing them over and over again, she's become desensitized to it all.

"Then came the infamous party that took place here on April 10, 1834. A fire broke out in the LaLaurie mansion. When the firefighters arrived, they discovered the fire had been started by a slave who was chained to the stove and left to starve. The servant woman confessed later that she set the fire as an attempted suicide, because she'd rather die than be taken to the attic," Ronnie says in an eerie tone, pointing up toward the mansion's top floor. Everyone's eyes follow his direction as he adds, "She said no one who was taken up there ever came back down."

A shiver runs up my spine, and I'm grateful when our tour guide tells us, "There's no one coming, so let's cross over real quick." And then he hurries across the street, our group following before stopping to turn and face the mansion. "This gives us a better view, so you can picture the horrors that took place that night."

"Oh, goodie. Exactly what we needed. A clearer picture of that shitshow," I murmur, and Erin giggles beside me again. When I look down at her, she gives me a lopsided grin.

"Pussy," she whispers, and I raise a brow at her, unable to make a comeback as Ronnie tells the rest of his story.

"As Marie scrambled to save her valuables, the townsfolk and people at the party tried to help her. But no matter the awful screams coming from the slave quarters, she wouldn't give up the keys, so they had to break the doors down to rescue all of them that were locked inside. The terrified slaves, finally being able to speak to guests in the pure chaos of the night, begged them to go up to the attic, to rescue their friends and family members inside.

"When they entered the attic, they found a scene from the most gruesome nightmare imaginable. According to Martineau, *Seven slaves, more or less horribly mutilated... suspended by the neck, with their limbs apparently stretched and torn from one extremity to the other.* The slaves who could speak said they'd been imprisoned there for months. Recounts of Marie's abuse have grown more fantastical over the years. You might've heard stories of the victims' limbs being broken and reset at odd angles and such. Not to mention how *American Horror Story* embellished the tale. But newspaper accounts paint a gruesome enough picture without any need for exaggeration. In fact, the rescued slaves from the attic were put on display, so the people of New Orleans could see the evidence of Marie's cruelty for themselves. This was not the work of a sweet and charming woman they all thought they knew. Oh no. These poor people had deep lacerations and scars from repeated floggings. They were skeletal in appearance from starvation. There was even a hole in one man's head wriggling with maggots."

At that, a woman in the group steps aside and gags, and I can't say I blame her. I'm feeling a little queasy myself, hearing that story while standing directly in front of the location where it happened. Even Erin, who'd been all smiles through the darkest of stories tonight, except for that one time during the boarding school tale, had a sorry look on her beautiful face.

Ronnie continues, "Slavery was already a brutal, dehumanizing practice during this time period. They used spiked collars, iron masks, and beatings on the regular, but even in the South, what they discovered at LaLaurie mansion was more than even they would tolerate.

"When word spread of Marie's cruelty, a crowd of locals *of all classes and colors* descended on the mansion and *demolished and destroyed everything upon which they could lay their hands.* After they destroyed most of the mansion, a local paper released articles stating there had been two more bodies found buried on the LaLaurie property, including one of a small child."

At that, Erin leans into me, and my arm automatically wraps around her as she shivers. I try not to look too much into her reaction. After all the wicked grins and giggles she's been sending me while listening to her city's dark history, it makes me wonder why this—the mention of two more bodies being found on the property—is what still gets a reaction out of her, even as she's heard these stories a hundred times over.

And then it dawns on me.

The two times she had this sad response were when small children were the victims.

What's up with that? I ask myself, and I make a mental note to pry later.

"Unfortunately, there is no great tale of justice being served. In order to get that, you'll just have to watch that third season of *AHS* and pretend it's real. In reality, Marie escaped with her driver, a slave named Bastien, where she lived out the rest of her life in comfort and freedom in Paris. When she died December 7, 1849, she was first buried at Montmartre—the area of Paris where the beautiful Sacré-Coeur is, along with the nightclub district, which includes the world-famous Moulin Rouge. Some people believe her body was later exhumed and returned to New Orleans, though it can't be proven."

"Is it true Nicholas Cage owns it now?" someone in the group calls out.

Ronnie smiles. "Sometime around the year 1888, the mansion was restored to its former glory. Over the years, it was used as many things. It's been a public high school, an apartment complex—twice, actually— and a halfway house for young delinquents. It's been a bar, a music conservatory, a furniture store, and yes, it was even previously owned by movie star Nicholas Cage, but only briefly and it's rumored he never even stayed the night. I know y'all are shocked to find out that it's terribly haunted." The crowd gives an uncomfortable laugh in unison. "In fact, it is named *the* most haunted house in New Orleans, which is a damn impressive title in a city known for being overrun by ghosts. But today, LaLaurie Mansion is a private residence; it's owned by an energy trader from Texas. It is closed to the public, but the owner frequently leaves all the lights on so tourists can get a peek inside."

"The final stop on our tour is a story of pure passion and love that turned into nothing but tragedy. A real-life Shakespearian tale that will live among these streets until the end of time. But before I begin—" Ronnie takes a look around the group, bobbing and weaving his body around to see between all the tourists before saying with a look of relief, "—good. No children amongst the crowd this time. Years ago, I made the mistake of telling this gruesome tale in full detail once, when I didn't realize there was an eight-year-old little ghost hunter here with her family. I will never forget little Elizabeth and her look of shocked fascination followed by all the questions she had until we parted at the end of the night."

The tourists chuckle, shaking their heads. Erin leans up to tell me, "I wasn't on that tour, but Ronnie told me about it later, asking if I had any advice. He said the mom of little Elizabeth friend requested him on Facebook and gives him updates. Apparently, it sparked a huge interest in the girl, whose probably like twelve or thirteen by now, and to this day she's determined to be a psychologist who helps survivors with PTSD. If she's still interested when she gets old enough, I'm funding a scholarship for her to attend college here in New Orleans at the same school I went to."

If I hadn't already decided before, then this would've been the final straw. Without a doubt in my mind, I know right then and there, Erin is mine. My yaya always told me that when I found the one, I would just know. There would be a woman out there for me who would check every single one of my boxes when it came to the perfect person to spend my life with, and Erin is all those things and more. And there's no way I'll ever let that go.

I wrap my arm around her back and spin her to face me then bury my hand in the back of her hair. Bending her backward, I seal my lips to hers before she can even make a sound of surprise to match the look in her eyes. And when I finally pull my lips away from hers, I say against her mouth, "You're the most incredible woman I've ever met in my life. How did my soul get so lucky to be mated to yours?"

She gasps, her eyes turning intense before her features soften. And like she's done frequently throughout the night, she makes a joke. But even it can't hide the fact that she's feeling the same connection I am. "I think these scary stories of ghosts, lost souls, and vampires have muddled your brain, *mon ami*. Either that or the Hurricanes are doing their job."

I grin down at her, where I've still got her dipped back and held securely over my arm. "You can '*mon ami*' me all you want, sugar. But we both know we're way more than just friends. Like I told you in the bar. Never letting you go."

A sad look crosses her face, and everything in me wants to whisk her away from the crowd to kiss all her pain away. What happened to my woman to make her so determined to close herself off? What has she gone through to cause pain to flash in her eyes at the mention of children and a chance at a happy ending with me?

And for the first time, she gives me a breadcrumb I immediately snatch up and store to later dip into the soup of Erin's past. "You say that now. But you don't know hardly anything about me. You don't know the whole truth. And when you find out, find out how broken I am, you'll leave me too, just like he did," she speaks quietly, and then with a side-eye to the crowd listening to Ronnie's story, she takes hold of my neck to help stand herself back up, but surprisingly, she doesn't close down or move away.

I situate us to where she's standing in front of me, and I wrap my arms around her middle, leaning down to whisper in her ear, "Whatever you think is broken about yourself, I'll spend a lifetime helping you fix. And if there are parts of you that can't be repaired, I'd be willing to bet the jagged edges and gaps fit together with mine just right. Our jigsaw pieces could make a beautiful picture, as long as we're together."

She doesn't say anything then. Just leans back against me, giving me most of her weight as she relaxes into my front. And I think to myself, *Well, that's a start*, as she doesn't make any joke to blow off my words.

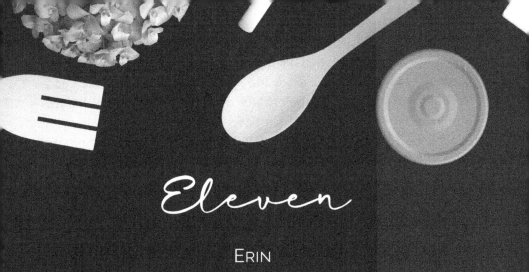

Eleven

ERIN

WHEN THE TOUR ends back where we started at the beginning of the night, it feels like a decade has passed since I stood outside this building, not just two hours. I feel like a different person, as if some of the weight I've been carrying around for the last several years has fallen off my shoulders. Those fortified walls around me don't feel quite as suffocating as I've allowed Curtis to chip windows into their stone, giving him a peek inside. And the more we talk and touch and kiss—oh God, his kisses—he's turning those windows into full-on doorways, passages into my heart.

"How about those beignets I promised you?" I suggest, feeling much different than I did passing the outdoor café on the way here. Before, I wanted to end the night as quickly as possible. I didn't want to give him the chance to wiggle his way beneath my skin, making it hard to get rid of him later.

But now… now, I never want this night to end. I want this night to last forever. Because as long as I never fall asleep, I won't have to wake up alone as I always do. I won't have to wake up and realize this was all a dream. I won't have to gain consciousness to the fact that everything I'm feeling with Curtis was nothing but a fantasy I conjured through a potent mix of adrenaline and alcohol.

Without thinking, I say out loud, "In order to make sure this night lasts as long as I can make it, I need coffee. Coffee with chicory to be exact, with a shitload of lait and sugar. Lots and lots of sugar. Sugar in my coffee, and sugar piled a mile high on my beignets. Sugar, sugar, sugar…" I chant as if it's a voodoo spell that will conjure the energy-boosting substances right before my eyes, not stopping until Curtis's arm halts my hurried pace. I hadn't even realized I was moving, and my hand goes to my startled heart when I see I nearly ran into one of the poles holding up the green canopy of Café du Monde.

My wide eyes lift to the sexy chef, his expression a little worried through his smile.

"You all right, sugar?" he asks.

"Uhhh… yeah. Yes," I state more firmly. "Sorry. I think I just need some coffee."

"I got that. As you said it about fourteen times between the tour place and here." He chuckles.

My face warms a little. "It's been an exciting day." At a little after one in the morning, the line for a table is minimal and we grab two seats within seconds. "The menu is tiny, but it's right there on the napkin holder. One side is the souvenir list and the other is the actual beignets and beverages available. But I suggest just sticking to the classics. An order of beignets and coffee. The café au lait is the best though."

"I am not too proud to let my woman order for me. You go ahead." He gestures to the young Asian man headed our way, his white paper hat sitting squarely atop his head, notepad in hand.

"What can I get you?" he asks, reaching behind him to grab a rag to wipe off the powdered sugar covering the top of the table.

"We'd like one order of beignets, two café au laits for here, and two to go, please," I reply, and he disappears into the building that houses the kitchen of the bakery. "When it comes, the coffee will be hot as fuck, so it's better to order your refill ahead of time so it can be cooling off."

"Noted," Curtis says with a smile. "So, while it's still fresh in my mind, I'd love to hear a psychologist's take on the last story of the tour."

I quirk my head. "That's a little dark for donut conversation, isn't it?"

He shrugs. "I just find all of it fascinating. And I find *you* fascinating. So lay it on me."

"You've already made me display all sorts of affection in public tonight, Chef. And I've totally decided to lay it on you… just not right here in the middle of the most famous bakery in the world," I admit, giving him a wicked look, and I love the expression on his face when he realizes what I just told him.

"See? Unlike any woman in the entire world, sugar. Most women would play it off like they didn't know how the night would end. They'd act coy or hard to get, even if they'd already decided how they wanted things to go. You just lay it out there. And you know what? It's fucking refreshing. Now we can just enjoy the rest of the night without the immature games," he states, reaching out to toss my ponytail behind my back that had fallen over my shoulder.

"Or… I've imbibed just enough alcohol to no longer have a brain-to-mouth filter," I admit.

He laughs at that. "Yeah, or that." He shakes his head. "Okay, let's hear it."

I roll my eyes. "Fine." I sit back in my seat as the waiter appears, setting our coffees and plate of beignets between us on the table. When he leaves, I grab the glass sugar dispenser, turn it upside down over my small mug of coffee in the center of its saucer, and prop my opposite elbow on the table, leaning my chin on my open palm. My eyes lift to Curtis as I begin to speak, his eyebrow lifting as his gaze goes from the sugar flowing into my coffee, up to my eyes, then back down to the sugar again. "Poor ole Zack and Addie. What a hot mess express those two were. The perfect storm. I mean, I know I'm not supposed to judge, and you should never speak ill of the dead and all that, but goddamn. For real. They didn't stand a chance. It's a miracle they lasted as long as they did—"

"Um… baby. Would you like some coffee with your sugar?" he interrupts, gesturing toward my cup.

I glance down, unfazed. I pooch my lips, righting the sugar dispenser for a moment, before tilting it once more for good measure. I begrudgingly hand the container over to Curtis, picking up my spoon as he chuckles, shaking his head. I stir my coffee, watching the steam rise for a moment before I lift my eyes to watch him.

He pours in just a little, what would equal maybe one packet of sugar, stirring and then taking a tentative sip. He makes a face, wincing a little, and I can't help but laugh. "Note to self," he starts, "listen to your woman when she tells you the coffee will be hot as fuck, and take heed when she pours in half the container of sugar. This is the darkest freaking coffee I've ever tasted in my life."

I grin. "Technically, it's still a light roast, so you'll still get an amazing kick of go-go. It's the chicory that makes it taste so bold. But add the right amount of sugar, and oh my Lord. Heavenly."

His eyes lock with mine and I can't help but jerk back a little at his possessive look. He leans forward, and I brace myself. "You just gave me the biggest boner of the day."

My brow furrows in confusion, but I immediately burst out laughing. "What the hell?"

"No lie, sugar. You have no idea how much you just turned me on," he admits.

"What'd I say? What'd I do?" I shake my head, a big grin on my face.

"Do you have any idea how many people think the bolder the coffee the more caffeine or kick they'll get? It's astonishing how many times I've had to explain during my lifetime that dark roasts come from roasting the coffee beans longer, which in turns cooks the caffeine *out* of the coffee. The darkest roast there is, is decaf," he tells me, shaking his head.

"Right? I always secretly chuckle at the people who order like 'Gimme your darkest roast,' thinking they're some kind of badass for being able to tolerate how bold and caffeinated their drink is. I'm like, bro. Order a large blonde roast and you're a true bad motherfucker." I giggle.

"Fucking. A. Yes. God, you're freaking amazing," he says, and my auto-pilot turns on momentarily to joke away his compliment.

"I mean, I have been known to order a grande or two of blonde roast." I flip my ponytail.

Suddenly, my hand is in his and my attention is on his handsome face as he pulls me closer across the table. "I mean it, Erin. You're amazing. And I know your joking is some kind of defense mechanism—hell, maybe it's even from that OCD of yours, a compulsion or automatic response when someone tries to get close to you. But just so you know, it won't push me away. I'll keep on complimenting you, telling you how goddamn wonderful you are, until you finally accept it, and thereafter too."

I nod, glancing down at my coffee and trying not to let the tears form in my eyes that want to fall so badly.

"But we'll delve into that later. Right now, I want some lighthearted donut talk. Tell me about Zack and Addie," he jokes himself, making me lift my chin to see the twinkle in his beautiful eyes.

I sniff once, getting my emotions under control before he allows me to extract my hand to take a sip of my coffee. "As I said. Hot. Mess. Express. They were doomed from the start really. I did a paper on them in college, so if you want, I can go into way more detail than Ronnie did on the tour."

He holds his hand out, palm up. "Please. I love hearing you talk."

I choose to ignore the compliment instead of making a joke. Baby steps.

"Zack Bowen was a charmer. He was a bartender here in the Quarter, a super good-looking young man who left an impression on everyone he met, according to people who knew him. He grew up in California as well, so he had the laid-back way about him, like you do. He married young, to a woman ten years older than him named Lana. They had two kids, and in order to take care of them, he joined the Army for the benefits. A lot of stuff happened overseas, and that's probably more tragic than what ended up happening at the end of Zack and Addie's story," I say quietly, leaning forward to take a bite of a beignet. I dip it in the powdered sugar that had fallen off onto the plate and hold it out for Curtis, but instead of taking it from me, he leans in a takes a bite, his eyes closing. How the man could still look so fucking sexy, even with white powdered sugar all over his face as he groans in delight, I have no idea. I smile at the simple pleasure.

"My God, that's delicious." He licks his upper lip, and my pussy clenches. "Why do you say that's more tragic? What happened while he was deployed?"

"Well, one of his fellow soldiers he was close to was killed, and then a child he befriended while he was overseas was murdered for speaking to American soldiers. It really fucked him up, understandably. And it may seem silly to add but is actually pretty important to the story— he developed a really painful case of hammertoe because of his army-issued combat boots. Seems like small potatoes, but physical pain on top of high emotional distress can be the straw that breaks the camel's back. It was all a terrible mix of shit that turned his once sunny outlook on the military into something he begrudged. Lana was sick with Hep C and alone with their two kids, and he was lonely, and in pain, and missed them terribly. So he started failing PT tests on purpose until he finally got discharged. This is the part that hurts my heart the most when it comes to Zack Bowen. No one helped him. No one took the time to care for the guy. No one made sure he got the medical attention, both mental and physical, that he so desperately needed. They just discharged him and sent him back into the civilian world with a slap on his ass, like 'Good luck to ya!'" I shake my head. I can't help but think about how if he'd just gotten treated for his depression and PTSD, there wouldn't be this awful story to tell all these years later.

"Anyway, enough about the depressy stuff. Because I could go on and on about shoulda-couldas and what-ifs, but there's nothing we can do for him now. I do what I can for people who come into my office with the same diagnosis, and in my head, that's my way of trying to make up for the people who failed Zack," I say, taking another bite of beignet before I move along the story. "So Zack comes back to NOLA, and he self-medicated the way a lot of veterans sadly do—with drugs and alcohol. He takes odd jobs to try to make money for his family, but eventually, Lana leaves him, adding to his depression. Until he meets Addie Hall."

"Dun-dun-duuuun," Curtis singsongs before taking a sip of his coffee, making me smile.

"Right? Addie was known as a free-spirited, feisty, and independent artist who found herself in the bohemian New Orleans lifestyle after a rough childhood in the Northeast. She was a poet, artist, dancer, and bartender here in the French Quarter with a lot of friends. She was hesitant about relationships with men—"

Curtis clears his throat at that, pinning me with a look. "Must be a NOLA girl thing," he murmurs with a playful lift of his brow.

I choose to ignore him. "—because of the abuse she experienced in her past. She was always looking for the perfect muse for her art, and then she finally found it in Zack, all the while battling her own demons and addictions."

"Oh shit. You weren't joking when you called them the perfect storm. Even if I didn't know how their story ends, I could tell you right there that these two would probably not be good for each other," he says with a wince.

"Seriously. So Addie meets Zack while they're both bartending in the Quarter. According to people who knew them, she liked to give him a hard time and play the mean girl as her way of flirting, but in all honesty, it was just a test to see what he could handle, to see just how far she could push him. Addie had an ugly side of her own. Her diagnosis included bipolar disorder, and taking the medication to treat her mental illness irregularly caused horrible, uncontrolled outbursts. Many of their friends remember their outrageous fights, saying they had a tumultuous relationship from the start, which was fueled by drugs and alcohol," I continue, taking a sip of my coffee.

"Fast forward a couple weeks, they were together a while before Katrina started making its appearance in the Atlantic. Zack had every intention of evacuating the city and holing up with Lana and their kids so he could get out of the storm. The thing about hurricanes is you can see them coming days and days ahead of time; you just can't tell how terrible and where exactly it's going to make land once it's here. But it was forecasted to be so disastrous that Lana even welcomed Addie to evacuate with them."

"Wow. That was… pretty fucking nice of her. You don't really hear about an ex-wife offering such a thing to the new woman," Curtis inserts, and I nod.

"Not too often. But Addie, being Addie, refused the offer. Her independence and need for a life all her own with Zack far exceeded any need she had to leave the city. On his way out of town, Zack went to check on Addie, and he ended up not being able to leave her, so they decided to weather the storm together in her apartment. The category five hurricane hit our city dead-on, leaving catastrophic flooding and nearly two thousand fatalities in its wake," I explain, shaking my head.

"You didn't stay behind, did you?" he asks, and I look up to meet his serious expression.

"Hell no. It was 2005 and we were fresh out of high school. Emmy and I hightailed our asses to Houston," I reply, seeing his look of relief.

But then he winces when he asks, "Was there a lot of damage to your home when you got back?"

"Miraculously, no. The majority of the French Quarter was unscathed, just fallen tree limbs, broken signage, and scattered debris. But back to Zack and Addie—they gathered the few people who waited out the storm, and they all made dinners together over campfires, drank booze, and stayed up late singing songs. Some of the survivors mentioned looking up and being fascinated by all the stars they couldn't see before because of the streetlights and brightness of the city. But our star-crossed lovers were so swept up in the romance of it all that they were completely oblivious to the chaos just blocks away at the Superdome and surrounding areas. They fell deeply in love and made a life for themselves in the weeks following the destruction in the empty French Quarter. They were inseparable from that point forward, made a name for themselves as they served alcohol and meals to their fellow survivors, and were even photographed for national magazines and newspapers, interviewed for their choice to stay in the city instead of joining the mandatory evacuation. They felt like King and Queen of the Quarter during those blissful weeks," I tell him.

"I mean, I can see that. It sounds like some kind of apocalypse romance movie or something. I can't believe this actually happened, and right here! Not like, in some other country. Right. Fucking. Here." He gestures out with his arm, and I can't help but look out across the street to Jefferson Square, the cathedral glowing beautifully behind the tall hedges and iron fence.

I nod. "Hell of a backdrop, huh?"

He gives a sad smile as he looks toward the Square as well, wiping his hands on his thighs and leaning back in his chair. "So what happened when they gave the all-clear for everyone to come back home?"

"Well, when the lights in the city turned back on and the stars disappeared once again, reality set back in and the clean-up began. Zack and Addie were forced back into their old life, a life neither were ready to have to live again. Bills, job schedules, responsibilities—all that replaced the bonfires in the middle of their street that they cooked on, the comradery with their fellow survivors, and all the time in the world to just sing songs and... be. And on top of all that, Addie just wanted Zack. She didn't want the responsibility of his children and ex-wife. Their time on a deserted island was over, and they dealt with everything as they always had, with vast amounts of alcohol and drugs, their addictions growing exponentially over the months to come."

"See, that just boggles my mind. You'd think that being in those conditions for that long would've been awful. Wouldn't it have triggered Zack's PTSD in some way, essentially living like the people he saw

---

while he was deployed?" Curtis questions.

"Everyone handles their diagnosis differently. In Zack's case, he thrived in those conditions. He had a sense of purpose, felt at home helping in ways he knew how," I explain, and he nods. "Zack wasn't triggered until the military vehicles moved in and the destruction Katrina left was finally revealed around the rest of the city. His PTSD was in full force then, and with the natural high of the hurricane gone, they had to look elsewhere for their next high. And unfortunately, violent fights erupted, and the couple began to drift apart. Their only solution to reignite their passion was to get a new apartment together and start over from scratch. That apartment just so happened to be above a famed Voodoo temple and was available immediately. The crazy thing was, though, reported later by the landlord, was they had barely even moved in when Addie came to him and asked that the lease be in her name only. Turns out, she discovered Zack was cheating on her, and that was the final straw. The landlord wrote a handwritten contract and asked Addie to sort it all out, hoping they would get back together. But once Zack learned of her deception, he became... let's just say really, *really* angry."

"Understatement of the century if this is where Ronnie's version of the story picked up." Curtis snorts.

"Yep," I say, popping the P. "That's when ole Zacky decided to strangle Addie, dabble in a little necrophilia, and go all Hannibal Lector on her ass."

"Oh fuck. He ate her?" Curtis grimaces.

"Well... actually no. I take that back. He put parts of her in the fridge, and other parts of her in pots on the stove and in the oven. But there was no actual evidence of him being a cannibal. I can't remember if he put it in his suicide letter to the police or if it was their assumption later on once they looked at all the evidence that he was actually trying to get rid of her body by cooking it, but the smell was so bad he gave up, just turned the AC on crazy high and got his ass out of there. Twelve days later, he jumped from the seventh floor of the Omni Royal Orleans Hotel."

"They never stood a chance. So sad," he murmurs, taking the last sip of coffee in the glass mug before pulling the paper cup full toward him to fix with sugar.

When he hands over the dispenser, I stir with one hand while pouring with the other, focusing on the swirling vortex the spoon creates. "Do you…? Ah, never mind."

"No, what? Do I what?" He leans forward, eagerness filling his every feature.

I pooch out my lips, contemplating my words first. "Do you believe in fate? Do you believe everything happens for a reason, is all part of some predetermined plan?"

He narrows his eyes a moment before answering. "I do. I suppose I always have." He nods.

"Then what do you suppose was Zack and Addie's purpose? Like, nothing good came from any of that. Their entire lives were nothing but tragic," I murmur, something that's always bothered me about their story.

He tilts his head. "Well, that's hard to say. But it could be tons of things. Zack's only purpose could've been to father those two kids. One of them could end up being the sole person to like… end cancer, or world hunger. Maybe Addie's art fell into the perfect customer's hands that inspired them in some world-changing way. Like, look how infamous their story is. Maybe it sparked a fire under someone's ass and could one day change the way veterans with PTSD are cared for. *Or…*" The way he breathes the word in excitement pulls my eyes to his, and I see the ah-ha in his features.

"What?" I can't help but smile at his enthusiasm.

"What if their purpose was for little Elizabeth to hear their story one day from the very tour guide whose friend is a psychologist, who would then, a decade later, fund her scholarship to college? What if little Elizabeth in turn becomes that person in the future who changes mental healthcare for all veterans in the years to come? That, sweet sugar, could be fate's plan. The whole reason for their tragedy," he tells me, and not even seven words into his explanation, my throat grows tight and my eyes fill with tears at such a beautiful thought.

I give a short laugh even as a tear spills onto my cheek, and I flip it away as I nod vigorously. "Yeah," I breathe. "Let's go with that."

Twelve

Curtis

I̲t̲ ̲t̲a̲k̲e̲s̲ ̲e̲v̲e̲r̲y̲t̲h̲i̲n̲g̲ in me not to reach across the table and pull Erin into my lap to swipe her tears away and comfort her. The only thing that stops me is seeing clearly that they are happy tears and somehow sensing what I said heals some part of her that was hurting. And knowing I've done that for her, that my words have made her feel better about something that's obviously bothered her for some unknown reason, is the best feeling in the entire world. So I leave her be and let her bask in the glow I see starting to spark inside her, and I decide right then and there that it'll be a lifelong goal of mine, for the rest of my goddamn life, to see just how bright I can get that glow to shine.

We sit in comfortable silence, finishing up our plate of beignets, until I can't hold it in any longer… literally.

"I made a mistake." I wince.

Her eyes immediately lose a bit of the light I put there before she shutters her expression, and I regret my words instantly.

I lean across the table a take hold of her chin, looking her square in the eye when I say, "I broke the seal earlier, and now I really, *really* gotta pee."

Relief overtakes her expression as she laughs, pulling back from my hand and then standing. "Goob. Come on, I'll show you the closest bathroom. It's down past these shops a ways."

I pull out my wallet and put two twenties under the napkin dispenser. The waiter deserves the huge tip for the amount of powdered sugar every-damn-where, which he has to clean up. We pick up our to-go cups of coffee and exit the canopied café, heading back toward the French Market. We pass several souvenir shops, a Harley Davidson store, another green-canopied café on our left across the narrow one-way street, and a bar, until we finally come to the public restrooms. They're situated back into a courtyard of sorts, and I in no way feel comfortable leaving Erin out here alone. Especially with the group of what look like gypsies sitting on the ground next to the building.

"I'll just wait here," she tells me, but I hesitate going into the men's room. "What's wrong?" she asks when I just stand there, looking between her, the four young men and women in ratty clothes surrounded by backpacks and a scruffy-looking mutt on a leash, and then the bathroom that's practically screaming my name.

Without giving it a second thought, I dip down, knowing she'd totally fight me otherwise, and pick her up over my shoulder, hauling her into the bathroom with me, her squawks echoing off the brick walls around us as she complains about me "almost" spilling her coffee.

Even though it's a three-stall bathroom, I close and lock the main door behind us. Everyone else can wait until I'm done, although I doubt we'll get much traffic back here aside from the homeless kids outside. This area of the Quarter isn't busy this late at night. It seems everyone else is several streets over on Bourbon. But I'm not taking any chances.

I set her back on her feet and give her a pointed look. "Don't. Open. That. Door," I order, walking backward until I reach a urinal.

She puts her empty hand on her hip and cocks it sassily. "I don't care if you're some big-deal, world-famous celebrity chef. You can't tell me what to do when I'm not naked, Curtis," she says with a huff, lifting an eyebrow.

And I stop my backward movement, my jaw dropping when her words register in my brain, and I burst out laughing at the same time my cock grows stiff for her once again.

"Goddamn it, sugar. Look what you did. Now I'm going to have to do a handstand in order to take a leak," I tell her, gesturing toward the tented zipper of my jeans.

"Yeah, well. Serves you right, going all caveman on me." Her eyes go from mine, down to my bulging dick, and back up to meet mine once more before she slowly makes a half circle, giving me her back, but not before I catch the little smirk on her sexy mouth. I set my coffee on the nearby sink and make quick work of facing the urinal, having to lean in such a way that I don't pee on myself, glancing over my shoulder and taking in the view of her perfect ass in those jean shorts. "Actually," she adds, "who am I kidding? That was hot as fuck. Thank you for saving me from having to stand out there with those people. Some of them can be really fucking mean, even when you go out of your way to be nice to them."

"I'd like to see them try while I'm around," I grumble, my hackles rising at the thought of my woman getting hounded by people she was trying to help.

When I'm done, I wash my hands then grab my coffee, unlocking the bathroom before taking Erin's free hand in mine and shouldering open the door.

"Holy fuck, that *is* him!" one of the homeless women says. She can't be older than nineteen or twenty. Her hair is in dreadlocks and her teeth are straight and white as she grins from ear to ear, making me wonder if the group isn't homeless after all.

"Dude. I fucking *love* your show!" one of the guys says. He's around the same age as the girl, maybe a couple years older, and he stands up, bringing his phone into view. He snaps a picture, the flash blinding in this dimly lit courtyard, and when he pulls the phone back down and uncovers his face, there's a look of awe in his expression. "Bro… did you just bang ya girl in the public restroom? That's just… gross."

I look down at Erin and then back into the face of this young man covered in grime from head to toe, a dog leash wrapped limply around his dirty hand, and realize his phone is the latest model iPhone. What the fuck?

I can't help it. I burst into laughter at the ridiculousness of it all. When I notice the group looking awkwardly at each other, I try to control my chuckles enough to tell them, "Thanks for watching. And no, I didn't 'bang my girl' in the public bathroom. We were in there all of what… two minutes, tops? Give me some credit. I'd last at least five… maybe six. Because look at her." I hike my thumb at Erin and wiggle my eyebrows. "Like a gentleman, I didn't want to leave her alone in the middle of the night in a dark… alley, basically."

The second woman, still sitting on the ground up against the wall, speaks up. "She wouldn't have been alone. We coulda looked after her for ya to piss, man."

Erin finally steps out from where she's been standing halfway behind me. "I appreciate that. That's not the case a lot of times though. Sorry for judging the situation incorrectly."

"Ah, you must be talkin' about Beau's clan," the guy with the iPhone says.

"That guy is a fucking *dick*," the second guy on the ground says before he stands up, walking toward us.

As I feel Erin take a tiny step back behind me, I stand my ground, pulling up to my full height as he approaches. And it's not until he comes into the light shining over the bathroom door that I notice… his grime isn't quite right. It almost looks like… makeup?

He holds his hand out to me. "It's a pleasure to meet you, Mr. Rockwell. Huge fan of your cooking. You actually catered one of my best friends' sweet sixteen birthday party back home a few years ago."

Before I can even try to put two and two together, Erin saves the day by blurting, "Okay, what the hell is going on? This cat has a phone as fancy as mine, and I *know* how expensive that shit was." She gestures toward the guy still standing near the two women, taking photos or maybe video of the situation. "That gal there is wearing ratty jeans, but they're freaking designer. She fucking bought them that way, and probably paid six, maybe seven hundred bucks for them! And you, sir—" She steps forward to look closely at his face, and I tighten my hold on her hand still in mine, yanking her back into my body. "—you are wearing stage makeup. I know, because I too am a cosplayer."

This makes me look down at her in surprise, and I smile, thinking about the beauty dressed up in nerd gear for Comic Con. If I wasn't in the middle of this completely weird situation, I would pop yet another boner.

"But the question is, what the fuck are y'all cosplaying? There isn't another convention around here for three more months," she points out, and I can't help but wonder who she likes to dress up as. I don't have time to ponder it though, because the other three kids stand up and make their way over to us.

"We're a group of students from UCLA… as in Los Angeles," the last girl finally speaks in a super Valley Girl sounding voice.

"They know where UCLA is, Cameron," the guy with the cell says.

She shrugs. "Well, I don't know that. The last guy we told thought the LA in it was for Louisiana."

"Back on course, y'all. What the french toast is going on?" Erin prompts, and I hold in a snort.

"We're here doing research for a movie we're producing. Thought we'd go undercover as homeless people a few hours a night. We have a couple days left out here, and after the first night, when we met Beau and his group, we've been mostly just trying to stay hidden from them while still getting the information and stuff we need. I'm Dominik, by the way." He puts his phone in his left hand and holds out his right for us to shake.

We do, and then the rest of the group introduces themselves, Cameron, Dominik, Andrea, and Carson all politely shaking our hands before Dominik leans down to pet the dog behind his ear, introducing him as Java.

Vaguely, I hear Cameron whisper to Andrea something about how much the photos of me and Erin will be worth when they get back to Cali, and Erin steps in, clearly having heard her too.

"How about we make a deal?" she asks, and Dominik looks up from where he's obviously recording. "If you delete the photos and video you're currently taking—" She glares at him until he has the decency to look a little ashamed and shuts it off. "—I will take you to a group of less fortunate people who would gladly let you interview them for your movie. They are kind and good-hearted and won't be assholes to you the way this… Beau person was. You'll get all the information you need, and then Curtis, who you clearly are a fan of and wouldn't want him to suffer any shit for being in an embarrassing tabloid magazine that'll definitely spread false rumors about him banging a mystery woman in a public restroom, can rest easy knowing that won't happen."

The group turns in toward each other, and after a moment of murmuring, Dominik holds out his unlocked phone, the Photos app on display, where we see at least a hundred photos and videos taken of this entire situation, which has only been a total of maybe five minutes.

"One condition. I'll let you delete everything so you can be sure they're all gone, but…" He pauses, and Erin and I glance at each other.

"Buuut…?" I prompt, giving in to what he so clearly wants.

"Dude. You gotta take a selfie with us. No one is going to believe we ran into Chef Curtis Rockwell in the middle of the night in New Orleans, man! This is so awesome!" Dominik exclaims, and I smile, nodding at his excitement.

"Deal," I tell him, and as I take his phone and delete all the photos, I hear him speaking to Erin.

"And if I can get your information, I'd love to put you in the end credits of the movie. If these people really are willing to let us interview them and get all the intel we need, that'll make our jobs so much easier than trying to gain it by pretending to be homeless. We're obviously not very good at acting, hence why we're studying to be the people behind the cameras." He chuckles.

When I get everything deleted, remembering to go in and permanently trash the Recently Deleted folder, I spin toward the bathroom door so the light above it is facing all of us. I pull Erin into my side, hit the front-facing camera button, and hold the phone up high so the entire group of us is in focus.

"Ready?" I ask.

"Ready!" all of them reply.

And I grin and say, "New Orleeeans!" as I hold down the shutter button, getting a burst of about thirty photos just in case someone blinks.

Thirteen

ERIN

THE GROUP OF students tagged along with us a few streets over until I found my old pal and pro bono patient Gunny and his buddies in their usual spot. After explaining everything to them, and after Dominik offered to treat them all by doing the interview in a nearby diner all on his tab, Gunny and everyone agreed enthusiastically. And Curtis and I left them to it, strolling down the narrow sidewalk hand in hand.

"Well, that was… interesting," he tells me quietly, shaking his head and smiling as he watches his feet.

"Yeah. Crazy shit like that happens every day here in NOLA. Keeps ya young and on your toes, I guess." I giggle. "You hear that?" I ask, glancing up at Curtis once more.

He cocks his head. "What is all the yelling?" He blinks.

"That, good sir, is the one and only Bourbon Street. We're currently walking parallel to it. It's just two blocks over. See the lights?" I point up over the building, where you can see the lights from all the bars, shops, clubs, and strip joints illuminating the sky.

"No shit?" he asks, his face suddenly full of awe.

I giggle once more. "No shit. You wanna go? After all the excitement, beignets, and coffee, I'm one hundred percent sober and fully awake."

"How about we change that to about seventy-three percent sober and still fully awake until after about the third… maybe fourth orgasm I plan on giving you?"

My eyebrow lifts and my feet halt, our arms stretching out as our hands stay linked because he takes a couple steps before he realizes I froze.

"What?" he prompts. "I thought we were skipping the whole playing coy, pretending we don't know what's going to happen at the end of the night thing."

"Oh, we totally are. I was just surprised by the goal you set. I have to warn you. I don't fake it. And I'm also one of those chicks who unfortunately can't get off with just a few pumps of a cock. I'm quite the handful," I admit.

"Challenge: Accepted, sugar," he tells me, yanking me to him by our interlocked fingers before he backs me up until I'm against the bricks of the building.

Being literally caught between a rock and a hard place sends a thrill through my veins, making my heart pump. And when he bends his knees and presses forward, allowing me to feel the thickness of him between my thighs, my head falls back against the wall and my eyes close with a groan.

"You sure you wanna go to Bourbon Street? I mean, we could just go straight—"

"I'm sure," he interrupts, and I whimper as he trails feather-soft kisses up my neck until he reaches my ear. "Not ready for this night to end. Won't be ready, and won't bury this cock deep in your tight little pussy, until I know for a fact that you understand it won't be the last one I spend with you."

"Curtis," I breathe, and he latches his teeth gently onto my earlobe.

"So I'm gonna need you to show me to the best place to get us a couple drinks on Bourbon, so I can get back to convincing you," he tells me, and I moan in agreement.

"Okay," I whisper, the closest I've ever been to an orgasm without being naked and thirty-minutes-deep into playtime. How the fuck did he get me this riled up with just a few kisses?

He takes a step back and takes my hand once more, and when we get to the intersection, I lead the way to Bourbon Street, stopping at the head of the closed off party area. Between certain hours on different days, cars can't pass through these few blocks, which allows everyone to drink and party in the street.

"Okay, so fun fact. I've never actually brought a guy to play on

Bourbon Street just the two of us before. It's always been like, a group thing or just me and my girlfriends. Sooo… what do you wanna do?" I ask, stepping into Curtis to let a few staggering women pass behind me on their way out.

"Well, what would you and your girlfriends usually do?" he prompts, holding me close and looking down at me with amusement.

I bite my lip, wondering if he'd really be willing to go to our favorite place on the street. "There's this club near the halfway mark up the street. They have great drinks and a cool upstairs area with a balcony. But you might not feel comfortable going."

"And why is that?" He lifts a brow.

"It's a gay club. We go because the people are awesome and they have a DJ who plays actual dance music instead of a live band," I explain.

He nods slowly. "Hey, babe."

I tilt my head. "Yes?"

"You remember I'm from California, right?" he asks, and he gives me a crooked smile.

I play along. "Sooo… you *are* gay. Therefore, you'd feel right at home at a gay club! Let's go!" I pretend like I'm about to run off toward it, but he yanks me back to him, making me cackle when he wraps me up in his arms before swatting me on the ass. It takes everything in me not to purr… or hump his leg.

"Does this feel like I'm gay, when I'm pushed up against such a fine-ass woman?" He takes my hand and slides it between us, pressing my open palm to the front of his jeans to feel he is rock-hard.

"Fuck my life. I guess my assessment in my kitchen was right. You are one virile fucking guy, Chef. How many boners have you had today? I've lost count," I tease, even though inside I'm more hot and bothered than I've ever been in my damn life.

"No clue. But I read somewhere that the average dude pops wood unconsciously about eleven times a day, so I'm right on track," he replies, and I throw my head back and laugh as he holds me.

It's the most relaxed and carefree I've felt in a long time, and it's all thanks to this amazing man who I just met *today*. How is it possible I can feel this close to someone, when I've known him less than twelve hours?

"So no, sugar. Not gay. But about 98.6% of my friends are, or at least rank themselves somewhere on the sliding scale of sexuality. So I have no problem going to a gay club. My only qualm is… I *am* a tourist, not a local, so I'd love to go somewhere more… authentic to New Orleans, if I have a choice," he tells me, and I nod, completely understanding.

"One question. Do we want to pretend like we just hit the legal drinking age, or do we want to acknowledge the fact that we're pretty much ancient as fuck and will be older than 87% of the population?" I ask, eyes wide, feigning innocence.

He rubs his chin for a moment, thinking about his answer. "How about a little of both? Pick two places. For the first one, make me feel like a frat boy on Spring Break, and for the second, take me somewhere we can rest our old bones and just chill."

I grin. "I have the perfect places." I slide away, keeping hold of his hand as I guide him between the two orange and white roadblocks and start weaving between people. A few yards in, and we're swallowed up by the crowd.

Music blares, echoing off the buildings as a huge group of partiers dance in unison to "The Wobble." I turn to face Curtis and walk backward as I take hold of his front belt loops and shimmy, giving him a flirty look. He smiles down at me, a heated gleam in his eyes, but there's more there than the usual lust most guys aim my way. No, there's so much more—a possessiveness I feel to the depths of my soul, chipping more windows into the walls around my heart.

His hands reach out to take hold of my waist, guiding my blind walk down Bourbon Street as I don't watch where I'm going, fully trusting him to keep me from running into anyone or falling off a curb. When I sense an intersection coming up, I spin around, feeling his palms glide around my body as he never lifts them away from me. My tank top bunches, pulling up from the waistband of my jean shorts, and as we pass over the crossroad, I feel his fingertips lightly trailing back and forth over the sliver of exposed skin at my hip. It sends tingles up and down my side, my nipples pebbling against the cups of my bra.

Normally, this place is sensory overload. The smells—good and bad, between the different restaurants battling with that unique NOLA aroma—the neon lights and people coming and going in all directions. Not to mention the music and yelling. It's always so… just so *much* and all at once. But for the first time ever, everything seems muted. I don't focus on the loud voices all around me, or the seizure-causing flashing lights, or the funk of the chick currently throwing up in the alleyway as we pass by, or the beads narrowly missing me as they're tossed from the overhead gallery to someone baring their breasts in the crowd next to us. No, my focus is on the man who overshadows all of that outside noise and narrows my every nerve ending on him, as if I'm a blossoming flower and he is the sun itself, everything in me wanting to stretch toward his warmth and light.

Finally, we reach his first request—frat boy central. "Here we are!" I tell him, and he glances up at the two-story building, it's beautiful classic wraparound iron gallery circling the second story of the corner lot. It's a crazy contrast, the gorgeous old architecture and the loud party scene going on inside, a big neon multicolored sign boasting **Tropical Isle, Original, Home of the Hand Grenade, New Orleans' Most Powerful Drink** above the door situated at the corner of the building.

"I think that's my favorite feature of this style architecture," Curtis says thoughtfully, and I glance up to see him looking at the entrance.

"The doors?" I ask, a little confused. There's nothing really special about the door here. It's just wooden and painted green.

He shakes his head. "Not the doors themselves. The placement of them. I don't think I've ever seen doors made right into the corner of a building before today. Like, right where two sides of the building meet, bam! That's where you go in. I bet that's a bitch to install when they have to replace the doorframes and stuff, trying to get it all aligned and level." When I raise a brow at him in question, he answers, "My yaya's husband has been a contractor since he retired from the military. When I was a teenager, it was my first job."

"Reeeally?" I trail my finger over his chest flirtatiously. "Not only could I fulfill my construction worker fantasy, but you actually know what you're doing? My very own Chip Gaines," I purr, rubbing up against him and watching his eyes flash. "See why Joanna is my idol? She's got it all figured out. Get ya a guy to do all your neck-down work and design biddings. Mwah-ha-ha-ha."

He chuckles at my evil laughter. Pulling me ever closer. "Sugar, I'll even walk around in just my tool belt, if it'll make you happy. Anything to make you happy," he murmurs just before he presses his lips to mine for a quick but oh so sweet kiss. "Now. Let's see if these Hand Grenades are better than the ones we had on the tour." He takes my hand and pulls me inside, walking up to the line at the bar.

When I can calm my racing heart enough to speak—damn this man for making me go all gooey when I was just trying to be my normal goofy self—I tell him, "That bar we got our drinks at was owned by Tropical Isle. Hand Grenades are policed like a motherfucker around here. They don't allow knockoffs. If they find out a bar or restaurant they don't own is calling a drink a Hand Grenade, they sue their asses in a heartbeat. So if you can walk in somewhere and get one in their signature green bomb cup, it's pretty safe to say it's always going to taste exactly the same."

"Interesting," he replies, and then smiles over my shoulder when the bartender asks what we'd like. "So do we want another one, or should we try something else?"

"Mine was on the rocks. You could try the frozen one. Or there's the Shark Attack. That's one's really good and they make a big scene when you order one. There's also the Tropical Itch and the Horny Gator," I supply, and his eyes twinkle at the name.

"Oh, the Horny Gator. I gotta try that one!" he calls over to the bartender, who nods. "What do you want, sugar?"

"Might as well match you drink for drink. That way you'll know when I'm reaching that seventy-three percent sober level you were talking about earlier." I shrug.

He laughs at that, turning away just long enough to tell the bartender to make that two Horny Gators. "I'm *sliiightly* larger than you, babe. I don't think our tolerance is the same."

"I don't know. I've got a liver of steel and live in New Orleans. My tolerance is pretty damn high," I retort, and he nods in acceptance.

We find a table a few minutes later, after I tugged Curtis out of a chair he plopped into, not realizing where he was sitting. Without verbally answering his question of why I made him move, I point to where he'd previously been sitting. He turns to watch as a group of drunk coeds attempt to throw the little green plastic hand grenade that comes in the top of the drink this bar is famous for into a net situated right over where he'd been. It takes them several tries to make their bombs into the net, the people cackling and falling all over themselves as they chase the ones they drop all over the floor before attempting to throw them in again. One of the girls even falls into the chair Curtis just vacated, and I'm happy I won't have to get into a bar brawl tonight.

That thought makes me sit up straight, my brow furrowing, and Curtis notices.

"What's the matter? You look… perturbed," he observes, taking a sip of his drink before glancing down into his green alligator-shaped souvenir cup adorned with little gator toys and licking his lips. "Damn, that's good."

I try to change the subject, uncomfortable with my jealousy. "Oh! Do your trick! Do your trick!" I chant, but he shakes his head.

"Nuh-uh. Not until you tell me what just made you look like you tasted something with arugula in it," he states, and I can't help but laugh.

"How did you know I hate arugula?" I ask, tilting my head to the side.

He smiles. "Because when we were at the grocery story earlier, in the produce section, I heard you say 'oh barf, arugula' when we passed by it," he informs me through a chuckle. "Now spill."

"I don't care what people say. It's arugula that's the devil's lettuce, not weed." I shiver dramatically.

"Uh-oh, do I have a little pothead on my hands?" he asks, taking another sip of his drink before moaning in approval at the flavor once more.

I shake my head. "Nah, while it does have many amazing medical benefits for both mental and physical ailments, it just makes me super hungry and then sleepy, and I wake up with the worst belly ache. So after the third or fourth time smoking it in college, I decided it wasn't for me."

"Sugar." He gives me a pointed look. "Spill," he orders.

And I sigh, sitting back in my chair and crossing my arms like a petulant child. "Hey, it was you who changed the subject that time. Not my fault." He lifts a brow, his lips going in a straight line. "Fine. That girl fell into the chair you were sitting in before. Which means she would've fallen right in your lap if I hadn't gotten you to move over here. The thought… irked me."

His nostrils flare, and I just know he's trying not to smile. "It *irked* you?"

I huff. "Yes. It fucking irked me! I had a momentary vision of a full-on cat fight where I took her by the hair and slung her across the bar, making her slide all the way down it and knocking over everyone's drinks."

He nods slowly, eyeing me. "So in this momentary jealousy-induced vision, you had adrenaline-fueled super-strength."

I shrug one shoulder, lifting my hand to look at my nails before buffing them on my tank then glancing at them once more, as if I don't have a care in the world. "Technically, it wasn't jealousy; it was possessiveness. And kinda like Black Widow, not quite Wonder Woman. I'm a badass in my coed slinging fantasies, not an Amazon."

He just stares at me. Deep into my eyes, all over my face, down my body before the rest of it disappears beneath the table, back up to my eyes. I don't know what he's looking at or for, but I feel… *seen* for the first time in my entire life. And instead of making me want to squirm under his perusal, I bask in the feeling, because there's nothing but awe in his expression.

"You truly are the perfect woman, sugar. Gorgeous, with a brilliant brain *and* you're a nerd? Fuck. You were made for me," he rumbles, leaning forward in his chair. "Which reminds me. What was all that you were saying to those college kids outside the bathroom? You cosplay and go to conventions?"

My cheeks heat a little. I forgot I said that in front of him earlier. It's one of my guilty pleasures. I groan, sinking into my seat and shaking my head. "It's something Emmy and I have done since I can remember. We get quite a few awesome nerd conventions here in New Orleans, and we dress up and go get autographs and photo ops with some of our favorite actors."

He bites his lip for a moment and then grins. "Who do you dress up as?"

I roll my eyes then look away, not meeting his eyes, because dear God, for some reason, I care about what this man thinks of me. And I don't want him thinking I'm too much of a geek, when he's this devastatingly gorgeous, super cool celebrity chef.

Be gone, stupid self-doubt! He's already told you you're perfect for him. Now see if he's perfect for you!

"My favorite to dress up as is Khaleesi," I finally reply.

His eyebrow quirks. "Daenerys Stormborn of the House Targaryen?"

I lean forward with a smirk. "The First of Her Name."

"The Unburnt? Queen of the Andals, the Rhoynar, and the First Men?"

I nod, flipping my ponytail over my shoulder. "Queen of Meereen."

He sighs dreamily. "Khaleesi of the Great Grass Sea?"

I put my elbow on the table between us and prop my chin on my knuckles. "Protector of the Realm."

"Lady Regent of the Seven Kingdoms?" he asks, his hand going to his chest like he's about to get the vapors, and it takes everything in me to finish the rest of the *Game of Thrones* character's title with a straight, serious face.

I throw my head back and my arm in the air, closing my eyes to call out, "Breaker of Chains and Mother of Dragons!"

When he doesn't burst out laughing like I expect, my eyes slowly open to focus on him, and his are full of an emotion I've yet to see directed at me by anyone before—not even my ex. Pure, unadulterated, undeniable, irrevocable, soul-shattering love. And it takes my breath away. Which is okay, because I gasp and gain oxygen once more when he says…

"Marry me."

Fourteen

CURTIS

AT THE LOOK in Erin's beautiful eyes, I snap out of the spell she put me under and joke to try to calm the panic my words put on her face. "I mean, after we date a couple weeks and then give you time to plan a wedding. So like, marry me in a month." I grin.

"You're like… joking, right? I can't tell," she squeaks, narrowing her eyes on me.

I look down into my drink for a moment, not really knowing how to answer. I'm serious as fuck right now. And if we were in Vegas, I'd throw her over my shoulder and haul her ass into the closest wedding chapel. But I know it sounds absolutely fucking crazy to want to marry someone after not even knowing each other for an entire day, so I… don't exactly backpedal, but I cool my jets a little while still being perfectly honest. "You are the embodiment of everything I've ever dreamed of in a woman, and more. You have qualities about you that I didn't even know I could ask for in a partner, and I'm pretty damn sure that after experiencing… well, you—just being around you, spending time with you, getting to know *you*—I'll never in my life be able to live without… you."

She glances at my drink then back up to my eyes. "Dafuck did they put in your Horny Gator? It's supposed to make you an insatiable lover, not… crazy," she murmurs.

I reach over and take her hand, pulling it to my lips so I can kiss her knuckles before enclosing my other hand around it too. "I know. I know

I sound absolutely insane right now. But you can't tell me you don't feel it too. You already admitted it earlier, and we already promised not to play stupid games. I'm just trying to be completely honest with you."

Her face looks thoughtful as her eyes drift back and forth between her hand enveloped in mine and my eyes, and just when I think she might jerk away and run out of here screaming, she relaxes a little, pressing her lips together before giving me a slight smile. "I feel it too, Curtis. I do. But there's something about me you need to know before you go wanting to make commitments, because in the end, I can't give you what you want out of life. I can't give *anyone* what they want in the end. Not even myself."

I squeeze her hand, pulling her closer across the table. "So why don't you take me to the more adult destination you promised me, and let's have a grownup talk about everything, and you let me decide just what I want out of life," I suggest gently, and she nods.

Without another word, she weaves her fingers through mine, picks up her drink with her free hand, and leads me out of the bar and onto the sidewalk. The street isn't as crowded as it was before, still full of life and partying, but not nearly as packed. It makes it a lot easier to travel down the walkway to the next place she wants to show me.

We walk in heavy silence. Not exactly uncomfortable, but with an air of anticipation of a serious conversation. I'm both excited to learn more about her, and anxious to hear what she seems to think is a deal breaker when it comes to herself. In my mind, there is nothing this woman could tell me that would make me not want to be with her. Not just in my head, but in my heart and soul as well. There's nothing we couldn't overcome. No demon I wouldn't fight for her. Whatever she has to say, I'll just have to convince her it doesn't matter. All that matters to me is her.

We walk until it seems like we're at the end of Bourbon Street. It's quiet down here, and dim, almost eerily so, after being in such a loud and bright environment. We come to a small brick building with several doors lining the front and sides, which are all open. I read the wooden sign hanging beneath the covered doorway, **Lafitte's Blacksmith Shop, Piano Bar & Lounge**.

It's dark inside, to the point I'm not really sure if it's still open, until a couple walks out one of the doors lining the front before heading in the direction we came.

"Lafitte? As in…?" I prompt, wondering if it's the same Lafitte her best friend made a huge discovery about a few years ago, and let Erin lead me inside the little building.

"Yep. According to the legends around here, this place is the oldest structure to be used as a bar in the entire United States. It was built in the early 1700s. So that means it survived all those fires we learned about on the tour. Later on in the 1700s, they say it was used by John Laffite and his brother Pierre for their smuggling operation. Their pirate friends would bring all their stolen goods and store them here to avoid all the government fees and shit. Jean used the building as a blacksmith shop, which was the perfect cover," she explains as we lean against the bar.

There are several people here, but nothing like the crazy crowd from earlier up the street. The atmosphere is almost soothing, even if it is a little creepy. The entire place is deeply dim, with the only light coming from candles on each table. There are dark wooden beams spaced out running along the entire ceiling, and dead center on the bar is an ancient brick double-sided fireplace that looks like it could crumble and collapse at any second. It looks like we're on the set of a period-piece movie, and I'm pretty sure if I glanced toward the other side of the bar, Jack Sparrow would be rallying a crew to go steal back his Black Pearl. I decide this is my favorite place we've been so far in all of New Orleans.

I pull Erin close as we wait for the bartender, nuzzling her ear when I lean down to tell her, "Thank you for bringing me here. This place is amazing."

She snuggles closer to me. "It's one of my all-time favorite spots. And wait 'til you try the drink."

Just then, the bartender makes it to us and asks what we'd like. "Two Voodoo Daiquiris please," Erin answers, giving me an excited wiggle of her eyebrows and making me smile.

"Coming right up," he tells us, and turns away to create our concoction using unmarked bottles before filling the rest of the large white plastic cups using a slushy machine. When he sets them in front of us, I hand over my credit card, signing the slip when he places it in front of me.

Erin glances behind me and around the fireplace, her face brightening when she spots what she's looking for. "My favorite table is open!" she squeaks, hurrying over to the rickety looking wooden table and chairs in the corner of the bar.

When we take our seats, I reach to pull her chair closer to mine by the leg but think twice. It looks like it could fall apart at any moment, so I decide to pick mine up carefully and move closer to her instead. "So what is a Voodoo Daquiri?"

"That's the thing. Nobody knows. But it's *provocative*," she breathes the last word, and I laugh, recognizing the quote from *Blades of Glory*. "I'm hoping you can finally solve the mystery with your taste-testing superpower."

"Dude. How shitty would it be if we lived in a world full of superheroes, and that's the only power I got? Fucking taste-testing," I gripe.

"Captain Taste Buds!" she exclaims in an announcer voice.

"Super Tongue!" I mimic her tone.

She bites her lip at that. "Well. That one makes me think of something completely different." And then she gets an overdramatic look of worry on her face. "Oh shit. If you're a super-taster, does that mean...." She shakes her head, flipping her hair over her shoulder. "No, no. I ain't got nothing to worry about. 'I have never had any complaints in the poonany odor department.'"

I hold up my hand, finishing the scene from *The Sweetest Thing*. "'High-five on the clean poonany.'" She claps her palm to mine and bursts into a fit of giggles, and I shake my head in wonder. "I swear, it's like we're the same person when it comes to the movies and shows we both love." With all our fun banter, I feel the weight of the conversation we came here to have lighten just a bit, especially when she takes a sip of her drink and turns to rest her head on my shoulder. "I can only imagine what our mouths are going to look like after we drink these. What the hell is it?"

"Well, Lil Wayne calls it Purple Drank. It's grape flavor is all anyone really knows. And it's supposed to make your clothes fall off," she says with a smile.

"Isn't that what tequila is supposed to be for?" I ask, referring to the country song.

"Could be what's in it, I suppose. Take a sip already! You're killing me," she urges, sliding my cup up to the edge of the table right so the straw is right in front of me.

"Why, sugar. Are you trying to get me drunk?" I ask, feigning offence.

She scoffs. "Duh. I wanna get you home and take advantage of you. And that's much easier when you're full of Voodoo juice."

I chuckle, finally leaning down and putting her out of her misery. And holy shit, it's delicious. "Yep, definitely grape. And even though my sense is slightly dulled from the Hurricanes and the Horny Gator, I'm tasting... Everclear and most definitely bourbon. Ha! I'm drinking bourbon on Bourbon Street."

"Whomp whooomp," she singsongs, shaking her head then taking a large swig of her daquiri.

I want to breach the subject of us, but I don't want this light feeling to end. I stare down into my big white cup, at the purple slush gleaming back at me in the candlelight of this amazing three-hundred-year-old building, trying to come up with a way to start the conversation without making Erin's spirits sink.

Just when I start to feel anxiety creeping up, she saves me, and I'm grateful to see she's still got a small smile on her delectable lips. "When you said you wanted one of our stops to be somewhere we could relax and rest our old bones, I immediately thought of this place," she says quietly. "This isn't my go-to bar, the one I frequent the most after a hard day at work or to just go out and meet new people, but it's like my... happy place. I save it for special occasions, and when I really need a pick-me-up. That way it doesn't lose its soothing effect. I came here after my ex-fiancé left me, and before that, I came here just to sit and regain some of my... zen, I guess you could call it, after I had my miscarriage."

My eyes that'd been locked on hers while she spoke shutter when I see the pain in her eyes. Her smiling lips tremble slightly, and I know she's trying to stay strong while she bravely just spits it all out for me.

"I've never told anyone about any of this, except for Emmy. Only my ex, my doctor, and my best friend know anything about it. Well, and my old therapist, but I don't really count her," she admits, and I tilt my head to the side.

"Why don't you count her?" I ask.

"Because she really didn't do much to help me heal from it. She doesn't use the same techniques and practices as I do, and after I laid it all out for her only to have no results in the end, I didn't bother finding another therapist. Didn't want to go through the pain of having to recap it all, so I decided—like an idiot, mind you—that I could be my own therapist, get over it on my own. As we know from earlier, I'm not the greatest at taking care of myself, and I save up all my energy for helping other people. Really, I've just been using other people's problems to ignore my own," she confesses, taking a long sip of her drink.

I nod, giving it a minute for her words to settle between us. And then what she told me before really sinks in. "You said your fiancé left you... but *before* then, you had a miscarriage? He left you after you lost your baby?" I rumble, my last sentence coming out testier than I meant for it to.

At her nod, things start clicking into place—the reason she seemed so sad during the tour when children were mentioned, when she snorted when Ronnie explained women were sent here because the residents needed wives to birth the next generation, and why she thinks she can't give anyone what they want out of life, including herself.

Not caring any longer about the furniture, I scoot back from the table and wrap my arms around the woman next to me, pulling her into my lap and cradling her against my much larger frame. She feels almost childlike herself when she curls into me, allowing me to comfort her broken heart. I feel her breathe me in, hear her sigh, and it makes me think of the many times I've seen my yaya bury her face in her husband's chest or neck to inhale his scent. She always pulls away from him with a look of blissful love on her face, seeming more relaxed and calmer than before.

I rub up and down Erin's back with an open palm, my hand seeming big against her small body. And when she melts into me, I know all her walls are finally crumbling down around us. In this moment, I feel a closeness with her I've never felt with anyone before, and I wonder if it's our souls finally greeting each other, after she finally let hers come out from the tower she had it locked away in.

She tilts her head, unburying her face from my shirt, so she can speak quietly in my ear. "It's not only that though, Curtis. Yes, it was super shitty that he left after one of the most heartbreaking experiences of my life. But I can't really blame him after what the doctor told us."

I pull away just enough so I can look her in the eyes while she talks. "What could he have possibly said that would make what your ex did forgivable?" My nostrils flare. I'm not a violent man. I've never really had to be. Any bad situation I've ever been in, the opponent would just look at the sheer size of me and back down. I've been grateful for my Nordic genes for keeping me out of too much trouble until now, but for the first time in my life, I feel the old Viking blood in my veins sizzle, wanting to go after this motherfucker for leaving this wonderful creature in my arms after she suffered such a painful loss.

"I have been blessed with a hostile uterus with an *un*healthy dose of random-ass leiomyomas for good measure, ensuring that the chances of conceiving and carrying my own child would be—for lack of a better word—a fucking miracle," she explains, and I narrow my eyes.

"I'm sorry, sugar. What is that lie-word you said again?" I ask, trying to take in all the information I can.

"Leiomyomas. It's the technical term for uterine fibroids."

I hold her closer, even as I reach out to take hold of her drink, pulling it up in front of her to take a big gulp before replacing it on the table. "Is that cancerous? My yaya had to have some pre-cancer cells frozen years ago, but that word never came up."

"No, not cancerous. At least there's that. They just… like, take up all the room in my uterus. Some can block the way for swimmers to make their way in and create the baby, but like I said, hostile uterus, so even when that miracle happened and I conceived, my body treated her like she was a foreign entity and rejected her," she murmurs, her lip trembling once again and her eyes filling with tears, and she tries to laugh away the emotion, shaking her head. "It was a long time ago. I'm fine, really."

"Clearly," I growl, my hand making its way into the back of her hair to tilt her head back so she can see deep into my eyes. "And you think that just because you might never be able to have a baby, you're unworthy of love, of having a relationship so fulfilling a man wouldn't even need anything besides you in his life?"

"That man doesn't exist. It's in men's very nature to want to spread his seed. It's basically their meaning of life, to put babies in bellies. I'm a psychologist. I know all too well the physiology of it all," she says heatedly, but not as if she's angry with me, just the hand she's been dealt.

When I let the silence stretch between us, I can't help but smile at the thoughts running through my mind. And when she sees the expression on my face, she narrows her eyes. "What? What could you possibly be smiling about right now?" She wiggles attempting to get away from me, but I just wrap my arms more tightly around her, not letting her go.

I pretend likes she's not struggling in my hold and hissing at me like a pissed off cat. "Not long ago, maybe a month or two," I begin, and she slowly settles back down, "I was hanging out with none other than your best friend's husband. We had a network meeting, and we sat together for lunch. We made small-talk, of course, shooting the shit like we always do, but then he asked me about my love life, if I was ever going to settle down."

She can't help herself. She gives in when I don't continue with my story. "And what did you say?" she prompts.

"I told him I wouldn't be settling down anytime soon, because there was nothing holding me to one spot. My travels and cooking and TV show were all I needed to have a fulfilling life. I never really craved the traditional marriage and two-point-five children and white picket fence life. That all just seemed so… claustrophobic. Almost… like a trapped feeling, you know? Literally feeling shackled down—which I suppose is why that term is used when referring to getting married, huh?" I smile.

"So what you're saying is you're happy being a bachelor with no responsibilities," she says with an accusing tone.

"Says the beauty in my lap who is one hundred percent the female version of me. Bachelorette pad, great job you love, not allowing yourself to get attached to anyone," I point out.

She turns her head and gives me a side-eye. "Touché."

"But as I said, that was a month or two ago. That was… before I met you. And somehow, in just one night, you've changed everything," I murmur, imploring with my eyes for her to believe me. "No, I still don't want the traditional two-point-five kids trapped behind a white picket fence. But you know what? Being shackled to a woman behind fancy wrought-iron gallery posts seems right up my alley."

She stares into my eyes for a full minute, and I watch, fascinated as her tear ducts seem to drain the tears from her once swimming golden pools. And the next thing I know, I'm breathing in her grapey breath as her lips lock to mine and she gives me the most heart-wrenching kiss I've ever experienced in my life.

Fifteen

ERIN

THE SIX-BLOCK walk back to my house passes in a blur, and not because of the drinks. We make several stops beneath random galleries to pause for kisses and sweet nothings, but the rest of the way is passed with hurried footsteps. When we reach the door, I can barely ring the hole with my key I'm so jittery with anticipation of what's to come and because Curtis can't seem to keep his hands off me. And when I finally do get the door unlocked, we've hardly made it inside before he slams it shut and my back is pressed against it.

The quietness of the room is deafening after the hustle and bustle we just came from. While Lafitte's was muted and intimate, we had to pass back through party central in order to make it home.

Curtis is so close, so big he's the only thing I can see, everything behind him disappearing at my height until I'm suddenly up, up against the door with my legs instinctively wrapping around his hips. Now that I can see over his shoulder, all I want to do is go up the staircases just feet away, lead him to my room, my haven. I've never allowed any other man into my room before. When my ex and I were together, we were waiting until marriage to actually live together, and while we were dating and engaged, I always stayed at his place. It felt wrong bringing him here when this wasn't my house, disrespectful somehow. But with Curtis, it's completely different. He feels like home just as much if not more than this building does, and I feel nothing but peace thinking about him joining me upstairs.

He presses me into the door, grinding his ever-present erection against the seam of my jean shorts once again, and my eyes roll back into my head before it thumps against the wood. It gives him access to my throat, where he licks and nibbles, sucking gently enough not to leave a mark, even though the death grip he has on my hips tells me he's restraining himself, holding back from doing everything as roughly as he truly wants.

"Upstairs, first room on the left," I tell him, and then I'm levitating. I'm lifted, spun, and hauled so swiftly to my room I don't have time to think about how he carries me as if I weigh no more than the fluffy beignets we consumed earlier tonight. He's not even breathing hard after the three flights of stairs, which is fucking impressive, seeing as there are sixty steps in total.

I'm flat on my back in the middle of my king-sized bed before I even have my shoes off, but he must read my mind, because I instantly feel him unlacing my Converse, hearing them thunk to the floor as my black no-show socks are whipped off my feet. And then his big, strong hands are sliding over my ankles, over my calves, between my inner thighs, and then over my jean shorts until he reaches the button there, which he pops open with ease.

My zipper is pulled down, and just as he's working the tight denim over my hips, my eyes pop open with sudden realization. And I'm so mortified by what he's about to see that I can't even move or speak to stop it from happening before it's too late. Up until this moment, since the second we entered the house, all our humor and easy nature with each other went out the window. It's been passion and ferocity, heated desire and desperation. That was... until my jean shorts are slid down and off and I open my eyes to take in what I hoped had miraculously disappeared at some point during the night. But alas, there they are, in all their stretchy, white, unflattering, as-far-from-sexy-black-lace-lingerie-as-you-can-get glory. My motherfucking surgery panties.

I hesitantly glance up at Curtis, who is frozen, my shorts gripped in both hands, paused midair over his left shoulder as if he was about to toss them behind him before he caught sight of the disaster wrapped around my hips. His face is almost comedic in its utter confusion, his brow furrowed, and he cocks his head to the side, obviously trying to figure out what the fuck I'm wearing.

I groan, covering my face, turning my upper half to the side and trying to pull my body into full-on fetal position in mortification, but he's got my legs trapped. "Fucking kill me now," I utter. "Whyyy me?"

He clears his throat. "Um… so, not exactly what I was expecting when I finally got in your pants, sugar."

"Fuuuck my life," I murmur.

"But… it could totally be worse," he soothes, pulling at my elbow to make me face him and uncover my eyes.

My fists slam into the mattress on either side of my body as I pout up at him furiously. "How? How could it possibly be worse than finding *those* inside my pants? I got caught wearing my freaking surgery panties while getting it on for the first time with the world's sexiest chef!"

He pinches my pooched-out bottom lip gently before hovering himself over me, one hand bracing him on either side of my head. "I mean… you could have a dick." He shrugs, and I'm so shocked by this answer that I let out a loud gush of laughter, the force behind it sending my hand into his chest, punching him there with my ineffectual fist. He continues, a mocking smile on his face as he teases me, "And while I totally believe in falling in love with the wine, not the label, as David Rose so eloquently explained, I don't really consider myself pansexual. I'm strictly non-dickly."

I groan once more before squeezing my eyes closed and letting out a pained laugh. "Couldn't have caught me in my cute lacy undies I wore at work all day, could ya? Nooo, had to be after I changed into my comfy stuff. And to think I go to that store because I never see anyone I know and can walk around in hermit mode without being embarrassed. Thank you for ruining that for me." I shake my head.

Without another word, I feel him crawling down my body, making his way to the offending item of clothing, kissing a shiver-inducing path. I open my eyes to watch him, suddenly entranced by the way his eyelashes fan out above his cheekbones, the way his brow lifts when he finds a particularly soft spot of skin next to my belly button, his deep inhale as his gets ever-closer to my center, sending goose bumps down my legs.

He hooks the ugly-ass panties with his pointer fingers and slides them down and all the way off, not saying anything else about them as he watches where he tosses them, turning back. And I see his eyes catch on my scar, the whole reason I have a drawerful of those panties in the first place. I'm shaved bare, so it's on full display, and I fight not to squirm under his stare.

Normally, I don't give a shit about it. I haven't been with anyone since my surgery. And even if I had, any other time, the lights would be out and everything so quick no one would take the time to look so closely at the other's body. But here with Curtis, my overhead light is still on from before we left the house earlier, and I'm completely presented for his perusal.

The scar runs from one side of my bikini line to the other, about four inches of pink slightly puckered flesh. It's been almost six months since my surgery, so it's no longer sore. But when Curtis reaches up to run a fingertip gently along the line, I involuntarily jerk, and he looks up to meet my eyes.

"Does it hurt?" he asks softly.

I shake my head, biting my lip as my gaze bounces between the scar and his expression. Until he leans down and kisses the pink line from one end to the other then running his nose back to the other side. I melt into the bed, my heart peeking out of the rubble that was its protective tower as Curtis soothes any embarrassment I felt before.

"What's it from?" he murmurs, tracing his finger over it once more.

"Myomectomy," I reply, and at his questioning look, I explain quietly, "I had some of the fibroids removed that were affecting my blood pressure. I was sleeping close to fourteen hours a day, and finally Emmy dragged me to the doctor. They did the ultrasound and found them, and I had the surgery almost six months ago."

"Did it help? You feel better?" he asks, concern in his eyes, and my heart starts throwing the rubble out of its way, clearing a path for its escape.

I nod, my lip trembling a little bit, and I inhale at the unexpected emotion. He's suddenly above me, looking straight down into me with his stormy eyes, and all I can see is him.

"That's all that matters, sweet girl. You could be scarred from head to toe, and wear nothing but those godawful… whatever those were, and you'd still be the most beautiful thing I've ever laid eyes on. It's your inside I'm completely falling head-over-heels for, and as long as that inside is feeling the way it should, then that is all I care about," he tells me, and my throat gets tight. "So is your inside feeling the way it should, sugar?" He leans down and nuzzles my neck, and my eyes flutter closed.

"Starting to…" I whisper. "Starting to feel a lot better than it ever did. I think—" My face grows hot at admitting this aloud, but he deserves to hear it, since he's been so open with me. "—you might be healing whatever it is inside me the doctors would never be able to. You're making my heart feel a lot better about things going on with the rest of my body that I never thought I'd recover from." A single tear slides down my temple and into my hair, and Curtis presses a kiss to its track before moving to my lips, letting me taste the salt as my tongue meets his.

After the most world-rattling kiss I've ever experienced, he thankfully lightens the intensity of the mood before I turn into a sobbing mess of emotions. "Now, how 'bout I make a different part of your insides feel good?"

I wrinkle my nose as he kisses his way back down my body. "Ew," I state, feeling him chuckle as he settles between my thighs.

"Yeah, that sounded a lot better in my head," he says, and then all words leave my mind as he takes his first taste of me, running his tongue from the very bottom of my opening to circle around my clit. I sigh at the teasingly soft touch of his lips as he presses a kiss to the bundle of nerves, but then my back arches as his grip on me tightens, and all hell breaks loose.

He growls as his control suddenly snaps, making me gasp as he covers me with his whole mouth and sucks. I let out a mewl of shocked pleasure as he releases his suction right over my clit, making a popping sound as if he just pulled a sucker out of his mouth. My thighs tighten around his shoulders as I try to grasp all the intense bolts of desire his mouth is provoking; it's almost like it's too much all at once, but he continues eating me like a man possessed, and all I can do is dive my hands into his thick blond hair and hold on for dear life, because there is no stopping him.

Fuck, the sounds he makes, his hums of approval and groans of ecstasy, as if he's the one on the receiving end of these expert ministrations, could send me over the edge alone. But I force myself to get ahold of my breathing, using every technique I can think of that I teach my patients to use during anxiety attacks, because my heart is in a panic it beats so wildly with every plunge of his tongue inside me, with ever nibble to my clit, with ever vibration of his growls of desire.

His big hands grip my hips, his fingers digging into my softness until his thumbs creep around to hold my pussy lips open, and I whimper, bracing myself for impact. I glance down to see him staring at my most secret place, and the look of animalistic possession on his face is nearly my undoing. I shudder under his heated gaze, and the movement of my body must snap him out of his trance just enough that his mouth lands on me once more, and I squeal at the force of it all.

I've never been eaten like this before. It's always just been a couple minutes of foreplay to make sure I was ready for the main event. But what Curtis is doing to me is a headline show all on its own. And that thought is solidified as my breath starts to hitch and I can no longer control my breathing techniques. A feeling of rapture starts to fill me up, building, building... building until I swear I will explode as he latches onto my clit, circling it with his flawless lips, and then massaging it incessantly with the flat of his tongue.

And then I do. I shatter into oblivion. I scream out, "Fuck, Curtis! Oh, God!" as my entire body convulses, my hands digging into his scalp to hold him against my pussy as I ride the wave of euphoria all the way back until I'm lying flat on a sandy beach of blissful release.

My limbs go limp and my hands fall from his head, my breath coming in deep pants as my heart beats wildly inside my chest. I can't move, but that seems to be fine with Curtis as he places one last kiss to my center before crawling up my body, where all I can do is stare up at him through eyes that are half-mast.

He smiles, but it's not cocky. It's one of love I've never seen directed at me before him. "How are those insides doing?" he whispers, nuzzling the flesh above my heart, and I blink when he meets my eyes once again.

"Empty," I reply. "Need you." And with the last bit of strength I can conjure after he's made me a limp, melted mess on my big bed, I hook my ankles behind his thighs and pull him to me, where his hips nestle right up against my still sensitive flesh. Which is when I realize he still has his pants on. "Please," I whisper, trying to use my feet to pull his jeans down, and he wastes no time. He's suddenly as naked as I am, and the head of his big cock presses right up to my entrance, making me shudder.

"Tell me if it hurts you in any way," he demands softly, and my eyes meet his concerned ones.

I nod, my arms lifting to bury my hands in the back of his hair, and I pull him down to me so I can kiss his lips, tasting myself there as he slowly starts to press inside me, filling me inch by gloriously thick inch. I whimper at being stretched like I've never been stretched before, his girth like nothing I've ever experienced, and when he pulls back, his eyes narrowed in worry, I bite my lower lip and sigh in pleasure before reassuring him with a whispered "So fucking good," and see relief fill his every feature.

He surrounds me then, his forearms wrapping under me to rest on his elbows beneath my shoulder blades, pressing my chest up to his, where I can feel my nipples getting lost in the hair he has on his chest. The light tickle there makes this suddenly a full-body experience instead of all the focus being right where we're connected, and it allows me to take yet another of his breathtaking inches.

When it feels like I won't be able to take anymore of him, as if he's reached the farthest depth of me, he pulls out slightly then sinks all the way in, making me gasp as the tip of his cock butts into my cervix. My back arches, trying to back away up the bed a little, because it's just… too… much, but his big palms grip my shoulders from beneath, not allowing me to move.

"Shhh… I'll take care of you, sugar," he whispers, holding his hips perfectly still as he kisses along my jawline to my ear, nibbling the lobe as he murmurs sweet nothings there, his deep voice and hot breath relaxing me until my slight pain and panic completely subside. "So fucking perfect. Your tight little pussy feels so fucking perfect wrapped around my cock, baby. I could stay like this forever, just buried deep inside you. Never felt so complete, like I'm where I'm supposed to be for the very first time."

He keeps on like that, telling me how beautiful I am, how perfect I fit him, how wonderful I feel wrapped in his arms, and I melt beneath him until I feel every single one of my muscles relax, including the ones gripping around his thick cock. And he must feel it, because he pulls up enough to stare into my eyes… when he finally begins to move.

It's like nothing I've ever experienced before. I'm filled to the very brim, my pussy stretched to its absolute limit, but there's no more pain. He's a master with his movements, thrusting just deep enough for maximum pleasure, never once pounding into my cervix after he found it the first time. With each thrust, the top of his crown slides along the top wall of my core, catching on my G-spot every time. I let go of the back of his hair, wiggling beneath him until he understands I want to wrap my arms around his back, so he once again braces above me on his hands on either side of my head. He's probably grateful I prefer to keep my nails short and shellacked instead of long and sharp, because I can't help but dig my fingertips into the muscles beneath his hot flesh as I hold on for dear life.

When I've grown as accustomed to his size as I'll ever be, I give in to my desire to meet his thrusts, digging my heels into the mattress to lift my hips as he plunges into me, and I hear him growl. I look up to see his face is more serious than I've ever seen it, his eyes the color of the ocean during a hurricane, swirling with possession and pleasure as he watches my own emotions play across my face. When my lips part on a gasp as he hits a particularly delicious spot inside me, he captures them with his, kissing me with so much passion I feel it to the depths of my soul. I purr as his chest hair slides against my nipples once more, sending a shiver throughout my limbs, and once again, I know the exact moment he loses a grip on his control, like when he was eating me alive. His growl turns almost ferocious as he grips around my small frame and flips us, and I discover I'm now on top, mounted above the most beautiful man I've ever had the pleasure of meeting—let alone make love to.

And that's exactly what this is. We're making love. This isn't some fast fuck with a stranger. This isn't some one-night stand to satisfy a basic human need until the next person comes along. This is a soul-deep connection, a heart-healing experience that will live in my blown mind for the rest of my days.

"You're a fucking goddess," he breathes, reaching up to trail the back of his knuckles along the underside of my breast, and I shiver, my nipples puckering. I throw my head back and rotate my hips, feeling his cock oscillate against the walls of my pussy.

I then lean forward, my palms flat on his top abs, my fingers spread wide to feel as much of his masculine flesh as I can. I tilt my hips, rocking back to watch his cock pull out a couple inches before I sink down again, mesmerized by the way he stretches my pussy lips around him.

Christ.

"Goddess?" I snort. "I must be a fucking superhero to be able to take all of you," I breathe, falling forward to rest my forehead on his chest as I raise my hips and glide down once more, whimpering at the fullness.

And that's when I feel his huge hands take hold of my ass and lift me effortlessly, holding me several inches above his hips as he rocks up into me, making my eyes cross before I shut them tight and cry out in pleasure.

"Fuck, I don't think I can be gentle any longer, sugar. You're making my control snap, baby," he rumbles from deep within his chest, and I feel the vibration against my cheek.

"Then don't be," I urge, and I delight in the feel of his fingertips digging into my ass cheeks.

"You think you can take it?" he asks, his voice teetering between a concerned question and a dare.

I take a deep breath, keeping my voice steady when I tell him, "Challenge: Accepted."

And I swear on my autograph collection, the next thing I know, I see fucking stars.

Dishing
~up~
Love

Sixteen

CURTIS

"CHALLENGE: ACCEPTED," I hear her reply, her voice calm, if not a little cautious, but that's all the encouragement I need to lose myself in her depths.

I grip her firm, round ass in my hands, hovering her above my cock, just the head of me left inside her, and then I fuck up into her, just once at first, testing her reaction. And when I'm gifted with her cry of pleasure, I allow myself to let go of the reins of my control and give in to everything my instincts are demanding me to do.

I begin pounding up into her, rough but steady strokes, until she braces her hands on either side of my head, her face twisted in immeasurable ecstasy. Her lips are parted as she pants with each of my thrusts, and I glance down, watching her tits bounce as my cock slams into her. The view of her, from her messy hair down to her smooth thighs straddling my hips, is the most erotic thing I've ever seen in my life. Never have I seen such a beautiful creature mounted above me, and I wonder for a split second how I got so lucky.

Her pussy grips me like a hot, wet fist, her juices soaking our connection, allowing my steel rod to slide easily with each lift of my hips. I can see my dick shine with slickness with every outward stroke before disappearing into her once again, and I remember the look of awe on her face when she looked at the place where our bodies were joined.

She's my own little porn star, shameless in the way she calls out my name, undeniable, real pleasure taking over her every feature. There's no way anyone could fake the concentration on her face, clearly set on working her way to a blissful finale as I fuck her. Plus, I believed her when she said she doesn't fake it.

And I give her my all, pulling out all the stops, using my very best skills to impress her, because I've never wanted anything more in my goddamn life than to make this woman melt. To make her fall for me in a way where she can't live without me. Can't think of being with any man after me, because no one else will compare to what I give her this fateful perfect night.

Because no one else will ever compare to her.

She's it for me.

This is the last pussy I ever want for the rest of my days.

That's the last fleeting thought I have before my mind is taken over by my physical pleasure. Her fingers dig into my chest as I pound up into her, and I feel her glutes flex in my palms as she starts to mewl. She's so close. Her breath hitches like it did right before she came in my mouth, and her expression turns almost scared, blissfully so.

I flip us quickly, keeping up my thrusts so she doesn't lose her momentum. She was honest with me before, stating it was hard for her to come. And I'm sure most men would puff up their chests and think they were God's gift with the skills to make it happen with the snap of their cocky fingers.

Me? Fuck that. I know orgasms aren't just physical for a woman. If they aren't in the right state of mind, if their thoughts are elsewhere, they can't get off. If you don't stroke them in just the right way, filling their mind with only what you're doing to them, bringing the perfect pleasure that makes all other thoughts cease to exist, it won't happen. And I'll do anything it takes to help her find her release.

With her once again on her back beneath me, I scoop my left arm under her hips, lifting her at the perfect angle for her pussy to accept every inch of me. My other hand wraps under her back, my forearm between her shoulder blades and my palm circles the delicate nape of her neck. And in this position, we couldn't be any closer, as my knees draw up, giving me more leverage as I pound into her, my grip around the back of her neck and around her hips keeping her perfectly steady to take all I have to give.

And finally, her body stiffens for a moment before she screams, "Oh,

God! Yes. Yes, fuck!" But I keep going, not letting up on my thundering pace and deep plunges inside her pulsing pussy. I can give her even more than this. One isn't enough. She deserves more. She deserves everything I can possibly provide her in these moments of pure bliss, when everyone and everything else in the whole world no longer exists. I will keep giving it to her until it's a physical impossibility.

She grips my biceps, letting her head hang back in my hold on the back of her neck, staring up into my eyes as I rock into her over and over. I memorize her every feature, never wanting to forget the way she's looking at me like I hung the fucking stars. And when she gets that slightly frightened look on her face once again, I know I'm about to send her over the edge once again.

"Why do you look scared when you're about to come?" I breathe against her ear, feeling her shudder.

"Be—because," she whimpers. "I've—oooh—never felt anything so... oh, fuck, Curtis!" Her pussy spasms around me, and I have to concentrate on my breathing in order to not come and end this night of ecstasy I wish to last for hours more. "Never felt anything as good as you. You... you build me up so high that it's scary when I finally reach the peak and it's time to jump off," she admits, and doesn't that make me feel like the King of the fucking world?

I pick up my pace once again, my cock reaching depths that had hurt her when we first started, but now she clutches at me, wanting me as deep as I can possibly go.

"Please, Curtis," she begs, but for what, I'm not sure.

"What is it, baby?"

Her eyes are pleading. "Please come. I can't take anymore. Please."

"You want me to come, sugar? I can keep going. Never let this night end," I promise.

"Yes, please come," she hisses, even as another orgasm makes her entire body convulse in my arms, and she cries out, this time weakly.

"I'll come for you. I'll fill you up, give you everything I've got if you let me," I tell her, and she nods vigorously in my grip, and I can't help but smile.

But then I close my eyes and rest my forehead between her tits, feeling the soft flesh against my face and I thrust into her at a punishing pace in order to come for her quickly, giving her what she wants.

She grips me tight with her hands, holding onto me like her life depends on it, and her legs wrap around my back, which she uses to lift herself into my thrusts, and at her determination to participate and give me pleasure, even when she's purely exhausted, I suddenly go from travelling up that roller coaster hill at a steady pace to shooting up to the top in record speed, growling into her breasts as my hold on her squeezes and I come harder than I ever have in my life. I spill every drop of cum I have directly up against the deepest part of her like a soothing balm, hoping it washes away any pain she's ever felt there. My body shudders, and I groan, falling to the side and taking her with me.

She collapses half on top of me as she slides into my nook, her head fitting perfectly in the crook of my arm and chest, my cock still semi hard as she disconnects her lower half. I could take her again right now, never having my fill, but the way she begged me to come, confessing she couldn't take anymore, is all the satisfaction I need for one night.

I hear her groan, and then she lifts her head up to look at me. "I gotta go clean up," she murmurs, and I try to pull her back down to snuggle.

"You just relax. I'll get you a washcloth," I say, but she holds firm, shaking her head.

"That's super romantic of you, but… I really have to pee. My bladder of steel is about to revolt," she admits, and I chuckle, letting her go. She gets out of the bed, bending down to grab something out of her purse she'd dropped earlier, and hurries out the bedroom door.

Seventeen

Erin

I MAKE MY way down the hall and into Emmy's room, then into her en suite bathroom. I've used it ever since she married Dean and is never here, because it's huge and gorgeous and just… better than the one two doors down from my room. Plus, I need to call my best friend, because I'm starting to minorly freak out at the moment, and I don't want Curtis to hear me.

She picks up on the third ring, wide awake even though it's only close to five in the morning her time on the east coast. "Rin? The hell you doing awake so early on a Saturday?"

"More like so late. I haven't been to sleep yet," I tell her.

"What?" Her voice is surprised. "I thought you were just going to get a pizza at the store and watch our show last night."

I groan, realizing the last time I spoke to her was at the grocery story before I even met Curtis. It feels like so long ago, months, instead of mere hours. "Oh my God, Em, I'm freaking the fuck out. So much has happened. So much. And I only talked to you like—" I try to math. "—thirteen hours ago or something." That ratchets my freak-o-meter up a few notches, remembering I've only known the man in my bed for less than a day. And it's not the fact that I slept with him in such a short amount of time that's making my heart pound and my hands shake. It's the fact that I opened myself up to him, let him stick his way into my heart like a splinter, where I have doubts I'll ever be able to tweeze him out.

"Okay, Rin, you're starting to freak *me* out, so why don't you tell me what happened?" Emmy's soothing voice comes from the other end of the line, and I plop down on the toilet, remembering how badly I needed to pee.

"So right after I hung up with you, guess who the fuck I *literally* ran into?"

She squeaks, "Who?"

"Apparently he's one of your husband's good friends. None other than Chef Curtis Rockwell. He was there filming his show, and he picked my hobo-lookin' ass to go home with!" I scoff.

She's quiet for a moment, and then she breathes out an "Ooohhh."

"Yeah. Well, I agreed, because... well, why the fuck not. YOLO and all that shit. Anyway. I felt this weird like... zing when he touched me. And he just smelled so good, and he's so... fucking... pretty. I mean, have you seen his eyes in real life? Wait, yes. You have. Apparently, you've met him tons of times. Shit, he's even been in a few places where I've been at the same time with you, and I never met him before yesterday! It's just crazy!" All of that comes out in one breath, and I realize I'm in a manic state of word vomiting, so I try to slow down.

"Anyway, we filmed his show, and we had this funny banter going on. And then like, we just... connected. Like, we love all the same shows and movies, and he listens when I talk as if I might be telling him the secrets of the world. He taught me how to cook the meal and then when the crew left, he made me go on a haunted tour with him," I tell her.

"He *made* you?" she prompts.

I roll my eyes. "Yeah, well, I didn't put up much of a fight. But still. You know I don't go on dates and shit."

It suddenly gets quiet in the background on Emmy's end, and I hear a door shut. "Sorry, I'm at the airport and just locked myself in the bathroom in the First Class lounge so I can hear you better, because this is all just... wild."

"Right? Absolutely insane!" I agree.

"No, no, Rin. It's wild, because I swear to God, every time we see Curtis, Dean always tells me when he walks away, 'That guy would be so perfect for Rin.' But I always blew him off, because I know how you feel about people trying to set you up, and also the reasons you never wanted to be in a relationship again. It's just... it's wild," she repeats.

"And hearing you talk about him now, I feel a little guilty for never introducing you sooner."

I clean myself up, still naked on the toilet, and then flush, shuffling over to sit on the side of her tub. "Don't you dare feel guilty about anything, Em. I could have met him at a different time and place and thought he was just a cocky asshole who thought he was God's gift to the world. But being stuck with him during the show, seeing him behind the scenes, he's really... not like that at all." The last part is whispered, as I think about just how kind and caring and gentlemanly he really is.

"So what the hell are you freaking out about, Rin? You sound like you're really happy," she points out, and I shake my head.

"That's just the thing! Being this happy is what's fucking with my head. And... I told him everything. Like, everything-everything. And he walked me home after we went to Bourbon once our tour ended, after he got me to really open up to him, and we had the most mind-blowing sex I've ever had in my life. My. Life. Amelia." I punctuate those last words, because she knows that's a big deal. "I lost count of the orgasms. And he told me he could keep going, and I had to beg his ass to stop. Because I literally felt like I was about to start having an out-of-body experience. Like, full on seizures."

She snorts at that. I've always told her in detail about my sex life, and it wasn't until she met Dean that she got to spill her own deets, when she no longer had to live vicariously through me. "I don't think you've ever told me a time when you had to beg a guy to *stop* giving you orgasms," she points out.

I shake my head. "That's because it's never happened before. The only other time I've ever told someone to 'please come' was when he thought he was doing a great job, going at it for a full ten minutes before I finally felt sorry for the guy who hadn't even made it inside me and was humping the space between the bed and my booty." I roll my eyes.

She giggles at that, but then a feeling of panic starts a ringing in my ears and I can no longer hear her laughter. I swallow thickly, immediately looking down at the naked place at the apex of my thighs.

"Oh, God," I whisper, looking over to the toilet and remembering it had taken a lot of toilet paper to clean myself up with. And it wasn't because of my own natural lubrication.

"What? What's wrong?" Her tone grows serious again.

"Em. I just remembered… he… he didn't use a condom." My heart pounds wildly in my chest.

"What?" she yelps.

"Oh fuck. Oh fuck! Oh my God, what if I now have some horrible disease to go along with all my other shitty health issues? Oh fuck!" As if I wasn't freaking out enough about the state of my heart, being all out in the open and vulnerable for the first time in five years.

"Okay, take a breath. Are you sure he didn't use one and you just didn't notice? He could've been discreet about it. They aren't the most romantic things to deal with when you're about to make love," she suggests.

But I'm already shaking my head. "No. Oh, God. That's what he was asking me there at the end. He said he'd fill me up and give me everything he's got if I wanted him to. And at the time, it was so fucking hot. I thought he was talking about his cock, not his jizz! Oh, God!" I run over to the sink, turning the hot tap on high, waiting for the water to heat up as I grab a washcloth and fill it full of antibacterial hand soap.

"Well don't panic yet, Rin. It's going to be okay. Curtis is a really good guy. I'm sure he wouldn't have even suggested that if he didn't know for a fact that he was clean. He's not that kind of man," she assures, and I close my eyes, nodding slightly. I know that in my heart.

This is Curtis we're talking about. Not just some random guy I met at a bar. No, this is the man who pulls me to the other side of him, so I don't walk next to the road. This is the man who holds me on his lap and rocks me soothingly while I spill my deepest, darkest, most heartbreaking secrets. This is the man who is determined to teach me to meal prep, so I get enough to eat every day, and gets mad at the thought of me not taking good enough care of myself. He wouldn't then turn around and do something that would hurt me.

But still, I stick the washcloth in the scalding water, lather it up, and scrub myself, knowing full well that antibacterial soap is hella bad for a va-jay-jay. But I'll suffer through a yeast infection if it means I won't catch something way worse.

When I'm all cleaned up, it's like all the adrenaline from moments before leaves my body all at once, and I slide down onto the bathroom floor, the coldness of the antique tiles feeling good against my overheated skin. I take a deep breath, letting it out slowly.

"You all right, bestie?" Emmy asks quietly from my cell.

I nod, even though she can't see me. "I think so. I just don't know what to do now," I murmur, pulling my knees up to my chest and resting my cheek on the tops.

"What do you mean? It sounds like you really like him and want to give this a shot."

"But in the grand scheme of things, I literally just met him. I haven't even known him for a full twenty-four hours," I reply, hearing her snort.

"Um… do you remember who you're talking to? A *lot* can happen in one night, Erin." And I lift my brows, remembering how she met Dean, getting trapped in the catacombs beneath our city overnight with the hottie adventure documentary host. "Fate doesn't play around. I think when two people are meant to be together, it's not like some slow buildup of pressure like a front coming in. It's like a freaking lightning bolt that strikes… like that 'zing' you felt. I felt the same thing with Dean, but it was just masked a little behind my misguided hatred for him."

I can't help but chuckle at that. She really had hated his guts for years before she ever actually met the poor guy in person. "Yeah…" A beat, and then, "I don't know how to do this, Em." I bite my lip, my throat suddenly tight. "I've been stuck in my mindset of living the rest of my life without being in another serious relationship ever again for so long that I don't even know where to begin." I blow out a breath. "Plus, how could this ever work? I have my practice here in New Orleans, and he travels the world doing his chef thing."

"Whatever is meant to be will be. I know you've already hit all the physical bases, but you still have time to take it slow emotionally. Y'all will figure it out organically. Take it one day at a time," she replies, and I take a deep breath, closing my eyes and nodding before letting it out.

"I mean. He's pretty much a keeper. We started getting naked, and he caught me in my goddamn surgery panties." I lift my arm to place my palm on my forehead.

She lets out a bark of laughter. "What? Oh no!" She cackles some more, sounding like she can't breathe, and I smile at the sound. "How many times have I told you it's time to get rid of those ugly things? It's been half a year since your surgery. You need to burn them. If they're so comfortable, go out and find some actual boyshort panties!"

"I've told you they don't make boyshort panties that stretchy! And up until about half an hour ago, no one had ever seen the bitches," I grumble.

"They're full of bad juju anyway. Get. Rid. Of. Them," she urges, and I huff.

"Fine!" I agree. After a moment of quietness between us, I ask for her reassurance one last time, "So you really don't think I have anything to worry about, about the whole no-condom thing? That scares the shit out of me. I can't believe I let that happen. I've never once done it without one before. Even when I got pregnant with shithead, we used a fucking condom; it just broke. But we were already engaged by then, so we didn't worry too much about it."

And then I let out a shriek of surprise, my knees drawing up to protect myself, when Curtis's deep voice echoes throughout Emmy's bathroom. "No, you have nothing to worry about, sugar."

"Uh-oooh," my best friend says through the phone. "I'm gonna let y'all handle this. Love you, Rin. Call me tomorrow. Bye!" And then the whore hangs up, leaving me alone with the towering giant staring down at me where I'm sprawled naked on the tile floor.

"Came to check on you, since you've been gone a while," he tells me, and a warm feeling spreads through my chest as I lower my feet back to the floor.

I narrow my eyes though when I ask, "Were you eavesdropping?"

He shakes his head slowly. "I wasn't. Just heard that last little bit and felt I needed to make it perfectly clear that you do not have anything to worry about. I've never done it without a condom either. That was the first time ever. And yet I still get checked out regularly, since I have to travel to other countries so often and get various vaccinations. But if you're worried about getting pregnant—"

I cut him off, my voice colder than I mean for it to be. "I'm not. I told you, it'd be a fucking miracle if that happened. I was just concerned about STDs."

His face softens, and before I know what's happening, he bends over and scoops me up. His hot flesh feels like it sizzles against my now cool skin from where I've been lying on the cold tiles. I allow myself to enjoy the feel of him carrying me bridal style back to my room, relaxing my head in the crook of his neck and breathing in his intoxicatingly male scent.

There's no more talking, both of us seeming to finally reach the end of our energy reserves as he lies us down, maneuvering my body the way he wants it until my back is flush with his front, his muscled arm draped around my waist as he holds me to him.

I relax, letting my body go limp and heavy as I succumb to my exhaustion, and the last thought in my head before I finally lose consciousness is to question, *Before I cut him off, what was he going to say if I was worried about getting pregnant?*

Eighteen

CURTIS

WHEN I AWAKEN the next… afternoon, I see, when I check my phone where I put it on her nightstand while waiting for her to come back from the bathroom last night, I'm alone. I roll over onto my back, gaining my bearings before looking around her room. She's nowhere in sight, but my surroundings are just so… her.

The rest of the house might be full of Egyptian memorabilia, but this space is completely Erin. It's tranquil, soothing, bright, and clean. It's all stark-whites and soft grays with black hardware on all the rustic furniture. The sun shines brightly through the white sheers over the windows, and it reminds me about what she said last night, how she never sleeps in, because it messes up her routine. Even as tired as we were early this morning, and how she even said she planned to, I smile at the fact that she couldn't allow herself to stay in bed this late. So she must be downstairs or in some other part of the house, doing whatever she normally does on a Saturday.

I sit up, swinging my legs over the edge of the bed, and find my jeans, pulling them on but leaving them undone as I go in search of the beauty, hoping I can encourage her to come back to bed so we can have a repeat of what we did when we returned to her house last night. Maybe we could spend the rest of the day curled up, after we're both sated, and veg out, watching TV and ordering take-out. There are all sorts of foods here I'm bound and determined to try.

I grab my phone before I head in search of her, seeing a reminder in my notifications. My original flight home for the weekend is supposed to depart in five hours. As soon as I find Erin, I'll call my assistant and ask her to rebook it for either tomorrow or Monday. If it were up to me, I'd stay long after that, take vacation time and spend weeks here getting to really know my woman, but I have obligations in California in a couple days, and it's not in me to break any prior commitments when people are counting on me with too short of notice for them to find a replacement.

I check the bathroom two doors down, but the lights are out with no one inside. I go to the bedroom I assume is Emmy's, peeking into the en suite there with my fingers crossed, hoping to find Erin bathing in the sexy claw-footed tub I saw last night, but no luck. It's empty as well.

I gallop down the stairs, ignoring the niggling feeling I have at the back of my mind telling me her presence is missing as I head into the kitchen. Nothing. Not even the lights are on. Frowning, I hurry back past the staircase and glance into the living room, stopping and holding my breath in order to listen.

Silence.

There isn't another soul in the house.

Maybe she went to get us some breakfast, I tell myself, as I go back into the kitchen, pulling out one of the stools to sit and wait for her. Surely any minute she'll come strolling back inside with a bag full of french pastries and a tray of coffee. Oh, or maybe even some Cajun boudin breakfast tacos. My mouth waters at the thought, and I force myself to relax, pulling up my Instagram feed.

My brows lift at the notifications. I have hundreds of tags, and my heart sinks into my gut when I see the candid shots of me out and about throughout the night, on the tour, on Bourbon Street, in the bars Erin took me to, and even a photo of us kissing beneath a gallery on our way back here early this morning.

I blow out a breath, trying to calm my racing pulse. "Okay, that's fine. Everything is fine. It may be all over the place, but no one knows who she is, so they're not going to bother h— Oh… fuck," I growl, seeing the comment under TMZ's post.

OMG! That's Dr. Bazzara! She's my therapist. Go on wit yo bad self, @ebNOLAshrink!

And I hold my breath as I click to see the seventy-eight replies beneath the comment.

There are comments ranging from **Lucky girl!** to **What's so special about her?** The latter making me want to reach through the phone and pop them in their blasphemous mouth before explaining every single wonderful trait Erin possesses.

I click on her handle that was tagged and suddenly find myself smiling, scrolling through the countless photos, mostly of her and Emmy together. I pause, staring at one of her best friend in a wedding dress as Erin uses a tissue to dab under Emmy's eye.

Can't let tears ruin this awesome makeup job, not even happy ones! #mybestfriendswedding, the caption states, and my heart thuds in my chest knowing we were in the same place at the same time all those years ago. I was down in the kitchen preparing everything for the reception dinner, but we were right there, breathing the same air.

Unlike now.

"Where have you gone, sugar?" I murmur, glancing at the time and seeing I've been scrolling through her feed for nearly forty-five minutes now. Surely it wouldn't have taken this long for her to just go grab us some food.

And then my gut sinks once again. I had been momentarily distracted, getting to look through all the pictures and reading the captions to gather her inner thoughts of what was happening in each shot. Now I remember what led me there in the first place.

What if she saw all the tags already? She seems to post something daily, so it's not a hard assumption to make that she checks her notifications throughout the day. Had she woken up to them, her Instagram having blown up over the hours we slept, curled up in her big bed? Had it scared her enough to make her run off, hoping I wouldn't be here when she got back?

Well she's got another think coming, because there's no way I'm leaving until I get to assure her she has nothing to worry about. I won't let anything bad come about from photos of us being all over social media. I'll protect her from anything that could possibly happen. I just hope her skin is thick enough to withstand the snide comments from keyboard warriors who know nothing about the amazing person she is.

I need to call my assistant to tell her to change my flight. I'll stay here all day and night and wait for her to come home if I have to. If I had Erin's phone number, I'd call over and over until she picks up and demand she come back right now, but alas, we never got around to that last night.

"Curtis! Have you seen all the—" Rachel starts, but I cut her off.

"I'm not worried about that right now. Can you change my flight from today to tomorrow evening sometime? I know I have appointments on Monday, but I need to stay in New Orleans as long as I can before then." My knee bounces in anticipation. This was not how I envisioned my day would go after falling asleep next to the woman of my dreams.

I hear her typing, and then anger fills me when she says, "I'm sorry, Curt. Everything is all booked up out of NOLA until Monday evening. There's nothing to switch your flight to."

I slam my fist down on the kitchen counter, closing my eyes before lowering my head. I try to calm the unfamiliar feeling of panic as I think about being forced to leave without seeing Erin first, and then I tell Rachel, "Okay, no worries. I'll be on my original flight." I hang up without hearing any type of response.

All I can do now is hope that Erin shows up before I have to leave for the airport. But as the minutes tick by, and a half-hour turns into an hour and then two, I realize she's not coming back. While I wonder where she's gone, where she could be staying on a Saturday to keep away from me, and exactly the reasons why she's not here, why she ran, I also don't blame her. Especially the more I check all of my social media outlets. Living a quiet life as a psychologist, a single woman in New Orleans, then all of a sudden having your face known worldwide and linked to one of America's most "eligible bachelors," as they call me, would make anyone want to hide.

After going back upstairs and getting all the way dressed, I leave a note for her on the nightstand before locking her front door from the inside and pulling it shut. I take out my phone and snap a picture of her house number and then the street name then use my app to secure a Lyft. She had to put all her information down in the paperwork she filled out yesterday while filming the show, but I don't want to risk anyone at the network telling me no if I asked for her address, since it's private information. This way, they also can't ask questions. I already feel like a complete idiot for not getting her number at any point during the night. Of course, I had expected to spend all of today and part of tomorrow with the woman who stole my heart in such an obscenely short period of time.

But you know what they say when you *assume* anything.

You make an *ass* out of *u* and *me*.

I leave with enough time to go back to my hotel, grab my few things scattered around the room, and then book another Lyft to the airport. I sit there in the seat feeling lonelier than I've ever felt before, waking up and not seeing Erin's beautiful face. Normally, I await my flights with excitement, looking forward and anticipating the meal I'm meant to prepare for the event I'm heading to. But this time, all I can do is look back, thinking about the woman I'm leaving behind.

Everything inside me screams not to go, to wait her out and once she comes back home assure her everything will be okay. But I can't, and it kills me, making me think about what the thoughts going through her head will be once she returns to her house. She'll probably think I gave up easily, that I found her missing, got my ass dressed, and hightailed it out of there, trying to get out before she came back in order to avoid an awkward walk of shame situation. But she couldn't be further from the truth.

And I hope the note I left is fair warning enough to prepare her for what I have planned for us.

Because she won't be getting away that easily.

Dishing
~up~
Love

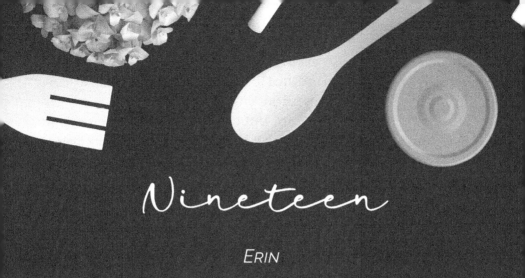

Nineteen

Erin

You can run, but hiding is futile.
I'll find you once again, sugar, and then I'll never let you
go.
Everything will be all right.
Because you're mine.
Love, Curtis

I READ THE note over and over again Saturday night, after finding it on my nightstand. If anyone else had left me such an ominous message, I would've been on my way to the police department and filling out a restraining order, but as I read it once more in Curtis's deep, hypnotic voice, I can't help but be soothed by the words.

I ran. I ran like a goddamn pussy. I woke up this morning with Curtis's muscular limbs entangled with mine, and I was fully prepared to spend the day basking in this new hope of having a happily ever after with the man of my dreams. But then… I shimmied out from under him, my bladder screaming at me to take care of business, and I grabbed my phone off the bathroom floor where I'd left it after my call with Emmy. Before I even unlocked my screen, my notifications popped up, and my eyes widened at the hundreds… no thousands of comments and mentions and tags.

Sally fucking Stewartson. The bane of my existence. If it hadn't been for her pointing out she recognized me in one of the photos leaked to the tabloids, I would've remained the "mystery woman" he was with all night and I could've lived in denial for just a little while, getting to know Curtis a little bit better before chaos ensued.

I would've been able to learn if it could be all worth the celebrity status, losing all my privacy. But as it is, I really don't know much about him. Yes, I spilled all my deep, dark secrets to him, and I got to know his protective and loving nature, but really… I don't know a thing about his past. I don't know if we'd mesh well as a couple. One date and a night of hot sex does not a relationship make.

I knew the moment he left. I know from my security cameras on the inside of the house and from the fancy doorbell Emmy's husband installed, since I would be living alone more often than not, that he paced the kitchen and living room. I saw devastation on his face when I assume he tried to change his flight and was told he couldn't. He wanted to wait for me. The hurt I saw in his expression nearly killed me and made me come running back home to him, but just then another slew of notifications hit my phone, reminding me why I couldn't do this.

Admittedly, I am not strong enough, with my medical history and past, to just get over what I've conditioned myself to believe—that I am not good enough, woman enough because I can't have kids—all in one night. I don't have the intestinal fortitude or the confidence in what Curtis and I felt so quickly in order to just ignore and blow off all the comments asking what makes me so special that one of America's most eligible bachelors would choose me.

What's so great about me?

What does he see in me?

Yeah, she's super pretty, but there's gotta be something else if he spent all night with her. He's never been seen making out like that before, just dinner dates, one comment reads. It's a much nicer version of the ones stating things like, **She don't look good enough for his fine ass *side-eye emoji**.

It made me want to reply, *I know. I know I'm not good enough for him. But he wouldn't listen to me when I told him that!*

So I held strong and stayed away, to save us both unwanted pain in the future, when he'd realize he does want a family with children and was stuck with a woman who couldn't give him that. Stuck until he left me for someone who could, at which time I'd be absolutely devastated after allowing myself to open myself up again.

It's just better this way.

Reading his note one final time, I toss it into the drawer of my nightstand and slam it shut, forcing myself to forget about his words. He'll forget about me soon enough. I sit on the edge of my bed and turn off notifications for all my social media accounts. If I ignore them, maybe they'll just die off and I'll be a nobody once again.

With all the attention my pages are getting though, I might as well do a little bit of advertising while people are looking through my profiles. I turn on a saved episode of *No Trespassing*, pausing it when my best friend and her husband are on the screen with the title of the show across the bottom, and snap a selfie with the TV. I post the photo with the caption **Miss you, bestie! Fantastic episode last night and can't wait for the next one on Friday! @notrespassing @adventurechannel @ RealEmmySavageman @RealDeanSavageman *TV emoji**

Before I even have a chance to close out the app, I have several comments, and I can't resist taking a quick peek.

jessYOGA: @hailienV Girl, look! She's best friends with Emmy from that show you like! I bet that's how they met.

I snort. "You'd lose that bet, Jess," I murmur, scrolling down.

Loolian: OMG, how do you know all these famous people and I've never heard of you before?!

I roll my eyes at that. As if celebrities are only friends with other celebrities.

There are a ton of **I love that show!** comments that make me smile, making me even prouder of my best friend and her sweet husband. And I give a yip in accomplishment at the replies about **I've never watched it. Looks cool though. I'll have to give it a try,** which have several responses from other fans saying things like **Prepare for a binge-watch**, or **You're in for a treat!** If I were to try to Like each and every one of the comments coming in, I'd literally be here all night, so I resist, but I can't help but to heart one that says **I was never interested in history. Barely passed the subject in high school. But this show made me love it and now I can't get enough!** because I totally feel that in my soul and laugh out loud.

The rest of the comments are actually rather sweet and uplifting.

OMG you're so pretty.

I love your TV stand! I love farmhouse décor *heart eyes emoji I wish my messy buns looked like yours!

And I can't help but shake my head and chuckle at **You're a psychologist? But you're so hot?!** And **Maybe I wouldn't have skipped my therapy appointments if my doc looked like you.** Which is a little worrisome, so I click on their profile and see he's a former Marine. So I make my one and only reply, because it's just not in me to not help someone who might need it.

@Jarhead421 If you live near NOLA, please book an appointment and I'll see you right away. If not, please don't hesitate to find any help you may need. I also do phone and video chat sessions.

That sparks another slew of comments, ranging from **OMG, she's so sweet! No wonder @ChefCurtisRockwell likes her!** to **Ooooh, she done did it now! People gonna be blowing her ass up at work trying to get to the hottie cook!** And I grimace—I didn't think about that.

I close out the app, suddenly feeling overwhelmed once again. I go into the master bathroom and take a scalding bath, hoping to relax away all the tension inside my body. It's starting to work, when my phone starts buzzing down on the tile floor. Since I turned off all the notifications for comments and such, I sit up, wondering what's setting my phone off, and that's when I realize I didn't turn off the setting for private messages.

I grab it up quickly, going into the app once more to turn those off too, ignoring all the new Follows and Likes and Comments, when I see in bold that the message is from one **ChefCurtisRockwell** himself, and my heart dives into the pit of my stomach.

I'm an idiot. Of course he found me on social media. Why didn't I think of the fact that we've been tagged in countless posts together all day? For some stupid reason, I thought I'd be safe from him being able to contact me, since I never gave him my phone number. I guess that's just how frazzled I've been.

I bite my lip, staring at the unopened message in my inbox. If I click on it, he'll see that I'm active on the app and read it. God only knows what he'll say then, after the note he left me.

But try as I might, I can't hold strong, and I give in to the urge to read it, because I cannot for the life of me get the devastated look on his face out of my head. I have to know he's at least okay.

ChefCurtisRockwell: Did you make it home okay? Please let me know you're safe.

My lip immediately trembles. I ran out on him, hid all day, leaving him upset before he finally left after waiting for me alone for hours, and instead of being mad at me, cussing me out for my bitch move, he messages to make sure I'm all right. Originally, I wasn't planning to respond, expecting something much different, but I can't do that to him.

Me: Home safe, hiding in Emmy's tub.

ChefCurtisRockwell: FML.

ChefCurtisRockwell: In order to not picture you naked, I'm now imagining you're literally hiding in it, fully clothed, with a butcher knife in your hand, peeking out over the edge of the tub. *monkey with covered eyes emoji

I sniff out a laugh, sinking down farther in the water.

Me: Yes. That's exactly what's happening on my end right now. *laughing emoji

ChefCurtisRockwell: Why are you hiding, sugar?

What a loaded question. There are so many things he could be referring to. Hiding from the unexpected media attention. Hiding from the feelings I have inside me. Hiding from *him*. I choose to respond to the former.

Me: In the span of twelve hours, I now have 126,435... no, make that 126,502 followers on Instagram. Yesterday? I had 2,330, and that was mostly my old high school buddies and nerdy cosplaying friends. THESE. ARE. NOT. MY. FRIENDS.

ChefCurtisRockwell: You can turn your page private, baby. There's a setting where you have to approve people to follow you.

Me: I don't want to do that though. I like to stay open and visible for my patients. It gains their trust, and they feel like they know me more and can open up to me more easily.

ChefCurtisRockwell: There's no one else like you, sugar. No one on this earth. You do know that most doctors and other professionals have their personal pages locked down tight, right?

Me: I'm aware. That's why I don't post anything majorly personal. Just things I'm interested in and enjoy. Like my geek conventions and food, pics with my bestie. What I'm not used to is going to my tagged photos and seeing a fucking close up of me

pushed up against a brick wall with my legs wrapped around a guy whose tongue is down my throat. That's waaay more personal than I've ever gotten on social media!

ChefCurtisRockwell: Aaaand I'm hard. Thanks for that.

I let out a squawk of laughter, shaking my head.

Me: Of course you are. *face palm emoji

Me: I'm just going to start calling you Chef Rock-Hard from now on.

ChefCurtisRockwell: LOL! Only for you, baby. Only for you.

ChefCurtisRockwell: Also, this is weird.

Me: What is?

ChefCurtisRockwell: I don't normally chat with anyone in my IMs.

I laugh once more.

Me: I can tell.

ChefCurtisRockwell: How?

Me: You called it an IM, old man. It's no longer an "instant message." The kids these days call it a DM, for "direct message."

Me: Come to think of it, does AOL even exist anymore? *thinking face emoji

ChefCurtisRockwell: As a matter of fact, it does.

Me: OMG do you still have your AOL account?? *laughing emoji

ChefCurtisRockwell: I mean, I never deleted it. But I know AOL exists because I did an exclusive recipe and interview for them a little while back.

And just like that, reality comes crashing down on me once more. For a split second, I forgot I was joking around with a celebrity. A person who is recognized wherever he goes. Which makes me wonder…

Me: Last night, was that a rare occurrence? Like, are you normally bombarded with fans everywhere you go? I honestly thought the only people who recognized you were the students. No one else said anything. I think that's why it was so shocking to see so many pictures of us.

ChefCurtisRockwell: To be perfectly honest, that's the first time I've ever gone out and not been completely aware of people sneaking pictures of me. Normally when I see someone trying to snap an incognito shot, I give them a goofy face or I approach them and let them take a selfie with me. They don't come up and bombard me, because either they're too polite, not wanting to bother me, or because they're too shy. I love my fans, and it always struck me as crazy to have fans for something I love doing so much… cooking. Like, how weird is that, for someone to be starstruck over you making food?

Me: What's funny to me is I've always assumed famous people can't even walk out their front door without being hounded, like paparazzi style.

ChefCurtisRockwell: It's different everywhere. In California, around where I live, I get it more like what you thought. Out and about in other states, because we don't announce where we're shooting before it happens, it's harder for people to make the connection. They're more like "OMG you look just like that chef guy" instead of realizing it's really me.

Me: Interesting. I'm sure there's something psychological behind that, but I just don't have it in me to shrink it.

There's a pause. As if he's thinking about what to say next. He's clocked me as a runner, so he's probably weighing every statement, every question, every joke in his mind, being careful not to say anything that could make me bolt again.

I hate that this is what I've made him believe about me. I have patients like that, people who have more flight in them than fight. And I've worked for years to help them get past their issues in order to stand up and fight for what they want after years of holding themselves back for whatever reason. I want to be all the things he saw in me last night. Everything he pointed out, I want to grasp onto and shove all my fears away.

All day today, I've been so down on myself, feeling sorry for myself, becoming this weak, fragile thing on the outside after I've worked so hard to make sure all those feelings stay hidden on the inside. I always thought that if I portrayed myself as this strong, single, independent woman who didn't need anyone else, then I would eventually believe it myself. Mind over matter. *If you believe it, then you can achieve it!* But I guess I've just stayed in denial this whole time.

Now that Curtis isn't here, where he isn't the only thing I see, breathe, feel, and taste, I can step back and assess how I'm truly feeling. If I were my patient, what would I say? What would I ask?

First, I would ask myself, *"Self, what are you afraid of?"*

That answer would be easy. I'm afraid of getting hurt again. I am afraid of what happened with my ex happening all over again.

And then I would ask myself, *"What is it that I want to happen?"*

I would reply, *"To live happily ever after in a relationship with a man I know for a fact would never leave me for not being able to bear his children."*

I would then ask myself, *"What could I do in order to obtain what I truly want?"*

Learn to trust him. And the only logical way to gain trust is to get to know the person, not just physically—because God knows I know him physically—but emotionally and on a soul-deep level. And the only way to do that is to talk, to ask each other questions, to be open with our answers, and to be completely honest with each other.

With that thought in mind, I send a message to end the silence between us.

Me: I'm sorry I ran. That's not who I want to be as a person. That's not who I want you to think I am. I want to be stronger than that.

There's another pause, and I hold my breath, having no idea how he might respond.

ChefCurtisRockwell: Sugar, we can take this as slow as you need to. I know that might sound silly after what we did before you fell asleep in my arms, but we can back up if you need to. We can go slow and build up that strength.

My eyes tear up at that, and then I laugh when he tries to lighten the mood.

ChefCurtisRockwell: You think I got this ripped overnight? Fuuuck no.

Me: LOL! *heart eyes emoji *flexing bicep emoji

ChefCurtisRockwell: And not only that, as much food as I eat—cuz you know a chef's gotta sample everything to make sure it's edible for his guests—you think I don't have to continue working on myself every day?

Me: Hey, who's the therapist here?

ChefCurtisRockwell: I may not be certified, but I've been to one

enough that I've got all sorts of advice to give.

My head tilts… something niggling the back of my mind.

Yesterday, when we were filming the show.

And then I remember.

Me: Is that what you were referring to, when you asked your director to cut it out during edits? Something about cooking starting out as a form of therapy?

No hesitation.

ChefCurtisRockwell: It is. I'm the product of teenage experimentation. My grandma raised me after the experimentation escalated from sex to drugs and we lost my mom. Dad was never in the picture. Anyway, most of my childhood was spent sitting on her counter, watching her while she taught me how to bake. She worked in a small bakery where we're from in North Carolina.

I eat up all the information about his past that he's feeding me, letting it paint a picture of his youth in my mind and how it molded him into the man I met yesterday. I keep the conversation light though, so I respond…

Me: Wait. Hold up. You're Southern?! My whole world is a lie!

ChefCurtisRockwell: LOL! We moved to California when I was a teenager, when my grandma remarried. You have to remember, Yaya was only 36 when I was born. She met this great guy who was in the Army, dated him for as long as I can remember. When it finally came time for him to retire, he wanted to move back to where he was from, and he asked her to marry him. Even asked my permission and what I thought about moving to California.

Me: Yaya didn't have any other children besides your mother?

ChefCurtisRockwell: No, and it's like… she blamed her parenting on how my mother's life ended up, and so she did everything in her power to not let that happen to me.

Me: How so?

ChefCurtisRockwell: I was super fucking sheltered. Didn't have many friends, because she didn't want me to end up hanging with the wrong crowd like my mom did.

Me: Is that what you went to therapy for?

ChefCurtisRockwell: Partly. My grades started dropping the second I hit high school, about a year after we moved to California. I started acting out, rebelling, and it freaked Yaya out. She started

thinking I inherited my mom's addictions and stuff, and at the same time, she thought she might've accidentally driven me to start being "bad." Also, she believed it was a big mistake moving us from NC to Cali, no longer in a quiet and small town but in a city with lots of colorful personalities. So she took me to a therapist.

Me: And what did the therapist say?

ChefCurtisRockwell: Pretty much I was just a normal hormonal teenager who happened to have ADD. I really liked my therapist, because she was on my side. She explained to Yaya that I needed to be given an outlet. Before, I was always awesome at school, because that's the only place I was allowed to thrive. But when my ADD decided to show up and I could no longer concentrate at school, it was really fucking frustrating and it made me feel like a failure. Hence the acting out. Once I got on my meds and my grades started picking back up, I was allowed to try out for different sports at school, since you had to have at least a C+ average in all your other subjects.

Me: So how exactly did you get into cooking?

ChefCurtisRockwell: Well, none of the sports really stuck. You'd think I'd be great at basketball, since I'm so tall. Not so much. I was really skinny and lanky, not very fast, so football and soccer were out. And baseball was just boring as fuck. But I remembered one time having to spend detention in the home ec room, and I spent the two hours flipping through the cookbooks and imagining what the flavors would taste like blended together. After watching Yaya bake for years, it was easy for me to picture measuring out the ingredients, the preparation of the different items, using the stove and the oven and such. I felt at home in that room, and I recalled that detention seeming to go by way too fast.

My heart swells for the young man years ago discovering his calling. I picture the moment it clicked in his head that culinary arts was something he could love doing, what he would eventually spend his life cultivating and making a name for himself for.

Me: That's awesome. So what happened next?

ChefCurtisRockwell: Well, Yaya switched me to home ec, and then when I maxed out my credits for high school, she was able to find a community college that allowed high school students to go ahead and start culinary training as an elective, which would also count toward a college degree.

I nod, even though he can't see me.

Me: We had that too! I was able to take College Psychology when I was a junior in high school, and it was a dual credit that counted as my science in 11th grade but also toward my college degree. I had an amazing professor, and it was him who truly sparked my love of the subject. It was easy to choose what I wanted to focus on once I graduated high school.

ChefCurtisRockwell: Same! After getting on my meds and kicking ass in school, I won a scholarship to one of the top culinary schools in the country. Once I graduated, I worked under some pretty amazing chefs all over California, and then finally got hired as the head chef at a restaurant on Rodeo Drive in Beverly Hills.

Me: Ah, is that where you were discovered to be the super-hot celebrity chef and got your own show?

ChefCurtisRockwell: Not quite. People who frequented the restaurant started hiring me to cater their events... weddings, Grammy parties, sweet 16s, as our friend pointed out last night. And I was discovered and asked to audition for this new show they wanted to pilot, *Chef To Go*, at Nate Berkus and Jeremiah Brent's daughter's first birthday party.

Me: OMGGGGGG! I freaking love their show!!!

ChefCurtisRockwell: Really? But their styles aren't farmhouse-y.

Me: Yeah, but I love THEM. They're so freaking adorable and funny. I love sassy Jeremiah, and Nate is so cute with his kids. *heart eyes emoji

Me: And that reminds me, you sure do seem to know a lot about design. You knew straight away what I meant when I said Joanna Gaines is my idol, and now you know Nate and Jeremiah aren't "farmhouse-y"? What's up with that?

ChefCurtisRockwell: LOL! I mean, I can be interested in more than just cooking, can't I?

Me: Well, that's true.

ChefCurtisRockwell: When I built my first home a couple years ago, the designer made me go through all sorts of books and magazines and articles, etc, to see what my tastes were. Just like the cookbooks in detention, it was super interesting to me. Not enough to make a career out of it or anything, but it was super-fun designing my entire house, and I'm told I have impeccable taste, so I've helped several of my friends decorate some of their rooms, and even Yaya let me design the bakery I bought her.

Me: You bought your grandma a bakery? *wide-eyed emoji

ChefCurtisRockwell: I mean... yeah. Why not? *laughing emoji

Me: Well, you did say you aren't frivolous with your money. And buying the woman who raised you a bakery of her own is a pretty generous gift.

ChefCurtisRockwell: Ah, see? I don't just blow my money on stupid shit. I don't drive the most expensive and flashy car. I don't buy sneakers that cost a hundred grand a pair. I don't own gold-plaited toothbrushes and razors. I drive a nice truck that can haul a trailer carrying a barbeque pit. My favorite tennis shoes are Asics Noosas. I use a sonic toothbrush I got from my dentist after the network got my teeth whitened when I started the show, and I use a Mach 3 razor, which I still believe is astronomical for replacement blades.

Me: Ah-HA! I knew your teeth couldn't naturally be that freaking perfect!

ChefCurtisRockwell: Sugar. It's called Zoom and it's available at like... any dentist office.

Me: Noted.

ChefCurtisRockwell: You don't need it though. Your teeth are gorgeous.

I wrinkle my nose.

Me: I live on coffee, and I've toyed around with the idea of that Invisalign thing, but I don't think I have the discipline for it.

ChefCurtisRockwell: Don't you dare.

Me: What?

ChefCurtisRockwell: You're not fucking getting Invisalign.

Me: Ummm... what?

My brow furrows.

ChefCurtisRockwell: If I ever find out you're trying to close that sexy little gap in your two front teeth, I will personally fly out there, break down your door, find the fucking teeth tray things, and melt them in your new Instant Pot. *red angry face

I know I should feel insolence at his bossiness, but really, I'm turned the hell on at the idea of him being so passionate about my annoying little gap. I always hated it when I was younger, when all my friends went through their awkward braces phase and came out with perfect, straight teeth. But then I didn't really think much about it as I got older, since no one ever seemed to notice it. I got made fun of for loving nerdy stuff more than I ever did for my gap, so I paid it no mind. That's why it's so strange to me for him to specifically point out that he wouldn't want me to close it. He'd obviously noticed it. Even called it "sexy." It makes me smirk and sit up a little.

I notice my water has grown cold, so I message him quickly.

Me: Gotta get out of the tub. I'm all pruny. BRB.

I set my phone on the floor outside the clawfoot tub then reach into the tepid water to pull the plug. I step out and wrap myself in a big-ass bath sheet, snatching my phone up off the floor right as it buzzes.

ChefCurtisRockwell: Ugggh… I had momentarily forgotten you were naked. I have a feeling being with you will be a lifetime of constant blue balls. *sobbing emoji

My heart stutters at this. He's still talking like he had last night, like it's a done deal, no doubt in his mind about me… about us. I wish I had even part of his confidence. In fact, a lot about him is inspiring. The way he's been so open with me, answering any and every question I've asked him, and without any hesitation, so I believe everything he's saying is the truth. He doesn't pause to filter his answers, not since I apologized and told him I wanted to be stronger and not run again.

So I take a deep breath and throw it out there…

Me: Is… there anything you want to ask me?

This time, there is a pause. But when I receive his response, I can't help but laugh.

ChefCurtisRockwell: Can I get them digits?

Me: LOL! Yes. As a matter of fact, you can.

I type out my number and send it through, and the next thing I receive isn't a DM in my app, but an actual text message from a phone number not programed into my contacts.

213-555-3808: Sugar, sugar… *music note emoji

I grin stupidly and save his info, sending him a reply.

Me: Ah, honey, honey. *music note emoji
Curtis: That's much better. *big smile emoji
Curtis: Now, can mine be a two-part question, or is it your turn again?
Me: I've asked several. You go ahead.

I dry off quickly, moving toward my dresser to grab a fresh pair of surgery panties and a nightgown, when my hand pauses above the drawer pull.

"They're full of bad juju anyway. Get. Rid. Of. Them." Emmy's voice echoes in my mind, and I bite my lip, narrowing my eyes as I grip the handle and slide the drawer open. There they all are, neatly laid flat in a stack ten-deep. Well, nine, since the pair I wore yesterday is still on the floor somewhere, where Curtis had tossed them.

I blow out a breath through pursed lips, my cheeks billowing, and then I straighten my shoulders, scoop all the surgery panties up, grab my phone off my bed where I'd tossed it, and hurry downstairs. Curtis's next text comes in, but I momentarily ignore it while I turn my video camera on.

"All right, Emmy girl. Here's documented evidence." I turn the camera around to make it forward facing, recording as I toss the hospital-grade undies into the kitchen's trashcan. "And to prove I will not change my mind and rescue them from the garbage—" I hurry to my fridge and grab a bunch of condiments I never use. I won't feel guilty for tossing them out before their expiration date, because it's for a good cause. I set the phone down on the counter after making it front facing once more, propping it so I can see myself. "—first, we'll add a jar full of… pickled green olives with pimentos in vinegar." I unscrew the cap and take a whiff, grimacing then making a gagging noise before dumping it on top of the panties inside the trashcan. "Next, we'll add some sweet and spicy barbeque sauce… and then the entire bottle of jalapeño mustard we bought because we thought it might taste like McDonald's spicy mustard sauce, but alas, it did not." I dump those in, shaking out the contents and doing a little dance for dramatic affect.

Forgetting I'm in nothing but a towel, it shimmies loose, and I catch it right before it hits the ground, wrapping it tightly back around me. "Hopefully you're watching this alone and Dean's not around." I slap my forehead. "Duh, when I send this to you, I'll just warn you not to let him see. Because I ain't taking the time to rerecord this shit or figure out how to use an app to edit it out."

I pick up my phone, pulling it up level with my face, and tell my best friend, "You were right. There's bad juju all over them bitches. Yes, they were comfy as fuck, but they were also a constant reminder of bad things that happened in the past. And I'm finally ready to get over those things and look forward to the future. I miss you, Em. So much. See you soon." And then I blow her a kiss, stopping the recording.

I immediately type out a text, **INCOMING! Beware, my boobs make an appearance, so don't watch around Dean!** I send that first as a fair warning, and then send the video behind it.

Just as the blue line showing the sending progress makes it to the very end, I receive a reply.

Isn't Dean in like... Delaware or something right now?

My head tilts to the side in confusion, my brow furrowing. Why would Emmy be asking *me* where her husband is?

And then I realize...

Me: Fuck. My. Life. That was meant for EMMY! Do NOT Watch!

Curtis: Too late.

Me: What do you mean "too late"?! You can't watch a video and be responding to me at the same time!

Curtis: I can if I'm watching the video on my 15 inch laptop screen and talking to you on my phone, sugar.

Curtis: *saves to spank bank

I squeal out in both embarrassment and laughter.

Me: You did NOT just save that! Delete it right now!

I shake my head while I wait for his response and start the long ascent, climbing the stairs in my bare feet. He still hasn't replied by the time I reach my bedroom, so I set my phone on my dresser while I grab a pair of much prettier bikini-cut royal blue undies out of the drawer. I slip them on, dropping my towel, and then pull my super-soft black sleep tee over my head. I pick up my towel off the floor and carry it to hang on the rack in the bathroom, and when I return to my room once again, I snatch my phone off my dresser then collapse on my bed.

Finally, after what seems like forever, I get a text from Curtis.

Curtis: First, did you remember to eventually send this to the person it was intended for? Just making sure, because I can't even

imagine how happy it'll make her. If not, DO NOT FORGET TO SEND THE NUDITY WARNING TOO. *narrowed eyes emoji

I sniff out a laugh and grin. For being so easygoing while he was here, he sure is all caveman-esque when he's not near me. I tell him so.

Me: You know, you weren't all bossy while you were here. Is that a proximity thing?

Curtis: I don't know. That's new for me. Just go with it.

I send Emmy the video, with the same boob warning ahead of it, and then switch back to Curtis's thread.

Curtis: I think it's because I'm not there to take care of you now. I'm not there to make sure you're safe, to make sure you're going to remember to eat and not walk too close to the edge of the sidewalk.

Me: You know I've survived this long without you, right? Almost 32 whole years. I've got this, honey.

Curtis: That may be. But everything changed last night. I'm not adjusting well to being away from you, now that I've experienced being with you. It's like... one hit and I'm already addicted.

Curtis: And just FYI, the video made me extremely happy as well. And not just because of the nip-slip.

I don't really know how to respond to any of that. I snuggle under my covers, and when I roll on my side, my head on the pillow, my eyes close as the light smell of his cologne immediately fills my senses. My heart beats inside my chest as memories of what we did early this morning flash through my mind. His head resting right where mine is right now, with me on top of him as he gripped my hips and looked up at me as if I was the most gorgeous creature he'd ever laid eyes on. His head resting here later, when I'd fallen asleep with him wrapped around me like he'd never let go.

I close my eyes, feeling myself start to drift off, twitching awake enough to see his text.

Curtis: You there?

But my eyes are too heavy to allow me to respond. I'd barely gotten three hours of sleep this morning before I ran and hid in Jackson Square all day.

I let out a grumpy huff when my phone starts to vibrate over and over, and I peek through one blurry eye so I can aim for the red Deny button. But my finger-to-one-eye coordination must be way off, because next thing I know, a swimmy image of Curtis's handsome face fills my screen, making me sit my head up and blink several times until I can see him clearly.

"You FaceTimed me?" I ask stupidly, because duh.

"You weren't responding. And you were naked," he replies, as if that makes any sense whatsoever.

I rest my head back down on the pillow. "What does one have to do with the other?"

He scowls, and it's so cute I can barely stand it. "What if someone broke into your house while you were in nothing but a towel?"

My mouth opens and closes like a fish before I can put together a sentence. Is he serious right now? "Are you serious right now? Honey, you need to put your crazy back in the box, mmkay?"

He lifts one brow. "Then why didn't you respond? Did I freak you out?"

I sigh. "No. I laid down, and the second I inhaled my pillow and smelled your scent, it's like I melted and can pretty much see myself being comatose for the next fourteen hours or so."

His face goes soft. "But you don't sleep in, remember?"

I close my eyes. "Then you better let me fall asleep so I can get enough hours in."

He lets out a small chuckle. "All right, sugar. Message me when you get up, okay?"

All the muscles in my entire body, including my face go lax as I breathe in deep and slow, taking him into my lungs and letting it soothe me like nothing has before. My voice is mumbled, and the last thing I remember saying is "Okay, caveman. Sleep yummy… or whatev—"

Dishing
~up~
Love

Twenty

CURTIS

I WATCH HER sleep for a good five minutes before she shifts onto her stomach, burying her phone beneath her. It kills me, but I end the call so I don't run her battery down. Before I hit End Call, I had the fleeting thought to prop my phone on my pillow just so it'd feel like she was sleeping next to me, but that would be like... one hundred percent creeper status.

Needy bitch status.

Stage Five clinger status.

Everything I've never been before status.

I shake my head at myself. "Get ahold of yourself, man."

But it feels like a piece of me is missing. Granted, it had felt like an entire half of me was missing all day, after realizing she was never coming home before I had to leave, while I was on my flight—which I refused to get the onboard WiFi so I wouldn't obsessively be checking my notifications—and on the drive home from LAX airport. It wasn't until after I showered and forced myself to eat something that I finally allowed myself to open Instagram.

I clicked on her profile, heat filling my chest when I saw the button read Follow Back instead of just Follow, and I clicked it immediately, hope springing up inside me and making my heart beat erratically. The first picture I came to was one she had snapped only a half-hour before, in front of her TV with our mutual friends on the screen. She was absolutely beautiful.

Her eyes were a little puffier than they were yesterday. Had she been crying, or was she just tired? I both loved and hated the idea of her crying over me. I wanted her to miss me, wanted her to want to be with me. The selfish part of me wanted her to be sad that I left, wanted her to be mad at herself for running and missing out on a day we could've spent together. But the bigger part of me, the part that wanted to protect and take care of the woman I never want to spend another day without, felt sick over the fact that she might've been upset all day, enough to bring her to tears. It made me want to fly right back to Louisiana and break down her door once I knew she was back home when she came out of hiding, and force her to see me again, force her to acknowledge these feelings between us.

And with these thoughts in mind, I took a breath for courage and messaged her privately. I just wanted to make sure she was okay.

As I lie here in bed now, a couple hours later, it's hard to believe how wonderfully the conversation went. I had expected her to ignore me, or to tell me to leave her alone, or to at least insist she decided she couldn't let this thing happen between us, at which time I was fully prepared to convince her otherwise.

But then she told me she was sorry for running. She wanted to be stronger and hated she left this impression on me of her being weak. It seemed to me she just needed us to get to know each other better. Which I'm all for.

For me, it's signed, sealed, and delivered. I know down to the marrow of my bones that she's the one for me. If I hadn't known when I saw her in the frozen pizza aisle of the grocery store, then I would've known the second I word-vomited secrets to her that I never told anyone. If I hadn't realized then, I would've for sure known when she stuck up for me and protected my privacy by taking those students to the guy she knew, so they could get the information they needed for their project. And finally, if it still hadn't occurred to me that I had found the one my soul wanted to reach out and cling to, then it would've slapped me in the face the moment I sank inside her tight heat and everything in the world disappeared but her.

But even feeling all this inside myself, I know we need to get to know each other. I know we need to learn each other's thoughts, likes, and dislikes. Each other's opinions and tastes. A long-lasting relationship can't be built on a soul-deep connection and physical attraction alone. And thankfully, everything I've learned about her thus far has only made me like her even more. Plus, the more she gets to know me, the more she'll trust me. Then, she'll understand I wasn't just telling her what she wanted to hear when I said it's her I want, and if that means never having biological children of my own, so be it. I've been to countless countries around the world, cooking for fundraising events involving homeless children. There are plenty of kids out there who need homes, and from what Erin told me last night, it was always her dream to someday become a mother. No one ever said she still couldn't be. It just won't be to a child who has our DNA.

Or maybe they could. Can't they like… take her egg and my swimmers and have someone else grow it? That's a thing, right? She never said anything about her eggs being bad. Just that her uterus was "broken."

It's with these wild thoughts of babies and laboratories and eggs and jizzing in a cup that I fall asleep, and all night I dream of Erin and a family we create, consisting of kids of different races and ages, and one with white-blonde hair and turquoise eyes, just like mine.

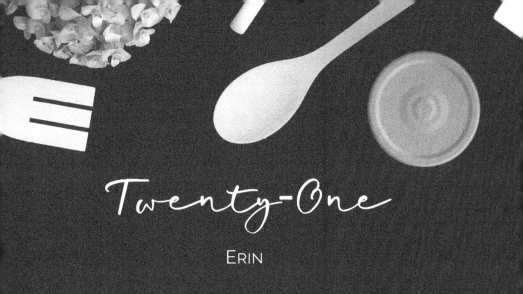

Twenty-One

ERIN

I'S BEEN A month. A whole month since that fateful day I ran headfirst into the man even my dreams couldn't conjure he's so fucking perfect. I've lost count of the hours we've spent messaging, talking, and FaceTiming.

Before, I never would've believed a long-distance relationship could work out so great. For us though, it's been exactly what I personally needed in order to heal on my own and also get to know Curtis without being swayed by the undeniable physical attraction between us.

At first, a week into waking up and falling asleep talking to him, it'd been frustrating. We both sat down with our calendars that night while we video chatted, and nothing lined up for us to be able to see each other anytime soon. He had chef obligations almost every weekend for events, and I had back-to-back patients who needed me during the week. On the one Friday coming up that I could've taken off, he had to film an episode of his show. By the end of the conversation, it had felt almost doomed, as if we'd never be able to see each other again.

But the very next day, Emmy called me, excitement pouring out with her every word. "We've been nominated for Best Documentary TV Series! Oh my God, Rin, please. Tell me you can take off and come be there for the award show!"

It was three weeks away, far enough in advance that I could maneuver my appointments around and be able to take a four-day weekend. So I told her, "I wouldn't miss it for the world."

Running on pure euphoria that I'd get to see my best friend for the first time in months, I immediately called Curtis as soon as Emmy and I hung up, telling him the news.

"Well how about that? I guess Emmy and I will have to fight over who gets to take you as our date. Because my show was nominated for the Reality TV Series category!" he told me, and my face grew instantly hot and my heart dove into my gut.

It had been one thing trying to make a plan to see each other, to be in his physical presence for only the second time since we met and had grown so close. Closer than I've ever been with another human being before. Closer than even Emmy and me. But it was a whole different ballgame when there was an actual date circled in hot pink gel pen on my calendar.

I had mumbled something stupid and obvious about Dean being her date, making him laugh, and apparently hearing the nervousness in my voice, he immediately assured me. "It's going to be okay, sugar. No reason to be worried. It's just me."

Just him.

Just *him*?

Him is the greatest thing ever created other than the bomb-ass Instant Pot gizmo he bought me—which he's taught me to cook several more meals in, walking me through it while we video chat, most of the time him in a hotel room or on a break at an event.

Him is the man who sets my blood on fire, sending hot waves of wetness with the simple attachment of a selfie.

Him is the person I see in my dreams every night, no matter the sometimes-flabbergasting stories I hear from patients throughout the day.

For the past three weeks, he's been trying to make me believe that the second we see each other again, it'll be like he never left. He's convinced that it's adrenaline from the anticipation making us feel all jittery and nervous. I can't count how many times I've used my "Hey, who's the psychologist here?" in these past twenty-one days.

And thank God for being a therapist, because as I sit on the plane, waiting for it to come to a stop at the gate in Los Angeles, I practice every breathing technique I can recall from my training. I feel nauseous with anxiety, and I close my eyes, wanting to kick myself for listening to

Curtis when he mansplained I needed to eat something before the flight, since it would be over four hours before I had access to real food again, and "the pretzels and crackers they pass out aren't good enough, sugar."

My temples grow wet with cold sweat as the plane finally parks and the door opens. I'm only in the second row back, because Curtis insisted on buying me a First-Class ticket so he could "see me a few minutes faster" than if I sat in Coach. I feel fidgety and worried as I grab my purse from beneath the seat in front of me and stand, side-stepping out of my row and into the aisle. I give the flight attendant and pilots a weak smile as they tell me to have a nice day and start to shuffle my way up the gangway.

God, what the hell is wrong with me? Is this a normal reaction to seeing a man you're pretty sure you've irrevocably fallen in love with after being apart for a month?

My psychologist mind tells me it's fine. I might be on the verge of an anxiety attack, a panic attack even, but the moment I see Curtis, it'll all be fine. The moment he wraps me in his big, strong arms and I inhale his scent once more, after it finally wore off my pillow a couple weeks ago, all will be right in my world, my serotonin will kick in, and all this craziness going on inside me that's manifesting these uncomfortable physical reactions will level out and disappear.

At the end of the tunnel, the light grows brighter as I step out into the airport. It's smaller than I imagined. You see all these tabloid photos of celebrities in baseball caps and sunglasses at LAX and you'd think it'd be extravagant or at least lined with countless stores and restaurants. But it's actually kind of dull, only a handful of stores and a couple food court style restaurants, at least in this terminal.

I glance up and see the sign for baggage claim, swallowing the saliva gathering under my tongue. My heartbeat feels fast and shallow, like the flapping of a hummingbird's wings as I make my way around the corner and out of the secured All-Gates area, and I see the circular conveyer belts up ahead.

There are benches next to them, and as the edges of my visions start to vignette, I tell myself if I can just make it to those benches without giving in to the full-on panic attack creeping up inside me, then I can reward myself by sitting down and putting my head between my knees until I can calm down.

I make it halfway there.

And stop.

Because stepping between me and my destination is the most handsome man I've ever laid eyes on. Even more handsome in person than I remembered. Even more handsome than in the countless FaceTime calls we've had over the last month.

And that handsome, excited, smiling face takes me in for a moment before his expression falters, and he rushes forward just as my knees start to wobble. He somehow catches me right as they give out, and just as I was hoping, with one deep breath, my lungs fill with the comforting scent of him, and it makes half of all the terrible nerves rushing through my veins pump their brakes as I melt into him. Letting him take my weight. Allowing him to just hold me up while I relax against him.

"You all right, sugar?" he breathes against my hair at the crown of my head, and I bask in the rumble of his voice against my cheek as it presses to his chest.

"I am now," I tell him, and we stay like that for I don't know how long as I soak up his strength.

When I think I can finally stand on my own, I pull my head back enough to look up at him, and his eyes dart back and forth between mine, making his own assessment before he lowers his head and kisses me gently.

This isn't the kiss I'd pictured thousands of times when I'd imagine what our reconnection would be like. I thought I'd spot him and run full-speed until I slammed into him, climbing up him like spider monkey, and latch onto his face with passion.

This though? This is a kiss of relief, of gratefulness, of love. This sweet, soft press of lips I feel in my heart, not my core. And *ahhh,* here comes that serotonin I was hoping for.

My eyes are still closed when we finally part, and when I look up at him, he's staring at me intently. "What is it?" I whisper.

"You look awfully pale, sugar. You feeling okay?" he asks, and I step back to grab and pull my purse back up on my shoulder after it had fallen to the floor when I almost collapsed.

Big mistake.

Just as I bend over to pick up my bag and am about to tell him, yeah, I'm fine now, that terrible tingling feeling starts in my chest and creeps up the back of my throat. My skin grows hot just as a chill runs through me, and the sweat that had dried on my temples starts to bead once more.

"Oh fuck," I hiss, glancing around frantically.

"Er—" Curtis doesn't even get my name out before I take off, leaving my purse behind as I bolt to the tall black trashcan near the bench I'd been aiming for just minutes ago.

"I'm sorry!" I cry out to the people standing nearby waiting for their baggage to be loaded onto the conveyor belt, just as I take hold of the black metal, put my whole head inside the open lid, and proceed to empty my stomach.

I hear who I hope is Curtis hurry up behind me and feel his big hands start pulling my hair away from my face. His fingers are so gentle as he gathers it all at the back of my head and holds it there with one hand, using the other to rub my back.

"She okay?" I hear in a familiar male voice, but I don't turn to figure out who it is.

"I've got her, bro. You mind running into the bathroom right there and getting some cold, wet paper towels?" Curtis asks quietly, and the guy must agree, because I hear his tennis shoes squeak against the floor as he walks briskly away from us.

Right when I think I'm done heaving—surely my stomach must be completely empty by now—I try to swallow and feel a chunk of my breakfast still hanging out. The feeling brings on another wave of bile until I'm dry-heaving, whimpering at the awful feeling and internally dying of embarrassment that this is how I greeted Curtis, literally the hottest man alive, after having a long-distance relationship with him for the past month.

"Here you go, man," comes the voice again, and when I groan in relief at the feel of the coldness hitting the back of my neck and feel another press into my hand, which I use to wipe my mouth, I peek up, seeing it's Carlos.

He waves at me sheepishly, the look of pity on his face as I try to give him a smile.

"Hey, Carlos. Thank you," I say through a sniffle, blinking away tears that filled my eyes while I barfed my brains out.

"Hey, sweetheart. You feeling better?" he asks.

I take a moment, still bent over the trashcan, hair still pulled back in

Curtis's hand, and assess how I'm feeling before I attempt to stand up straight. When all I feel is emptiness in my gut, the queasiness gone, I nod and push up from the can, and Curtis lets go of my hair, wrapping his arms around my waist to keep me steady.

"I feel much better now," I murmur, feeling bashful. "Sorry, guys."

"I didn't realize you were that worried about seeing me again, sugar," Curtis says, and when I look up at him, he uses the knuckle of his pointer finger to trace my jawline gently. My eyes flutter closed at the sweetness of the touch, and then I meet his gaze.

"I think it had more to do with the breakfast you insisted on me eating before the flight. And then we hit a spot of turbulence about halfway here that made me pee a little," I inform him.

He chuckles. "So what you're saying is you need a shower that includes a toothbrush. Got it. Let's grab your bag and get you home."

And that's exactly what we do. He drives me straight to his house, which is a gorgeous two-story expanse that embodies everything I imagine Curtis to be. All the walls are bright white with a mix of masculine and modern furniture and splashes of color in the artwork on the walls. We don't take the time to go see his kitchen, because I want to wash off that plane smell and the gum he gave me in the car isn't doing anything to make my mouth taste better. I don't think anything will until I'm able to scrub it with my charcoal toothpaste and gargle the hell out of an entire bottle of mouthwash.

At first, it seems like he wants to give me privacy, unsure if I want to take a shower alone, but when I leave the door open to his en suite and give him a playful wink as I pull my shirt over my head, that's all the invitation he needs and he closes us into his bathroom.

"You sure you're feeling okay, sugar?" he asks as I reach behind me and unhook my bra, letting it fall to the floor.

I give him a smile, looking up into his turquoise eyes as I watch his nostrils flare when he takes in my breasts. "I'm feeling much better, thank you," I reply, stepping out of my sparkly moccasins and pulling off my leggings.

When he glances down then, I can't help but giggle at the look of relief on his face when he sees I'm wearing a pretty thong instead of a pair of surgery panties I might've rescued out of the trashcan.

I take his T-shirt over his head, him helping to get it all the way off, since he's so tall and I can't reach. And then I unbutton his jeans and unzip the fly, hooking my fingers into his boxer briefs and pulling it all down at once, where he steps out of them apparently having already taken his shoes off before we came into the bathroom.

When he leans down to kiss me, I smack my open palm over my mouth, shaking my head. As he rears back, giving me a questioning look, I tell him, "There is no way in hell you're kissing me until I brush all the nastiness out of my mouth."

He nods begrudgingly, and so I hook my thumbs into my thong and pull them down my legs, spinning around and tossing them at him over my shoulder as I step into the shower that's big enough for ten people. I had every intention of turning the water on and getting it all set for us, but I can't quite figure out how. I look around for a knob, a faucet of some sort, but there's not one to be found.

Instead, I hear him chuckling still outside the shower door, and I glance through the glass to see him lift his hand to press buttons on a touchscreen. I have just enough time to glance up at where he points at a place above me with a wink before the water cascades down from the ceiling, as the biggest showerhead I've ever seen turns on. It has to be a good two feet wide by three feet long, taking up most of the ceiling space inside the stall, and the water comes out as if it's a rain shower. There's just enough space around the perimeter for you to stand in order to be able to lather up, and it has to be the most relaxing shower I've ever been in, in my life.

"Oh my God, I could seriously live in this thing," I tell him as he finally steps in after watching me, seeming mesmerized, while I enjoyed the soothing hotness of the water.

"You could if you wanted to, sugar," he replies. "Just say the word and I'll move your sexy little ass out here at the drop of a hat."

My breath doesn't even catch when he says things like this anymore, because he's so often said them over the past month. It no longer shocks me when he talks about the future as if he already knows it's going to happen.

Most of the time, I choose to change the subject, like I do now. "We need to hurry. We still need to pick up Emmy and Dean when they get to the airport."

"You know, they have drivers for that, or they can call an Uber, and then we could spend the next few hours making up for lost time," he teases, kissing the back of my shoulder, and it immediately sends a shiver down my breasts, making my nipples hard.

I look up at him over my shoulder, raising an eyebrow. "You do realize that I've seen *you* since the last time I saw my best friend, right? There's no way in hell I'm letting her get an Uber when I can tackle her at the airport... like I had fully planned on doing to you before I puked my brains out in front of God knows how many famous people." And then it dawns on me, and a worried look comes across my face. "Oh, God, famous people. That means there were probably a shitload of incognito paparazzi there, huh? Which means the next time I look at my Instagram, there's going to be eighteen thousand tags of me barfing in a trashcan with my hot boyfriend holding my hair back. That's sooo attractive."

He wraps his arms tightly around me, and it instantly calms me down. "Well, if there's no time for hanky-panky, then I guess let's hurry up the shower, so I have time to feed you before we get your bestie."

My stomach rolls at the thought, but I know I should probably put something in it, because it is definitely empty. Even though we don't end up having sex in the shower—we'll just have to christen it later—it's still a sensual experience allowing Curtis to take his time lathering up every inch of my body. And when his huge, masculine hands take hold of my head, massaging shampoo into my scalp with his long, skillful fingers, it's almost as satisfying as an orgasm anyway. So after he rinses me off and I treat him to the same pampering, we get out of that heavenly stall feeling sated.

After getting dressed, leaving my hair up in a towel, we go downstairs and I finally get to see his kitchen. I've been looking forward to it, because I imagine the personal kitchen of a chef would be astounding. And I wasn't wrong. Everything is white stone and stainless-steel appliances. The backsplash takes my breath away, and for a moment, I wonder if it was already there over a month ago.

Of course it was. There's no way he would have remodeled anything about his precious kitchen just for me.

"If you're wondering if I already had the white subway tile backsplash, the answer is yes. That's why I kind of chuckled when we first met and you said you love Joanna Gaines. I thought it was ironic that the one thing in my house decorated in the farmhouse style you love was the kitchen, since when I met you, you were in the frozen pizza aisle and don't know a thing about cooking."

"*Didn't* know a thing about cooking," I emphasize. "I can now make almost ten different recipes thanks to a certain chef giving me private lessons over the phone."

He smiles. "True story, sugar. Now, what do you feel like eating?"

I grimace. "Nothing really, but if you're going to make me, then something starchy. Super-duper starchy. Like super potatoey starchy."

"I take it you want some carbs?"

I gave him a cheesy grin and nod.

"All right, I'll allow it, but there's got to be some type of protein in your starchy potatoey starch. You think you could handle some cheese… maybe some bacon in a baked potato?" he asks, coming closer to trace the line of my cheekbone with the gentle tips of his fingers.

The look in his eyes takes my breath away and all the words right out of my head. Have I ever seen love so openly naked in someone's eyes before? Never. Has anyone shown me such selfless care before? Only Emmy, her grandma, and my parents.

God, I love him, I think, giving a dreamy sigh inside my head as I soak up the feeling of finally being in his arms once again.

His eyebrows shoot upward, nearly hitting his hairline, and only when his eyes twinkle and the corners of his mouth lift a little do I realize—

"I sure hope the 'him' you're referring to is me, sugar. And in that case, him loves her too," he says softly, and it confirms what I suspected. I hadn't thought those words to myself. He made me so dumb they had come out of my mouth without me meaning for them to.

I swallow thickly and nod, my cheeks heating furiously. "Yeah. Him is you. That… that wasn't supposed to be my outside voice. You just make me stupid."

"You are a lot of things, sugar, but stupid doesn't come even close to being one of them," he tells me, and I melt a little more against him. "But now that it's out in the open, can we try that again, properly this time?" At my nod, he smiles as he leans down, his lips a whisper away from mine, and I can feel his breath as he says, "I love you, Erin."

The words and use of my real name make me shiver against him, and my eyes tear up as I reply something I never thought I'd get to say to another man for the rest of my life. "I love you too."

"I know," he sing-songs, giving me a cocky grin, and I'm grateful for his playfulness. He kisses me thoroughly then, and right when I'm just about to point out that yes, Emmy *could* get an Uber, he pulls away, giving me a swat on the ass and making me yelp before rounding the giant island in the center of his kitchen. He grabs a huge russet potato out of a basket on the counter, and I pull out one of the stools under the lip of the island to sit and watch his handiwork.

"For time's sake, I'm going to do it in the microwave," he says absently, almost like it's a habit from speaking all the steps while he's filming his show. All I can do is stare, watching his masculine grace as he fixes me lunch, the look of concentration on his face making my heart swell, knowing he's making it for me with such care, even if it's just a baked potato.

When he slides it across the white stone countertop, my jaw drops at the starchy masterpiece, and as the scent wafts up my nose, I feel hungry for the first time. He pulls out a drawer and hands me a fork then wipes his hands on the white towel slung over his shoulder.

I groan at the first bite. This isn't some cheap steakhouse stuffed potato. I watched him grate this cheese, watched him whip up this fresh sour cream as the potato cooked in the microwave, and the butter came out of an unmarked container, hinting it wasn't something he just bought from the grocery store. These bits of bacon didn't come out of a package or a shaker. I got to witness his awesome knife skills again, like that day in my kitchen, as he diced a couple slices he pulled out of a block wrapped in white butcher paper.

"This is the best starchy potatocy starch I've ever eaten in my life," I mumble around a mouthful, breathing in and out through my mouth to try to cool it off as I attempt to chew it. So unladylike, but goddamn. It's fucking good and I don't want to wait.

He grins, coming around the island to kiss me on the top of my head. "Lemme taste."

I narrow my eyes up at him, shaking my head. "My carbs," I growl.

He widens his eyes. "Woman, gimme a taste, or I will take it myself."

I sit up straight, shifting in my seat haughtily. "Oh yeah, and how will you do that?" I challenge.

He leans over me, his towering height allowing him to look down on me even with me sitting on his bar stool. "Before you can even blink, I'll have you across my knees and I'll spank that tight little ass then use your back as my dining table."

My eyes widen at that. "Kinky. I read an erotic novel like that once." I dip my fork into the potato, making sure to get a little bit of each topping into the one bite before lifting the utensil to his lips.

"You like to read dirty books?" he asks before opening his mouth, using his perfect lips to slide the food off and onto his tongue.

I snort. "Is there a woman out there who doesn't? Have you ever read one? Hotter than watching porn, because you can imagine for yourself what the people look like, even putting yourself in their place if you want."

His eyes twinkle as he chews and watches me take a bite. "Men are more visual creatures, aren't they, Ms. Psychologist?"

I shrug. "This is true."

"Maybe they'll make it into a movie and then we can both enjoy…?" he prompts, and he must mean the title of the book.

"Oh goodness. I don't remember the title, because the author, Red Phoenix, has like eighty-four thousand hot-as-hell stories, but yeah. If they made them into a movie or series, I. Am. Here. For. It." I emphasize each word with a tap of my finger to the end of his nose.

"So you like the potato? I think it needs salt," he adds, reaching to the center of the island to grab the grinder full of pink salt crystals.

I use both my hands to make a shield over the potato, shaking my head. "While it's adorable that my big, strong, handsome man has pink salt—"

"It's Himalayan," he grumps.

"—this is perfect the way it is. The salt from the bacon is just enough. I needed something a little bland to settle my tum-tum. I think adding anything else would send it into the 'too flavorful' category," I finish.

He sniffs out a short chuckle. "Yes, let's settle that 'tum-tum.' Because I have plans for it later."

I screw up my face. "Do I take that as you wanting to rearrange my guts with your dick, or are you cooking something special for me?"

He barks out a laugh. "Both." He smacks a kiss to my lips before circling the island once more to clean up the little mess he made while making my potato.

Dishing
~up~
Love

Twenty-Two

CURTIS

I DON'T THINK I've ever witnessed pure joy with my own two eyes until I got to watch the moment Erin spotted Emmy coming around the corner at baggage claim at the airport. Even their ear-drum-bursting squeal as they collided in the exact same spot I caught Erin before she nearly collapsed earlier today couldn't lessen the delight I felt inside my chest getting to see the love of my life so completely happy. It's the same reaction I had hoped for when she spotted me when I picked her up, and I'm one hundred percent positive it would've been had she not felt so awful.

I swear I lost at least four years off my life when I saw her knees give out, and thank God for my long legs and the adrenaline rush that shot through my veins, because I was able to catch her just before she hit the floor. If that's her normal reaction to flying, we're going to have to figure out a regimen of motion sickness meds and breathing techniques or something. Because I will never go another month without seeing her again. Hell, it'll be a miracle if I allow a week between visits. Especially now. Now that she's admitted not only to herself but out loud to me as well that she loves me.

After giving Dean a bro hug, pulling each other in and slapping each other on the back, we stand back with stupid grins on our faces as we watch the girls roll around on the floor, refusing to end their hug and laughter. Neither of us gives a shit as people look at our group weirdly, and I give someone a goofy face and a peace sign when I see them whip out their phone for either a video or photo. I'm sure my woman won't mind that someone caught this moment on camera. In fact…

I take out my own cell, and turn on the video recorder, using the button near the bottom of the screen to take some snapshots while it's still filming. When the girls finally sprawl on their backs, trying to catch their breaths as they look at each other, they let out a fit of giggles once more.

I feel honored to get to witness such a wholesome moment, two of the closest friends reconnecting after months apart. It makes me want to speed up the process of Erin and me living together even more. I see Dean and Emmy several times a month because of our work at the same network, which means Erin could see her favorite girl way more often than she does now. I just don't know how she'd feel about giving up her practice in New Orleans, since there's no way she could take off as much as she'd need to in order to make all that happen.

And if she expresses she doesn't want to leave her job, then what?

That's easy. I'll do whatever it takes to be with her, not just officially, but physically. It would be a shitload of travelling on my part, but I would make my home base in NOLA in a heartbeat for her. I'd do anything for her.

When Dean and I are finally able to pull the girls up from the floor and grab their luggage from the conveyer belt, we all pile into my truck, the two women choosing to sit in the back seat together. The only thing that keeps me from huffing over my girl not sitting next to me is the fact that she's in the seat behind me, so every time I glance into the rearview mirror, all I see is her gorgeous smile. She catches my stare every few miles and sticks out her tongue, her little nose wrinkling the way I remember it doing the first night we spent together, reminding me exactly what made me fall in love with her.

We've almost made it home, and I'm deep in conversation with Dean about the next location their going to be filming *No Trespassing*, when from the back seat I hear, "You okay, Rin?" and my eyes immediately dart to the rearview mirror. Erin's face has gone pale like it had when I picked her up today, and I've already turned my blinker on before she can ask me to pull over.

We're in my neighborhood, so it's nothing to jump out my driver seat at the same time her door opens, and I reach in and scoop her up, carrying her swiftly to the grass on the passenger side of my truck. I set her down on her feet and she spins away from me, bending over just as I wrap my arm around the front of her waist. I hold her up, taking her weight as she throws up, the most pitiful whimper coming out of my girl and breaking my heart.

"I'm… sorry," she manages to get out between heaves, and I rub her back, shushing her worry.

"Don't apologize, baby. I've got you," I soothe, just as Emmy comes up beside me to pull her hair back from her face.

"It's okay, Rin. Let it out," she tells her, and her confused eyes meet mine.

"Second time today," I reply to her unspoken question, and she nods, her brows furrowed.

As Erin catches her breath, I pick her up, and Dean hops out of the front passenger seat so I can set her there. "Maybe she's car-sick. I know some people can't ride in the back seat without getting nauseous," he suggests.

I tell him and Emmy as I buckle the seat belt around Erin, even as she weakly swats at me, "At first, I thought maybe it was all the excitement of seeing each other after a whole month. Like anxiety or something. But she said she hit turbulence on the flight, so she thought maybe it was motion sickness." And then I direct a question at my girl, "Sugar, do you normally get car-sick? Motion sickness? Shit, even sea-sick?"

She shakes her head. "No, not normally. It's always Em who needs all the Dramamine and stuff. I've usually got a tummy of steel."

I see Emmy nod in the backseat as Dean shuts the door behind him. "It's true. She can go on any roller coaster and not be fazed by the loops and twists, while I feel like I'm going to die."

I frown at that, closing the passenger door and rounding the front of my truck before hopping back in the driver seat.

When we get home, I help Dean carry in their luggage as Emmy wraps her arm around Erin's waist, walking with her inside. I hurry to the fridge and pour her a glass of Sprite, and she gratefully gulps it down.

"You want some crackers or something, baby? Another potato?" I murmur, wrapping one arm around the small of her back and pushing her hair behind her ear.

She shakes her head vigorously, sneering a little. "Not right now, but thank you. I think I just need to lie down for a little bit."

I nod and give Emmy a look, and she silently agrees, taking Erin's arm in hers and leading her up the stairs. She knows the layout from the couple times she and Dean have been over for dinner while in California for either network meetings or if they're filming an episode nearby.

"She all right?" Dean asks as he comes in from grabbing the last of their bags.

"I think so. I hope it's not like a stomach bug or something. I'd hate for her to have to miss the award show if she's sick," I tell him, and he follows me into the kitchen, where I ask if he'd like something to drink. I crack us open two bottled waters, and after he takes a big gulp, he looks at me.

"She seemed perfectly fine at the airport. I think if it was a stomach bug, she wouldn't have felt like wrestling with my wife in the middle of the floor for all to see," he points out, and then his face grows pensive. "You said she threw up when she first got here too?"

"Yep, poor thing," I answer.

"And then she was fine up until just then outside?" he prompts.

I nod. "Exactly."

"So it's like… coming in waves of nausea?" He lifts a brow.

And when I narrow my eyes, giving him a drawled, "Yeeeah," he rubs his chin in thought. "What is it?" I ask impatiently, wanting to know what he thinks might be making my woman feel like shit.

"I was just thinking about how my wife did the same thing before we found out she was pregnant. Perfectly fine one minute, and then puking her brains out the next. They may call that shit morning sickness, but we can vouch it was morning, noon, and middle of the night," he says, giving a little chuckle as if he's reminiscing the experience.

But I'm already shaking my head. "I'm sure you know, since our women are so close, that Erin can't have kids. Plus, we've only had sex one time since we've been together."

"Bro, don't you remember sex ed? It only takes one time. And she can get pregnant, it's just highly unlikely. And if she does, it's even less of a chance she won't miscarry," he tells me, a worried look in his eyes, even though I can tell he's trying to hide it for my sake.

I shake my head once again in denial. "There's no way, man. She said it'd be an absolute miracle if she ever got pregnant again. This can't be that. She's gotta have a bug or something." But even as I say the words, something niggles the back of my mind and my heart gives an exaggerated thump at the possibility.

What was it I read when I researched Erin's condition? Something about the surgery she had seven months ago now. I can't remember.

I meet Dean's eyes. "But it can't hurt to find out for sure, right?"

He gives me a tentative smile. "Right, bro. I'll hold down the fort," he tells me, sensing exactly what I want to do.

"Thanks, man!" I call over my shoulder, jogging to the front door and waving over at him. And then I hop in my truck, trying not to speed as I drive to the nearest drugstore.

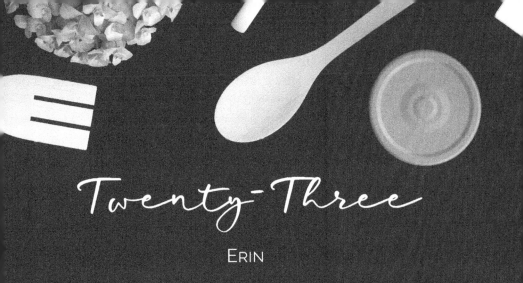

Twenty-Three

ERIN

"WHY AM I dyiiing?" I whine, snuggling into my best friend, where I have my head on her soft tummy as she rubs my back. "I finally get a long weekend with that fine piece of ass, and I can't stop puking my brains out. What's wrong with me?"

"Well, we've already established what it's not. You don't get motion sickness. You feel relatively fine one minute, and then vomit the next. You didn't eat anything out of the ordinary, did you?" she asks.

"No. I just had a sausage, egg, and cheese biscuit before my flight. Nothing tasted off about it." I think for a moment. "It felt almost like an anxiety attack, so I thought I was just nervous about seeing Curtis again."

"Maybe," she replies, but she sounds doubtful.

"And then all the excitement of seeing you," I add.

And she placates, "Maybe."

I sit up, narrowing my eyes on her. "All right, spit it out. Quit babying me with all the maybes and tell me what you think."

Her nostrils flare as she takes a deep inhale, and I brace myself for her response. "Okay, so don't freak out," she tells me.

I close my eyes, already knowing what she's going to say. And somehow, in my heart, I know she's right.

"It's possible, Rin. Y'all didn't use a condom."

But I shake my head, wanting to be in denial for a little longer before I have my heart broken once more, knowing I'll soon have two angel babies in heaven instead of one. One is more than enough.

"No." My lip trembles, my eyes filling with tears. "The doctor said it'd be a miracle if it ever happened again."

She tucks my hair behind my ear, giving me a small smile. "Miracles happen, babe."

"But… but I'm going to lose—" My voice hiccups, and my hand presses to my still-flat stomach.

She shakes her head. "You don't know that, Rin. Remember, you never had morning sickness last time," she whispers. "Dean always reminded me while I was praying to the porcelain gods, trying to make me feel better, that morning sickness is a sign that everything is all right, that the pregnancy was going how it should. You've already been sick twice today."

And then my eyes meet hers with worry for a different reason. "Oh, God. Curtis. He's going to think I lied to him, that I trapped him on purpose because he's a super-hot, rich, famous celebrity!" I cry, and my head whips around at the sound of my favorite voice in the whole world.

"Curtis is *not* going to think that, even though I appreciate the fact that you think I'm super-hot." He gives me a smile, although I still see worry in the lines at the corners of his eyes.

I glance down, seeing a Walgreens bag in his hand, and I understand he must have his own suspicion of what's been going on with me today.

"You want to do it alone, sugar?" he asks, stepping up to the side of his bed, and I shake my head.

"No. I mean, yes, for the peeing part. But I want y'all here for the test part," I murmur.

He reaches across Emmy and scoops me up, and she slaps my ass when I'm midair above her right before he holds me against his body.

"You got this, babe. Remember, miracles happen. And everything will be fine," she tells me as he carries me to the bathroom, setting me on my feet before handing me the plastic bag.

Before I turn away to head toward the toilet, he yanks me to him, his arms engulfing me before he kisses me like his life depends on it. When he finally pulls away, I'm wobbly on my feet and love drunk.

"I love you," he whispers. "No matter what happens, no matter how everything turns out. Whether everything goes smoothly or whether it's not meant to be, I love you with everything in me. You will always be the one I want. Only you, sugar."

With my heart in my throat, all I can do is nod. And then he spins me around and gives me a little nudge toward the toilet. I hear his and Emmy's unintelligible voices going back and forth as I shut myself inside the little room with the toilet.

My heart pounds inside my chest as I unbox the test, taking great care to aim correctly and pee on the stick, slipping the cover back on the end of it before wiping and pulling up my leggings. I don't look at the test as I open the door and carry it with me to the vanity, where I wash my hands, refusing to even peek at the window that will give me the results. I dry my hands on a towel hanging next to the mirror and carry the test out into the bedroom, where there are three sets of eyes now staring back at me, as Dean has Emmy pulled onto his lap, his back against Curtis's headboard. Curtis is sitting on the end of the bed, his knees jumping up and down a mile a minute as he waits for me to approach him.

And in this moment, as scary as my near future could turn out to be, there is nowhere I'd rather be than in the company of the people in this room right now. I've never felt so safe in such a terrifying situation in my life.

I walk up to Curtis, and he pulls me between his legs, turning me sideways and tugging me down to sit on his thigh. I still refuse to look at the test, unsure what I want the results to be. I haven't even had time to think about any of that.

I grab hold of his wrist and turn his hand over so his palm is facing up, and I lay the test in the center of it. Then I rest my chin on his shoulder, looking over his back to lock eyes with Emmy. She can't hide the emotions on her face. They're bouncing between excitement and worry, but anticipation is always there in her eyes. And when I feel Curtis's head bow, knowing he's looking at the test in his hand, I close my eyes, praying for… I don't know what. Do I pray it's positive? Even at the risk of losing our baby? Do I pray it's negative, so we don't have to worry any more about it?

So I pray for everything to just work out the way it's supposed to.

I wobble on Curtis's thigh as I feel the bed shift, and I open my eyes to see Emmy crawling as fast as her hands and knees can move over the thick covers as she reaches Curtis's back. Her hand wraps around the back of my head and into my hair to hold me tight in a hug as best she can as she looks over my guy's shoulder.

And I hear her gasp.

Just as Curtis turns his head more in her direction.

"What does that mean? Two lines side by side. Is that two minuses? Like negative? Would it be a plus sign for positive?" he asks, his body starting to tremble beneath me, and I hear my best friend's giddy voice respond as I bury my face in the side of his neck, tears welling in my eyes as I already know the answer.

"No! Two lines means positive! You're pregnant!" she squeals, and I pull my eyes up enough to watch as she stands up on the bed and starts jumping, chanting with each hop, "Miracle baby! Miracle baby! Miracle baby!" And then "Belle's getting a cousin! Belle's getting a cousin!" And her enthusiasm is contagious as I allow myself ten seconds of hope that this will all work out okay.

Curtis's arms encircle my waist and he falls back on the bed, hauling me with him as he lets out a whoop, and Emmy plops down on her ass before—gently—dogpiling on top of me. I feel her smack a kiss to my cheek before I peek up to see Dean picking her up off me, a huge grin on his handsome face. He gives me a wink as Emmy tries to wiggle out of his arms, but when he tells her, "Let them have this moment, love," she settles down and melts against him with a nod. They disappear out the bedroom, and I hear the door close behind them.

CURTIS

I FEEL HER trembling against me, and I don't know whether she's crying or laughing. I wrap my arms even more tightly around her, holding her to me. "Are you okay, sugar?" She nods against my chest and I relax a bit until I hear her soft voice.

"We need to go to the doctor. What time is it?" she asks.

"It's 6:06 p.m.," I reply.

"Shit," she says, "they won't be open again until tomorrow."

I chuckle. "Baby, if you wanted to go to a doctor right this minute, I could make that happen."

"How?" she questions. "The doctor's offices stay open later here?"

"This is LA. Doctors don't set office hours; dollar bills do." I smirk.

"I never thought I would be grateful for your cockiness," she tells me, looking at me with hopeful eyes.

"So do you, baby? You want me to find a doctor right now?" She nods, her gaze turning pleading, even though she doesn't need to beg. I would literally give her anything she wants in this very moment. I reach into my pocket, not letting her go with the other arm, and I make a call to my assistant. Within minutes, Rachel is sending me an address with an appointment to be there within thirty minutes.

Dean asks us if this is something we would like to do on our own, giving us the option for him and Emmy to stay here while I take my woman to see the doctor, but at Emmy and Erin's simultaneous "No way!" that's all the answer I need. We all pile back into my truck, thankfully making it to the office without Erin getting sick on the way, and when we arrive, Dr. McNealy meets us at his locked door, opening it up and allowing us in before locking it behind us once more.

A few minutes later, Erin is up on the exam table with me and Emmy sitting in the chairs along the wall, Dean choosing to stay behind in the waiting room.

"So what's going on?" Dr. McNealy asks, and Erin holds out the pregnancy test, allowing him to see that it reads positive. "Well, congratulations are in order!" he says with a smile on his face that I see as I come to stand next to her.

Then I listen as the love of my life word-vomits her entire medical history onto the doctor. She explains to him in detail everything that went on from her miscarriage all the way until seven months ago, when she had her fibroid surgery. I watch the play of emotions across his face as I see the understanding with every slight nod of his head, and then his eyes alight, twinkling with mirth when he seems to put it all together in his head.

"Well, dear girl, I can tell you exactly what happened. Your myomectomy was successful in ridding your uterus of all the fibroids that would've been blocking any sperm from being able to enter the uterus through the cervix and into the fallopian tubes. Nevertheless, being diagnosed with a hostile uterus, you are still susceptible to miscarrying once again. But luckily there are now medications you can take in order to keep that from happening. And as long as we, or whoever your OB/GYN is, keep a good watch during the pregnancy, there is no reason why you shouldn't be able to carry this little one full-term and have a healthy and happy baby." He claps his hands, which give away he's much older than what his plastic surgery enhanced face portrays.

A healthy and happy baby.

A healthy and happy baby.

A healthy and happy baby.

Those words circle my mind over and over again, the world seeming to finally slow down enough that it hits me what we're actually doing here. It all seemed to happen so fast from the second in the kitchen when Dean suggested the idea of the pregnancy test to here, in this moment, with a medical professional telling us that it's possible for us to have *a healthy and happy baby,* it repeats once more.

I look down at Erin, and although she's a little paler than normal, looking a little green around the gills, I've never seen her look more beautiful than the second it all occurs to me.

I'm going to be a father.

Twenty-Four

Erin

"So the question is now, what would you like to do? Do you want to wait until you can see your own OB/GYN before being placed on any type of medication? Or would you like to have me call in for your medical records and get you those prescriptions here?" Dr. McNealy asks.

I feel Curtis's eyes on me as if he wants to talk about the decision, but I've already made up my mind about it before the question is all the way out of the doctor's mouth. "Here. Now," I say. "I have my medical records stored in my phone. I'm a therapist, so I know how handy those can be. If what you're saying is true, then I don't want to take any chances of losing the baby before I can get home to New Orleans on Monday. So go ahead and sign me up for these meds."

I know I've made Curtis happy with my decision, because the soothing smile he's kept on his face for me through all of this craziness turns into a huge grin and he nods before leaning down to kiss my cheek.

The next hour and a half is a whirlwind. Dr. McNealy runs another pregnancy test and the next thing I know, I'm pulling into Curtis's driveway with a white paper bag of prescriptions.

Dean drags Emmy into their own room after we make plans to go to dinner in half an hour. This gives us all time to freshen up before we're seen in public.

Curtis and I are in his bathroom. I don't exactly know what to say, and for the first time ever, our silence is awkward. I grab my toiletries

bag and set it up by the vanity, pulling out my makeup to put on. I hadn't bothered before we went to get my best friend and her hubby at the airport, because I figured I'd cry it all off with happy tears anyway. Little did I know I would be crying it all off while having morning sickness in the middle of the day.

Morning sickness.

I'm pregnant.

With a baby.

A real, living, so-far healthy little bean that's been growing inside me for almost five weeks now.

I'd never had morning sickness before. I hadn't even known I was pregnant the first time, until I lost it.

I don't realize I've frozen in place with my thoughts, my mascara halfway to my lashes, until Curtis's arms wrap around my waist and his front presses against my back. My eyes focus on him in the mirror, and I replace the mascara wand into its tube. He has the most serene look on his face, as if he's the happiest man alive, and I spin in his arms to look up at him, all awkwardness disappearing.

"I hope you're okay with my decision about the doc—"

"I've been begging you to move in with me for almost as long as we've been together, sugar," he interrupts.

I raise my brows. "I mean, there've been a ton of different ideas that come along with that, honey. You've asked me to move here with you. You've asked to get a place together in NOLA. You've even suggested us selling off everything and getting an RV to live on the road, wherever the events may take us." I can't help but giggle.

"I'd be happy doing any of those things. Because all of them put you and me together. That's all that matters to me. I'd give up everything for you, baby," he tells me, squeezing me a little tighter with that last part, but I'm already shaking my head.

"I don't want you to give up anything. I never want that. And I don't want to have to give up anything either. I love my job," I reply, and the light dims in his eyes just a bit, so I continue on, getting to the good part. "But as soon as that doctor told me it's possible for us to have a full-term healthy pregnancy, it all clicked into place."

His nostrils flare, and I see hope in his every feature. "What did?"

"There is nothing in the entire world I've ever wanted more than to be a mom. Nothing. I threw myself into my work, making it my world, allowing it to take over my entire life until I wasn't even taking care of my own self in order to care for other people, nurturing them as if *they* were my babies. But now—" My hands move to my stomach and I close my eyes, imagining our little miracle there. "—I know I wouldn't be giving up anything. My dream is actually coming true."

"So what are you saying, sugar?" he prompts, his voice a soft whisper as if he's almost afraid to ask.

"That my answer is finally yes. I will move in with you. Here in California. I love New Orleans and will be sad to leave, but my parents live there, so I'll still get to visit as often as I want. But I want this to be our home," I tell him, and I swear to God I think I see tears fill his eyes before they close and he slams his mouth down on mine, cutting off any more talking.

He devours me as if his life depends on it, and I let him, my nose tingling with tears this moment is so beautiful. I've never made a person so happy before. I feel his joy rolling off of him as if it's a tangible thing, and it crashes into me in waves, filling me up until I feel like I'm going to burst with glee.

He picks me up, setting my ass on the vanity, and the loud clattering of all my makeup falling into the sink pulls us out of our haze before the party even gets started. "Fuck, I'd do anything to make love to you right here and now," he breathes against my lips and then rests his forehead against mine.

"I'd love that too," I whisper, "but one, we don't have time before we're supposed to go to dinner. And two, you'll be happy to know I'm actually feeling a teensy bit hungry."

He pulls back at that, searching my face, and when he sees whatever it was he was looking for, determination takes over his gaze. "Right," he rumbles. He looks around me into the sink, grabs my blush and shockingly the right brush, and opens it up the compact. He dabs a little on the brush, and then to my utter amazement, he strokes it gently along my checkbones. At my wide-eyed look, he prompts, "What?" And then finishes off the other cheek.

When he closes up the blush and reaches around me once more for the mascara I hadn't finished, he tells me to close my eyes, and I do as he says, too flabbergasted to do anything more.

"You're… you're doing my makeup right now," I point out stupidly.

He applies the mascara flawlessly to my lashes, not a smudge out of place, and when I open my eyes, I see him reaching for my lip gloss. "Open," he orders, pulling the wand out of the tube, and my jaw drops without question. He smirks at that. "Gotta remember that for later. Such a good girl when I order you around, huh?" When my face never morphs from my astonishment, he finally gives in to my unspoken questions. "Sugar, I've gotten my makeup done nearly four or five times a week for the past decade. You don't think I've picked up a few things with that many hours in a makeup chair?"

When he lifts a brow and demonstrates me pressing my lips together, I mimic his action. At his, "There. Fucking beautiful," I turn around on the counter to peek into the mirror. Subtle highlights of color, just enough to take away my paleness from being queasy most of the day, make me look like I have a healthy glow, and I whip around to stare up at him once again.

"Is there anything you're not good at, honey? Cooking, designing, now makeup?" I shake my head in wonder. "How did I get so lucky? You're like a gentleman, an alpha, and like, the coolest girlfriend ever wrapped into one."

He frowns at that, narrowing his eyes.

"Of course, you *are* from California," I tease, and then I'm squealing as he scoops me off the counter and carries me out of the bathroom to the bed, looking as if he wants to drop me there. But instead, he lays me down gently, trapping my hands above my head.

"You're lucky you've got my baby in you, sugar. Or there would be hell to pay for all that," he growls, but I see the playfulness in his eyes.

I soften at the mention of our baby and stop struggling against his grip on my wrists. "I love you," I whisper, and after a moment of just looking at me, he lowers his face to the side of my neck, nuzzling me there, before whispering in my ear, "I love you too. More than anything."

My stomach growls then, and his head pops back up. "I had a surprise dinner planned for you tonight, but I'm thinking it would be way too flavorful for what your belly can take today. What would you like instead?"

I narrow my eyes. "First, what was the surprise?"

"What if I want to save the surprise for a different day?" he counters.

"What if your surprise happens to be just what I'm looking for?" I volley.

He tilts his head to the side. "Italian," he hints, and I groan.

"Oh ma God, yaaasss. Super buttery breadsticks. I'm in," I tell him, and he thinks about it for a minute and then finally gives in.

"Whatever my sugar wants, my sugar gets." He stands then, pulling me up when I reach my hands out. "You bring that little black dress I requested?" he asks, and I nod. "Good. If you feel up to it, wear that. I've gotta change." And with that, he disappears into his huge walk-in closet.

My dress is comfy as hell, a bodycon dress that's made of pure stretch, so I have no qualms wearing that bad boy to dinner. And then it dawns on me, and I burst out laughing. It makes Curtis peek out of his closet, and I see he's buttoning up a sexy-as-sin black shirt that fits his torso and biceps like a second skin, making me drool a little as I wiggle into my dress. His eyes flare with heat, but he manages not to attack me, asking, "What's so funny?"

"I was going to say something about this dress not being able to hide my food baby, but then I remembered... there's a *real baby*," I sing-song, threading my arms through the straps, and then I cease all movement. My head drops and I stare at my mostly flat belly, my hands raising to press there. "A real baby," I whisper, and the next moment, Curtis's hands are cradling my face as he tilts it up for me to look into his eyes.

"A real baby. Our real baby," he breathes. "She's really in there, sugar."

My lip quirks. "She?" I whisper.

He shrugs. "Or he. Either way, I'd be happy. I just... have a feeling. Every time I picture the baby, it's a girl."

My bottom lip trembles at that as more love than I've ever felt in my life fills me up for the man before me.

At his "No crying. Don't ruin my awesome makeup job," I huff out a laugh and nod, sniffling back the tears.

"Fuck, these pregnancy hormones are no joke," I reply, and then I stand up on my tiptoes and drop a peck on his lips before spinning to grab my shoes.

Twenty-Five

CURTIS

HALF AN HOUR later, I meet Dean's eyes in the rearview mirror, since he's sitting in the backseat behind me. He gives me a subtle nod of encouragement, and I exhale quietly, not wanting to freak Erin out with my anxiety. God, I hope she likes the surprise.

I see her sit up straighter in the passenger seat as we get closer to the restaurant, seeing the crowd out front, the bright lights spotlighting the red-carpet backdrop where my handpicked, invitation only guests pose for the reporters with cameras. Rachel is on the sidewalk, and the minute she spots my truck in the line of cars letting out high-profile patrons for tonight's event, she gives a signal, and all the reporters turn to face the street.

"What is going on there?" Erin breathes in awe. "Is that… it that your assistant?" She turns to look at me, her eyebrows high on her forehead.

"Yeah, sugar. We're here," I tell her.

Her eyes widen. "I… I just wanted breadsticks," she squeaks, and I press my lips together to keep from laughing as she spins to look out the window once again.

When I pull up to the curb, I meet Dean's eyes in the mirror once more, and he gives me a grin and a thumbs up before I look over my shoulder when I feel Emmy squeeze my shoulder in support. She smiles excitedly, and I nod, reaching for my door handle and opening it up. As I circle the hood, I let out a growl when one of the valets reaches for Erin's door, and he hops back, giving me room to open it myself.

Her eyes are full of wonder as she looks up at the restaurant, obviously trying her best to ignore all the cameras now flashing like crazy around us.

I reach in and pick her up by her hips, gently placing her on her feet on the sidewalk and plastering her to my side. Dean and Emmy are next to us seconds later, and I vaguely register my truck pulling away.

"This is a hell of a surprise. Is it always like this at restaurants in LA?" she asks, looking up at me, her face a little nervous with all the attention.

"No, not always. Just when there's a big event, or… a grand opening," I tell her.

Her eyebrows raise at that. "Oo! Is that what this is? Did a celebrity just open this place up?" she asks, excitement filling her voice.

I smile softly. "Something like that." I look at Rachel, giving her a nod, and she hurries over to give me a small black remote, which I hand to Erin. "See that white curtain?" I ask her, pointing at the top of the building we stand in front of.

"Uhhh… yeah," she replies, shifting from one foot to the other with nerves.

"Aim this at it and push the button," I say, and I watch as she looks at her best friend, a questioning look in her eyes as if she's trying to figure out if Emmy knows what's going on. The huge grin on Emmy's face and the way she's practically vibrating, Dean's arm the only thing apparently keeping her from jumping up and down, lets Erin know she's in on the surprise.

"Do it!" she squeals, and hesitantly, Erin lifts the remote, aiming it at the white curtain.

We all hold our breath as she pushes the button, and the curtain falls away, revealing the name of the restaurant.

"Sugar's," Erin whispers, and all eyes in the crowd watch her, silence having fallen over the hundreds of people except for the sound of cameras flashing the moment I handed her the remote.

Finally her head whips around and she stares up at me. "Did you open a restaurant?" she hisses in shock.

I smile down at her. "I did."

"And did you name your restaurant… after me?" she clarifies.

My grin takes over my whole face. "I did… sugar." I wink at her, and her eyebrows practically hit her hairline.

"You opened a restaurant and named it after me, after only knowing me a month?" she prompts.

"Technically, I only knew you a week before I decided to name it after you, but the restaurant has been in the works for several months now," I explain. And I barely have the words out of my mouth before she leaps at me, her arms encircling my neck the best she can with our height difference, so I bend at my knees and lift her up, allowing her to have access to my face, where she plants kisses all over my cheeks, nose, forehead, jaw, and then finally my lips, the crowd bursting into applause and cheers as the flashing around us crescendos.

Minutes later, when she's finally let me go, we all bark out in laughter when she asks our small group, "Okay, now can I have breadsticks?"

Dishing
~up~
Love

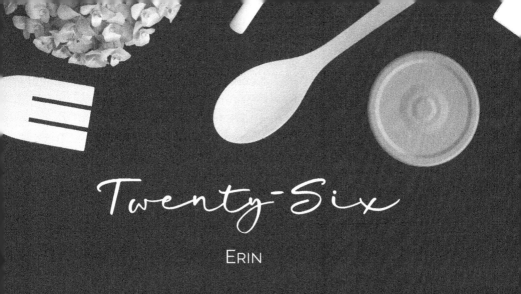

Twenty-Six

ERIN

I COME AWAKE to a hot, wet feeling between my legs and instantly go into a panic. It's mostly dark in the room, just a teensy bit of light coming in through the tiny crack in the curtains. My hands dive to the apex of my thighs, and I know—I just *know*—I've lost our baby. I sob out, lifting my fingers to try to get a closer look at the wetness that I pull away, fully expecting it to be an ugly red.

And that's when I feel Curtis whisper against my thigh, "It's okay, sugar. It's only me."

When my eyes focus, I see my hand, my fingers only shiny with clear wetness, and my head falls against the pillow in relief. Tears sting my nose at the roller coaster of emotions I've been on in only the few moments I've been awake, and when I sniffle, Curtis crawls up my body, circling his arm beneath my back to hold me to him as he shushes me, trying to soothe away my fears.

"I'm so sorry, baby. I only wanted to make you feel good, wake you up in the best possible way. Made sure to wake up before you, so I could convince you not to run this time. It was the first time we would ever wake up together, and I wanted it to be special. I didn't mean to scare you," he says against my lips, pressing kisses between each sentence.

I let out a weak laugh and brush away my tears that have fallen out of the corners of my eyes. "I'm not going anywhere, honey. I promise. You never have to worry about me running ever again." I lift my hands to cradle his face. "I guess we both have a little PTSD to work through, huh?"

He nods. "I guess so, Ms. Psychologist." He kisses me passionately then, and my hips instinctively begin to move against him. "Is… is it safe for me to make love to you?" he asks tentatively, and I smile, closing my eyes, nodding slowly.

"Yeah, honey. It's safe. Just be gentle," I reply, and when I open my eyes, he looks a little worried.

"Gentle because I might hurt you?" he clarifies.

I shake my head. "No, gentle because I don't want to risk crazy acrobatics bringing on my morning sickness in the middle of the bed."

"Oh," he pushes out through a laugh. "Got it." With that, he kisses his way down my body.

And we make sweet, slow love, managing to stave off any nausea until way after my second orgasm.

"So what's the schedule today?" I ask, sitting at the island next to Emmy as I nibble on a piece of toast Curtis buttered for me while he flips a pancake flawlessly midair.

"Well, the team will be here around three to start getting us ready for the awards show. They're going to bring you girls several dresses to choose from, and us guys a couple tuxes," Curtis replies.

"Hawt," I say, taking another bite.

"Blow on it first, baby," he says, his eyes turning to me over his shoulder.

"No, you goob. You in a tux. Hot," I tell him, shaking my head.

Emmy giggles next to me. "Get used to that shit, Rin. If you thought they were annoying before with their overprotectiveness, you ain't seen nothin' until you're knocked up." And then she squeals, "*You're knocked up!*"

I chuckle with the toast up to my mouth, leaning my head over to rest on her shoulder for a minute of loving companionship before I sit up when Curtis slides a pancake on my plate.

"Eat," he orders, and I roll my eyes.

"I'm just going to throw it up," I argue.

He puts his fists on his hips. "Yeah, well. At least your body might have enough time to soak up some of the nutrients before it makes its reappearance. I packed in some extra protein in that pancake. Eat."

"All right, all right, bossy britches. Gimme some syrup," I tell him, propping my elbow up on the countertop, my palm up as my fingers wiggle for him to hurry up.

He grabs a glass bottle out of a cabinet and hands it to me. "Not too much. Internet said a lot of sugar can set off nausea."

I pout my bottom lip. "Awww, you researched pregnancy stuff for me, honey?" Emmy and I share a look that agrees that's super dreamy.

"Of course I did. I gotta know what I can and can't feed my babies," he says, coming around the island to press a kiss to my lips before I dump syrup on the pancake. He growls, stealing the container away.

"Why is all your stuff unmarked? If I ever try to cook anything, I'm going to have to smell and taste everything trying to figure out what each item is." I cut up my food, placing a square of the flapjack on my tongue. I close my eyes and moan around the bite. "Oh, that's gooood."

"I buy a lot of my stuff from farmer's markets or make it myself," he explains, confirming my suspicion he probably churned the butter himself. Maybe that's why everything he makes me tastes so much better than anything else I've ever tasted before.

"So anyway, what happens after we pick out our dresses?"

"Then our team will do everyone's hair and makeup and all that crap, and then we'll head to the awards show. After the awards, we'll go on to our after party, which we'll have whether we win or lose."

"Oh my God, Rin! This will be the first party you've ever been to where you didn't drink you-call-its," Emmy says, nudging me with her elbow, and I stick my tongue out at her.

"I will make you whatever virgin drink your heart desires," Curtis counters, and I blow him a kiss.

Dean comes downstairs then, stopping next to Emmy to kiss her on top of her head before circling the island, standing next to Curtis. "Your protein pancakes?" he asks, and at Curtis's nod, he whoops. "Hell yeah, man. I'll take three."

"Coming right up," Curtis replies and pours more batter into the skillet.

"How you feeling, Rin?" Dean asks, taking the stool on the other side of his wife.

"Good so far. The doctor said I have to take this medication with food, so I'm hoping to keep a little bit of this down," I reply.

"Curt, you'll have to get her some of those sea bands they use on cruises for sea sickness. They have this little bead that pushes on a pressure point in the wrist that helps with nausea. Oh, and what was that stuff that worked for you, love?" Dean prompts.

"Oh, Unisom Sleep Tabs. I would ask Dr. McNealy if it's okay to mix those medications, but it's just an antihistamine that has a side effect of curing nausea. It's the only thing that got me through the first trimester. And then later on, when you start having pregnancy insomnia, it'll help you sleep a little better," Emmy explains.

"Are you getting all this?" I asked Curtis, and he uses his pointer finger to tap the side of his head, letting me know he's making mental notes, and I smile.

Knowing what a crazy-busy night we're going to have, we decide to have a day of lounging around Curtis's house—well, I guess it's *our* house now—until the team of stylists arrive later that afternoon. We binge watch the entire first season of *Schitt's Creek,* the four of us laughing our asses off at the Rose family's antics.

Several hours later, I look at myself in the mirror and can't believe the woman staring back at me from the reflection. There's no denying I look damn hot whenever I dress up for Comic Cons as Khaleesi. But even that doesn't compare to the way I feel in this cobalt blue gown. It hugs me in all the right places with a sweetheart neckline that does amazing things for my cleavage, chiffon crisscrossing over the bodice, and an intricate beaded pattern makes a thick belt around my waist. The skirt is straight but flowy, and the strappy pumps hugging my feet make my legs look they go on for days as I stick one out through the slit in my dress.

I have never looked better in my life, and as Curtis walks up behind me and I see the reflection of him in his tux, I can't help but think we are one damn fine-looking couple. While the thought of all the paparazzi taking our pictures gives me anxiety, there's no doubt in my mind we'll be in the tabloids as one of the best dressed couples.

Curtis wraps his arms around me, one hand resting low on my belly. "You're absolutely stunning," he tells me. "And all mine," he adds.

I spin in his arms, my heels making me a little taller, but he still towers over me. But when I tug on the lapels of his tux, he gives me what I want and bends down, his lips pressing to mine gently so he doesn't smudge my lipstick. When he pulls back, I smile and use my thumb to wipe away the color left behind on his lips.

"You ready to do this?" He lifts a brow.

"Ready as I'll ever be." I shrug, and we make our way down the stairs.

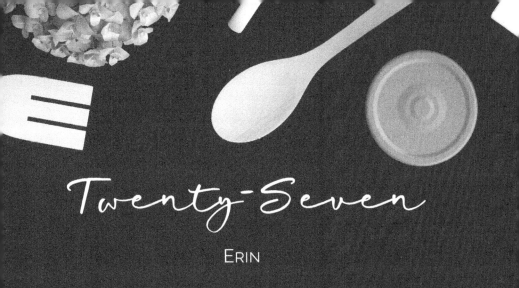

Twenty-Seven

ERIN

IN THE LIMO on the ride there, worry fills my gut and I look over at Curtis. "Can I ask a favor?"

"Anything," he replies.

"If you win, do you promise not to say anything about the baby in your acceptance speech? I don't want to jinx anything, and it's bad luck to announce a pregnancy before the ten-week mark," I explain.

"Of course, sugar. We won't say anything until you're ready," he tells me, and I give him a relieved smile and nod just as we pull up to the curb at the end of the red carpet.

Hours later, we pile into the limo, laughing and whooping in celebration. Both Curtis and Dean and Emmy's TV shows won for each of their categories, so there's definitely something to celebrate as the driver takes us all to the after party.

I managed to only have to excuse myself once during the awards ceremony in order to hurry to the bathroom, the smell of so many colognes and perfumes making me nauseous in the theater. Now, I'm absolutely ravenous, and Curtis assures me there will be tons of stuff I can choose from on the buffet at the party.

I'm settling in at a table marked with our names with a plateful of crackers, cheeses, and different deli meats, and Curtis sets a glass of Sprite on the table in front of me. I thank him just as several people come up to our table, and Curtis starts introducing everyone from the network. After the first two, they all start to blur together, but I smile

KD ROBICHAUX

politely, shaking everyone's hand, making sure to say things like "nice to meet you," as I try to nibble on the crackers while still looking like I have manners.

Curtis must see how badly I need to eat something, because in the most charming way possible, he looks at everyone and tells them, "If y'all wouldn't mind, my woman had a nervous stomach before the awards show and really needs to eat something, now that all the excitement is over." He grins, and everyone nods in understanding, calling out "of course, of course" before waving and heading toward their own tables.

Several minutes later, Emmy and I are in the middle of an intense yet hushed conversation about maternity jeans, when Carlos approaches, giving us all a wave. He slaps Curtis's shoulder, giving him a wink, and I narrow my eyes as he walks away.

"What was that all about?" I ask, and he grins, pointing up at the screen we are dead center in front of with the perfect view. Suddenly, the screen fills with a video image of Curtis, and my eyes dart to him, but he only grins and points back up at the screen again.

"I'm Chef Curtis Rockwell, and this is *Chef to Go*. I'll be surprising one lucky shopper with a chance to take me home with them, where I'll teach 'em how to cook a gourmet meal."

And then the feed cuts to Curtis as he starts walking up and down the aisles like he always does during every episode, searching out his latest victim. I smile as he gives the camera wide eyes, shaking his head vigorously as the little kid kicks their mom and takes off in the opposite direction. And then I lay my head on his shoulder, seeing at a distance when Carlos zoomed in on little baby feet sticking out from beneath a blanket. Curtis makes a sweet face at the camera and then holds his pointer finger over his lips for the international sign to stay quiet as he tiptoes to the next aisle.

Finally, he stops, and a look comes over his face I've never seen before. It's a look of awe, as if he can't believe his eyes. And then the footage looks different, unedited, almost like a behind-the-scenes reel. It's no longer perfect, the way it is when you see it on TV.

The camera is a little shaky as I hear Carlos ask, "Yo, Curtis. You good, bro?"

Curtis, not seeming to say it to anyone in particular, replies, "Yeah, I think she's the one." And if I hadn't already recognized the grocery store, I would be one jealous bitch over whichever person Curtis had laid eyes on.

Finally, the camera refocuses down in the distance in the frozen pizza aisle, and standing there is the hot mess express that was me on that night one month ago. I'm leaned up against the freezer door, finishing the telephone call I had with Emmy that night, and when I end the call, I start toward the camera.

I watch the screen, transfixed on Curtis's back as he heads toward me, and I bite my lip, knowing what happens next. But still, I laugh when I see us collide. That's when I realize the entire audience around us laughs as well, and then a moment later, everyone lets out a collective "aaawww" as the camera zooms in the moment Curtis's and my eyes meet for the very first time.

I feel that moment to the depths of my soul, as if I'm feeling it once again for the very first time. Butterflies set off in my stomach, flying up to my chest, their wings tickling my heart as I lean my head on Curtis's shoulder once again, and he kisses the top of my head.

I ask him quickly, "Is this a viewing of our episode before it airs?"

He winks at me then gives a chin lift toward the screen once more. I huff out in frustration that he won't answer my questions until I see the next thing on the screen is us walking down the sidewalk toward my house. That answers my question, because if it was our episode, the whole grocery shopping part of the show wouldn't have been cut out.

I rest my chin on the palm of my hand, my elbow propped on the table, as I smile, my eyes tearing up the moment I watch Curtis take hold of me on the screen, pulling me to the other side of him so I'm walking next to the building instead. I feel his hand come to rest on my thigh beneath the table, and I slide my fingers through his, tightening them to try to help control my emotions.

The screen cuts back to the grocery store, in the middle of our conversation. "But what's interesting, at least to me, is the majority of the people from here sound almost like a perfect mix of Southern and working-class New Yorkers," I tell him, and after a pause, he smiles and replies, "Now that you mention it, that is exactly what they sound like. Hm!" He stops, looking back at me. "Lafayette really nailed the accent on *True Blood*, huh?"

I see myself pout. "Rest in peace, Nelsan Ellis. He was seriously my favorite character," and then my eyes dart to Curtis's response.

"Right? That actually made me really sad when I heard he passed away. Like, most of the time you hear about a celebrity dying, and it's like, aw, that sucks, and you kinda just go about the rest of your day. His made me genuinely sad that we wouldn't see him around anymore."

"Same," I breathe, and then we stand there staring at each other.

And stare at each other.

And stare at each other.

And the audience around us starts to giggle, and then everyone bursts out laughing when Martin yells off camera, "Cut!" and our eyes turn toward him in confusion.

There are a couple of cute scenes of us in the kitchen, and there's no denying how in sync we were with each other from the very beginning. I watch as I hand him utensils and things before he even has a chance to ask for them, our time together in Emmy's kitchen seeming more like a choreographed dance than learning to cook.

But then the screen goes white for a moment, and suddenly Curtis is speaking directly into the camera. I can tell from the background that he was in his living room when he recorded this part, and it must've been on his phone, as he adjusts it where he's got it set up before sitting a little farther back on his couch. He rests his elbows on his knees and claps his hands together, a nervous smile on his face.

"Erin… sugar… um… hi," he stutters out, chuckling, and next to me, I feel his hand squeeze mine. "You'd think this would come easy to me, talking to a camera as if it's a person, but this… this is for *you*. You. *Hello, you*, as Joe would say." He does an actual face-palm, making me laugh. "Aaand now I'm quoting one of our shows. No. No quoting, Curt. This has gotta be original. It's gotta be special. Because it's your girl."

I turn to look at Curtis sitting beside me, and this time he meets my eyes for a moment, a sweet look on his face before he nods at the screen.

I dutifully watch as he says, "In about ten minutes, I'm headed to the airport to pick you up. I haven't seen you in what seems like a lifetime, and my heart feels like it's going to come like… tearing out of my chest *Alien*-style." He grabs the center of his chest and closes his eyes for a moment while he blows out a breath. When he opens them again, he looks a little calmer. "I have something for you," he says from the screen, and he reaches into his pocket, pulling out a royal blue box and opening it to show a gorgeous diamond ring.

I gasp, letting go of his hand to cover my mouth, my fingers steepling as my eyes go wide. I don't take them off the screen, dying to see what he says next.

"I want to be able to relive this moment over and over, so I'm asking you to marry me out in public, in the middle of LAX, where tens, even hundreds, of people will be able to see and record if they want. And all the better, because then they'll tag us on social media, and I'll be able to enjoy the moment from all different angles." He chuckles, shaking his head. "I mean, that's if you say yes. Please, dear God, say yes, or I'm gonna look like the biggest freakin' tool."

The audience laughs around us, but I barely hear it I'm so focused on the video playing before my eyes, even knowing how the airport played out.

"But just in case no one decides to care for the first time like... ever, our good buddy Carlos is meeting me, gonna catch it all for me, and he's gonna make this cool little video that... well, I guess you're watching now." He opens his hand up toward the camera in a gesture showing it dawned on him I'd be watching this after he filmed it. "So, uh... yeah." He glances at his watch then claps his hands together. "Time to go make you my future wife." And he reaches toward his phone, turning the camera off, and the screen goes white for another moment.

The next thing I see is me in the distance over Curtis's shoulder before I got to baggage claim. There's just a moment of me registering his handsome face before my knees visibly wobble, and then my man takes off like a bolt of lightning, catching me before I hit the floor. The screen goes white.

Curtis's face fills the screen once more. "Well, that didn't go as planned." He chuckles, rubbing the back of his head nervously. "That was not the special moment. Not the right time to ask you to marry me, sugar. But I'll think of something." He looks off to the side, and I hear my voice off screen growl out dramatically, *"Breadsticks!"* And then Emmy yells, "Woman, calm your tits! We're leaving in like two-point-five seconds." Recorded Curtis shakes his head, chuckling to himself once more. "That's my woman. That's my future wife right there. Mark my words." He winks at the camera then, and the screen goes black.

That's when I realize real-life Curtis is no longer sitting beside me. When I glance around, trying to spot him, I see he's kneeling behind me, holding out the ring from the video, and tears fill my eyes once again as I let out a mix of a sob and a laugh.

"Sugar, sugar," he sing-songs, lifting one brow as he smirks.

I sniffle. "Ah, honey, honey," I squeak out, wiping my nose with the back of my hand.

"Will you make me the happiest man on this whole damn planet and be my wife?" he asks, his eyes pleading.

I bite my lip, trying to rein in my emotions, my pregnancy hormones adding to the chaotic beat of my heart. I can't stand the fearful anticipation in his gaze for a second longer, so I let out a cry of happiness. "Yes!"

He stands up then, pulling me out of my chair and onto my feet, and slips the ring onto my finger just as everyone in the audience cheers, a roar of applause erupting around us.

I laugh as he picks me up, spinning me in a circle before kissing the hell out of me, and when he sets me back on my feet...

I wobble a little.

"Ah fuck," I repeat the first words I ever spoke to him.

I hear the laughter in his voice when he asks, "What is it, sugar?"

I swallow thickly, pulling my lips between my teeth, trying to make the feeling go away, but no luck.

"I'm gonna puke," I get out, right before I bend over and vomit in front of every fucking person who works at my fiancé's network.

Dishing
~up~
Love

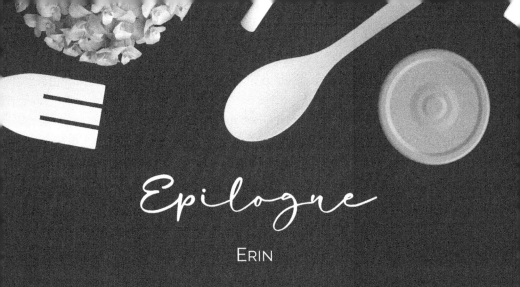

Epilogue

ERIN

Five years later

"DAAAD, DO WE gotta watch it again?" Louis, our twelve-year-old son, whines. "It's so gross, and not just because Mom barfs. You're so mushy." He plops onto the couch between Curtis and me, and I thread my fingers through his, admiring the way our hands look like a work of art as our flesh tones go back and forth between light tan and dark chocolatey brown. We adopted him from Burkina Faso, a West-African country, two years ago after completely falling head-over-heels in love with him when we visited an orphanage during one of Curtis's fundraising events. All the kids spoke pretty good English thanks to the missionaries who ran the home. And when we looked into those midnight eyes, we knew Louis was meant to be our son.

"It's not gross, Lou-Lou," Alexis scolds in her sweet little voice, coming around the couch to hop up in my husband's lap, their matching light-yellow hair shining beneath the overhead light as two pairs of turquoise eyes turn toward me. "It's romantic."

"Hm," Curtis says to our four-year-old. "That's quite a big word for such a little nugget." And he tickles her ribs, making her squeal.

"I learned it on *The Aristocats*," she explains when she finally catches her breath.

"Ah, those are smart kitties," Curtis agrees, and they both nod at each other.

"And the answer is yes, we have to watch it again," I tell Louis, pulling him closer to me as I wrap my arm around his narrow shoulders and kiss the top of his head.

"Ugh, fine," he says haughtily, but then he snuggles against me, ever the momma's boy.

The video starts playing, the same as it's always been. The day we met. The thwarted proposal. And then the addition of the night of the awards, when Curtis finally got to ask me to marry him. There's a clip from our wedding, and us dancing at the reception. And the moment the doctor held Alexis up over the curtain during my C-section.

Not long after we brought her home from the hospital, I had to return for a hysterectomy. But we were grateful for the little miracle we were given, and one day Curtis told me about a dream he had when we first started dating. One where we had a huge family with lots of kids, all different races, and how the little girl on my hip looked just like him. I agreed to his unspoken question in a heartbeat.

Which led to the tear-jerking moment on the screen now, when Curtis and I stepped off the plane with Louis, as Emmy, Dean, my parents, and Curtis's Yaya held up signs welcoming him to our big family.

But then comes the new addition, the one we recorded this morning when we got the news. At the same moment, Curtis and I look at each other, our eyes locking for a moment of secret joy, and then together we watch the kids' reaction.

"Wait... what does that say?" Louis prompts, the excitement in his African accent making the hairs on my arms stand on end.

He reaches for the remote and pauses the screen, his eyes going wide as his jaw drops.

"What is it?" Alexis asks. "Lou-Lou! What's it say? I can't read!"

He stands up, taking her hand, and like the amazing big brother he's been since the day we brought him home, he tugs her over to the screen, his finger pointing to each word as he reads out loud. "It says, 'Rockwell Party of Five, established 2026."

She shakes her little head, her blonde pigtails whipping around her face. "What does that mean?" she asks.

Curtis grabs my hand, squeezing it before lifting it to his lips to press a kiss to my knuckles.

"It means we're getting a brother or sister!" Louis yells with glee, and at Alexis's precious gasp, they jump around the living room while we watch on.

THE END

Note from the Author

My greatest fear I ever had as an author was that after I wrote my first trilogy—which was the 100 percent real-life story of how my husband and I met—I wouldn't be able to write a completely fictional book. My Blogger Diaries was easy. I didn't have to come up with characters, a plot, a happy ending, etc. I just retold exactly what happened.

But then one night I dreamed the entire storyline of *No Trespassing*. It was my fourth book, and even after writing nearly twenty now, it's still the one I call my favorite when I'm asked that question. New Orleans is my favorite city on earth, and I got to put in all sorts of useless NOLA fun facts my brain stores for absolutely no reason. I've always wanted to give Erin, the BFF, her happily ever after, but she needed the perfect hero, a special man who was just right for her, and I'm so happy Curtis volunteered as tribute.

It was such a blessing for me to get to write this story and revisit some of my all-time favorite voices in my head. And if you enjoyed Erin's happily ever after and would like to see just how her crazy bestie Emmy found the love of her life, please check out *No Trespassing*, an enemies-to-lovers rom-com treasure hunt adventure beneath the streets of New Orleans.

Keep up with all things KD Robichaux in my reader group on
Facebook: KD-Rob's Mob.

Follow Me:

Facebook.com/authorkdrobichaux

Instagram.com/kaylathebibliophile

www.kdrobichaux.com

Acknowledgements

First and foremost, thank you Boom Factory Publishing for this amazing opportunity to tell Erin's happily ever after. Thank you for making this small fry feel like the whole damn bag of potatoes. You'll never know how much your encouragement and belief in me means to me.

Thank you to my hubby face and kids for being so supportive and understanding, and for always telling me what a big deal I am. Mama's trying her best, y'all.

Thank you, thank you, thank you to my Barb, my awesome editor. And Stacia, my alpha reader. I'm keeping you two forever. Eighteen books and counting.

Thank you also to the rest of the editing team at BFP. It was weird being on the other end of the process, but I didn't hate it LOL!

Last but certainly not least, thank you to my girl squad, lovingly named by my CC "Kayla's Titty Gang." I couldn't life without y'all. #DesperateHousewives2020

Other Books from Boom Factory Publishing

Beauty and the Badge by Ella Fox (http://mybook.to/beautyandthebadge)

Love At The Bluebird by Aurora Rose Reynolds and Jessica Marin (http://mybook.to/loveatthebluebird)

Surrendering To Him by Hope Jones (http://mybook.to/surrenderingtohim)

Aurora Rose Reynolds's Happily Ever Alpha World (https://boomfactorypublishing.com/)

About Boom Factory Publishing

Aurora Rose Reynolds and her husband, Sedaka Reynolds, created Boom Factory Publishing to use their experiences to expand and promote upcoming and existing indie authors.

    With over six years in the industry, and millions of books sold worldwide, we know what it takes to become a successful author and we will use this knowledge to take our authors to the next level.

    "As a successful hybrid author in this ever evolving industry, I know that you're only as successful as the team that is promoting you!" – *Aurora Rose Reynolds*

Please check out Boom Factory Publishing's website to see all of our talented authors and the books they have published.

https://boomfactorypublishing.com/

Made in the USA
Monee, IL
06 January 2021

56766641R00152